CU00942432

Nick Richardson has been a journalist for three decades and has worked on newspapers and magazines in Australia and England. He has been a Margaret George fellow at the National Archives of Australia and a research fellow at the Australian Prime Ministers Centre. Nick has a PhD in history from the University of Melbourne and is adjunct professor of journalism at La Trobe University. He lives in Melbourne with his family and works for the *Herald Sun*.

MARIBYRNONG LIBRARY SERVICE

In a time of war,
Australian Rules became…

THE GAME
OF THEIR
LIVES

NICK RICHARDSON

MACMILLAN
Pan Macmillan Australia

Imperial measurements have been used in this book as they were in documents from the First World War. Exceptions to this are measures of explosive yields, which were measured in kilograms; and Olympic races are measured in the metric system.

1 inch	25.4 millimetres	1 centimetre	0.394 inches
1 foot	30.5 centimetres	1 metre	3.28 feet
1 yard	0.914 metres	1 metre	1.09 yards
1 mile	1.61 kilometres	1 kilometre	0.621 miles
1 pound	0.45 kilograms	1 kilogram	2.2 pounds
1 stone	6.35 kilograms	1 kilogram	0.16 stone

First published 2016 in Macmillan by Pan Macmillan Australia Pty Ltd
1 Market Street, Sydney, New South Wales, Australia, 2000

Copyright © Nick Richardson 2016

The moral right of the author has been asserted.

All rights reserved. No part of this book may be reproduced or transmitted by
any person or entity (including Google, Amazon or similar organisations),
in any form or by any means, electronic or mechanical, including photocopying,
recording, scanning or by any information storage and retrieval system,
without prior permission in writing from the publisher.

Cataloguing-in-Publication entry is available
from the National Library of Australia
http://catalogue.nla.gov.au

Typeset in 12/15.5 pt Bembo by Midland Typesetters, Australia
Printed by McPherson's Printing Group

The author and the publisher have made every effort to contact copyright
holders for material used in this book. Any person or organisation that
may have been overlooked should contact the publisher.

MIX
Paper from
responsible sources
FSC® C001695

The paper in this book is FSC® certified.
FSC® promotes environmentally responsible,
socially beneficial and economically viable
management of the world's forests.

To the memory of Private Charles Henry White,
No: 1252, 15th Battalion AIF
(1892–1987)

Contents

Contents

Prologue

The crowd pressed forward as the train pulled in to Sydney's Central Station. A hum of expectation mixed with the smoke and whistles. Railway porters moved through the curious mass of onlookers to help organise luggage and clear a path for the city's visitors. Beyond the congested platform, 15 horse-drawn coaches were waiting to take the train's passengers down Pitt and Park Streets, bound for a reception at the Town Hall.

It was late morning on Tuesday, 4 August 1914, a mild and clear day in Sydney. The train had started its journey three nights ago, on a chilly Saturday evening in Adelaide, farewelled by 5000 boisterous supporters. From there, it wound its way to Melbourne and on to Sydney, picking up passengers as it went. But they were not the usual mix of tourists who made the trip north, with their sturdy suitcases and holiday hopes: this was a special train, carrying young men with skills in a unique Australian game. They were footballers, selected as the best of their state to compete in a national showpiece of Australian Rules football starting the following day at the Sydney Cricket Ground.

They made a congenial throng on the train as they grabbed their hats and coats and moved towards the carriage doors to catch a glimpse of the onlookers. Sydney, with its stunning harbour and warm winters, was about as keen on football as it was on frost and fog. But few of the footballers from the rest of the country knew the city: they had not had any reason to visit, until now. But curiosity was piqued by the carnival's pomp. It was just as well, the carnival would be the latest effort to spread the word about Australian football to a state seemingly impervious to the game's charms.

There had been numerous attempts during the previous few years to get Sydneysiders interested in the indigenous game; the Australasian Football Council put £200 aside in 1911 as propaganda money to sell the game north of the Murray. Two of the big Melbourne clubs – Collingwood and Fitzroy – had gone north too, and played for premiership points in front of 20,000 spectators. But in all the build-up to this carnival, there was a hope among the men who ran the game that it was going to help cement football's place beyond the southern states. Football was going to rival and then overtake rugby. The doubters would be converted.

The platform for this push was established with the jubilee carnival in Melbourne in 1908, which not only celebrated 50 years of football but also included a New Zealand team. Enthused and perhaps moved by the occasion, the then prime minister Alfred Deakin told an audience at one of the smoke nights organised around the carnival that 'when the tocsin sounds the call to arms, not the last, but the first to acknowledge it will be those who have played, and played well, the Australian game of football'. It was a prescient prophecy from Deakin, a politician with an interest in spiritualism. He could not have known how accurately he had pinpointed what would become a critical issue in the years to come. At the time, the prime minister's sentiment affirmed the view that somewhere at the core of football was an Australian nationalism trying to burst through. Another national carnival in Adelaide in 1911 tried to build on the notion of a 'federated' football code, but getting the game established in New South Wales was always fundamental to spreading the Australian football message.

The footballers on the train didn't see themselves as the game's missionaries. Far from it. All of them knew there were problems with football — gambling, incipient professionalism and violence at the grounds made it appear to be evolving into something far less noble than its originators had hoped. The problems were identified in the newspapers every day, in every town where football was played. But these young men had grown up with the game and just loved playing it, whenever or wherever they could.

That's why Dan Scullin, a rangy, jug-eared 23-year-old, travelled from Boulder in Western Australia to join the Adelaide train. Scullin hailed from an Irish-Catholic family in the gold-fields. There were six kids — four boys, two girls — Mum and Dad, plus two uncles from the old country in the one house, just a short stroll away from the Boulder Recreation Ground, where football was played on Sunday afternoons. The boys took to the game. Scullin was one of nine players selected in the Western Australian team from Goldfields League, a competition known for its toughness and eccentricities at a time and a place when football filled a need. There wasn't much to do outside of working down the mine — you either played football or watched it. One of Scullin's teammates was 'Poet' Smith, a gangly miner with knobbly knees, who always played in a hat. No one was quite sure where the nickname came from but the man christened Walter Smith had an enviable record that included kicking 20 out of 25 goals in a match against the Boulder Stars.

Football in the Goldfields League had more than a touch of the Wild West: you needed speed and skill to survive. Dan Scullin had both. He and his older brother Jack played senior football with the Mines Rovers, but it was Dan who outstripped his brother when he won the club's best footballer award in 1913. The club gave Dan and a couple of his state teammates a send-off before the carnival at the Shamrock Hotel in Boulder City. Ten days later, Scullin found himself in Sydney for the first time, accompanied not just by his mates from the West but also by a range of footballers he didn't know and some he had barely heard of. But whatever gloss the administrators had applied before the carnival quickly wore off when it became clear who was actually playing.

The South Australians were not quite the team they could have been: the Port Adelaide and South Adelaide clubs were sending teams elsewhere, even though they were on the train too. Port was going to play matches in New South Wales, and South Adelaide was heading further north, to Brisbane, for another football carnival. The Perth Football Club would join them there while Norwood, from South Australia, was going in the other direction, headed to the West to play some matches. The train was also carrying the Cananore team, from Hobart, and Collingwood, dubbed 'the Fighting Magpies on tour'. Both clubs would be part of the Brisbane carnival. The absence of some quality players, such as Collingwood captain Dan Minogue, compromised the carnival's determination to present a showpiece of the game's finest exponents. It was not an ideal start. And travel arrangements meant that not everyone could be at the official welcoming ceremony: the Queenslanders arrived the previous day but the Tasmanians didn't show up until opening day.

The Victorians were always the ones to beat, even if South Australia had won the title three years earlier. The Victorians were proud of their state's reputation as the home of the game and had created a competition that featured the game's best players. The Victorians arriving at Central Station carried themselves with the confidence that comes with talent and success. There were plenty of name players in the squad: Collingwood's mercurial forward Dick Lee, ruckman Hughie James from Richmond, the long-kicking Dave McNamara from St Kilda, Melbourne's

Charlie Lilley, the gifted all-round athlete Jack Brake, and Jack Cooper, a 1913 Fitzroy premiership player. But there was one fellow in particular who was developing a handsome reputation for South Melbourne – 25-year-old Bruce Sloss.

Sloss was a solid man for his era – just on five feet 11 inches and almost 12 stone, with a broad face and a mop of fair hair that fell across his forehead. He was an old-fashioned gentleman, mindful of his obligations and responsibilities to his family, his church and his football club. He started his career with Essendon in 1907 but transferred to South Melbourne for the 1910 season. He was an engineer by trade but more of an artist in temperament, with a strong tenor singing voice. As a youngster, he was often emotional. As an adult, he was serious, keen to show how responsible he was. His job references spoke of a man who was 'attentive . . . industrious and in every manner straightforward'. It translated into how Sloss played football. He went about his game with the air of a man who had a job to do. His calm, workaday attitude to excellence brought reliable performances on the field. It was no surprise that Sloss was picked for his state; he was becoming an outstanding player. Maybe, the wise observers in Melbourne thought, he could become a great player.

The official carnival program released ahead of the event featured an opening address from the governor-general, Sir Ronald Craufurd Munro Ferguson. One Sydney newspaper helpfully suggested to the viceroy that he make it clear in his remarks that the 'visiting warriors' should 'deal gently' with the New South Wales team, 'otherwise the Rocks Push and the Botany Battlers may join forces with the Woolloomooloo Wowsers and get to them'. The carnival opening was to be one of a long list of official duties the governor-general was scheduled to fulfil during a month-long trip to Sydney. As with all matters of state – federal or colonial – Melbourne was the capital. It was where Munro Ferguson took up residence when he and his wife, Lady Helen, arrived in Australia on Monday, 18 May 1914. The timing could not have been more propitious: as the Empire's man in Australia, Munro Ferguson was the key link with the discussions, deliberations and plans in London to deal with the rapidly escalating conflict in Europe.

Munro Ferguson was a Scotsman who had been a Liberal member of the House of Commons and a junior lord of the Treasury. But, increasingly tired of the yoke of party discipline, he sought other appointments, turning down the governorship of Victoria and South Australia respectively before finally assuming the vice-regal role in 1914. Outside of politics, he was absorbed by agriculture and the arts. He was a cultured man, a noted arborist and a waspish correspondent about his new home. But Munro Ferguson was also shrewd and insightful. He embraced the new experiences with gusto, and although his detractors described him as 'choleric' there were few instances of such irascibility in the early months of his tenure. Lady Helen, the daughter of the former British viceroy to India, was a renowned philanthropist with a deep understanding of pragmatic politics. But she had a withering manner that generated behind-the-hand disapproval among some Australian women who encountered her.

Perhaps there was not much else to do in the first week of being the nation's new governor-general. It might just have been a local novelty, like fraternising with other indigenous curios, such as koalas and kangaroos. But, most likely, Munro Ferguson was told that football was the cornerstone of the state's recreation, so going to the game struck him as a powerful way to connect with the Victorian community. Five days after he arrived in Melbourne, he watched St Kilda and South Melbourne with federal Labor leader Andrew Fisher. This was a radical choice for the new viceroy, whose understanding of sport and games was negligible. Exercise, for the King's Man in Australia, was more likely to be cutting down a tree than running after a ball. Fisher, who shared a Scottish heritage with the new governor-general, assured him that football 'was a bonny game and that he would like it fine'. At half-time, Munro Ferguson and Fisher went into the rooms, and the new viceroy was heard to remark on the extent of each footballer's preparation – a safe observation for the novice.

Munro Ferguson was beginning to see how important sport was in his new home. Two weeks after attending the football, the vice-regal couple went to the Caulfield races. Munro Ferguson shrewdly observed, 'We have been to the Races, which in this country is tantamount to saying we have entered society . . . The crowd is very sporting and the arrangements perfect.' All of this before Munro Ferguson had even set foot in Sydney.

The governor-general was nervous about making the trip north because of lingering resentment towards the vice-regal office in Sydney. He confided to London, 'If any part of what one hears is true neither the Government nor the Governor of NSW [Sir Gerald Strickland] are likely to welcome me with both hands. I fixed up as many functions as possible for the first week so as to get quickly in touch with everyone in order if possible to make my visit a success.' Macquarie Street remained vacant but unavailable, forcing the vice-regal to look elsewhere for Sydney accommodation. Instead, the governor-general stayed at a property on the Parramatta River owned by the philanthropist Edith Walker. The absence of a central grand address was an indication of the early tensions Munro Ferguson identified. Even the Sydney press called it 'inhospitality'. But once Munro Ferguson met his obligations to the federal government – which included an urgent constitutional resolution to allow Prime Minister Joseph Cook a double-dissolution election – he headed north, his formidable wife in tow.

The couple arrived in Sydney on 11 July to a diary packed with social events, from polo matches to official dinners and receptions. The initial plan was to stay for about a month before going to Brisbane to open the city's show and then returning to Melbourne in August. But events took a turn.

The hopes for European peace after the assassination of the Archduke Ferdinand and his wife, Sophie, in Sarajevo on 28 June had evaporated by July. War was imminent. Britain was plunged into the gloom and anxiety of mobilising an army to help the French repel the German menace. Munro Ferguson was in regular cable contact with the Colonial Office in London. This would be a war between empires, and there was no doubt on whose side Australia would be. But the nation was in the middle of an election campaign. Prime Minister Cook's government was in caretaker mode, and his Cabinet was spread across the country on electioneering duties. When news broke of the escalation in tensions between Britain and Germany in late July, it was almost impossible to relay the message to any Australian politician of significance. But London knew where to find Munro Ferguson and he was alerted about the looming danger by cablegram.

On 31 July, Munro Ferguson cabled Cook, who was campaigning in the Victorian town of Ballarat. 'Would it not be well, in view of latest news from Europe, that ministers should meet in order that imperial Government may know what support to expect from Australia?' he asked with a veneer of politeness not disguising the urgent command contained in the message. Cook understood. Coincidentally, he and Opposition leader Andrew Fisher both made statements later that day that chimed in unison — whatever happened, Australia would do its duty. 'Remember that when the Empire is at war, so is Australia at war,' Cook told an election gathering at Horsham. Fisher uttered his own version at Colac: '. . . Australians will stand beside [the Mother Country] to help defend her to our last man and our last shilling'.

Cook ordered a Cabinet meeting in Melbourne for 3 August. The governor-general knew his place was back in Melbourne as the conduit between the government and London. The accommodation on the Parramatta River was too far away to be a practical headquarters at such a dire time. 'It is impossible to conduct business in times of crisis from this inaccessible place,' he told London. 'I have felt for the last three days I could not remain here longer.' Munro Ferguson initially planned to take his car, with Defence Minister Edward Millen and Attorney-General Sir William Irvine, to Melbourne. But there was a last-minute change of plan, and Munro Ferguson, the two ministers and several officials boarded the express train to Melbourne on Sunday night to ensure they would arrive for the next day's Cabinet meeting. Before he left Sydney, Munro Ferguson let it be known that all of his engagements in Sydney would be cancelled until at least 13 August. There would be no appearance at the nation's football carnival.

While Munro Ferguson was travelling south, the train carrying some of the country's best footballers was making its way north. The players were still en route when Cook's Cabinet meeting resolved to put the Australian fleet at Britain's disposal and pledge 20,000 volunteer troops to the war effort. Germany had declared war on France. The dominoes started to wobble and waver. Belgian neutrality was inviolable, England warned Germany. There appeared to be no way to avoid war now. And the footballers, whether they liked it or not, would be caught up in it.

In Sydney, almost 500 footballers trundled from Central Station to the Town Hall for the official welcome. Hugh Denison, who had made his fortune from the family tobacco manufacturing business and had started his own newspaper company four years earlier, was on stage to welcome the players in his role as patron of the New South Wales Football League.

It was shortly after 2.30 pm on Tuesday, 4 August. Denison admitted that the shadow of war cast a pall over the carnival. But he had no doubt that sportsmen would inevitably be the first to defend their country. Denison loved sport and, although most of his passion – and money – was spent on four-legged pursuits, he wanted to see New South Wales football prosper. His comments inadvertently echoed Deakin's sentiments from six years earlier. Both believed that footballers would not be found wanting when the time came.

Judge Alfred Backhouse, a man of long legal standing in New South Wales, followed Denison onto the Town Hall stage. After years on the bench, the judge knew how to deliver a message about right and wrong. War was one thing; honour was another. In an environment where being paid to play was considered something of a blight on the noble notion of competition, the judge urged all those interested in Australian Rules to keep the game clean. It was, he added, important to discard the money element. After a couple of other speakers, the reception wound up with the national anthem and loud cheering for the King. The next day would be the start of the carnival.

The Tasmanians arrived in Melbourne after the mandatory rough crossing of Bass Strait, a perilous stretch of water that tested the constitution of travellers for generations. Jim Pugh, originally from Trafalgar in Victoria but Tasmanian by choice, spent several years on the island, carving a niche for himself as a professional footrunner and footballer. He was strong, broad-shouldered, blessed with an easy grin and a determination to make the most of his sporting abilities. Pugh made regular appearances at regional athletic gifts in Victoria and Tasmania, appearing in the final of Shepparton Gift, without capturing a title. But he carried himself with the athlete's confidence, and locals described his physique as 'straight as a rush'. Pugh's decision to play football with his adopted state gave him the ideal chance to distinguish himself; he was no longer lost in the deep talent pool of Victorian football. He played with the City club in Launceston, where he was regarded as one of the team's most consistent performers. His form justified his selection in the carnival team that joined the overnight train to Sydney on the evening of 4 August.

Germany's ambitions couldn't be contained or shamed by the growing outrage at its aggression in Europe. It declared war on France on 3 August. When Germany invaded Belgium, Britain responded. The little country's neutrality was a point of honour and interest to Britain. It insisted that Germany recognise Belgium's neutral status. But events were so advanced – and Germany's ambitions so clear – there was little doubt that Germany would ignore the ultimatum. At 12.30 pm on Wednesday, 5 August, Munro Ferguson was cabled news that the British Empire was at war with Germany. 'The Government is full of zeal and there is a cheerful disposition to discharge obligation and expedite preparations,' a resolute Munro Ferguson told London of Australia's reaction.

Half an hour after the cable's arrival, the New South Wales football team, led by Ralph Robertson, began its carnival campaign at the Sydney Cricket Ground against Queensland. Robertson was one of the first Australian sportsmen to join the Australian war effort. Three months after the carnival, he was in Rabaul (Papua New Guinea) as a member of the Australian Naval and Military Expeditionary Force that Britain asked to take over the wireless station in German New Guinea. At the Sydney Cricket Ground, though, he led New South Wales to a 77-point win. The host state turned out to be the surprise of the tournament, winning its first two games, which included defeating Tasmania, a state with a superior football pedigree.

On Thursday, Victoria took on Tasmania in what turned out to be a one-sided game. Sloss and Cooper performed well enough to be considered among Victoria's best, and Pugh stood out for Tasmania, but Victoria coasted. More one-sided games followed – South Australia thrashed Queensland, and New South Wales's easy win over Tasmania franked the game's improvement in the northerly state. One of the showpiece games was Victoria against Western Australia, which Victoria won by 14 points.

In the midst of this, a busy social program was rolled out to entertain the visitors and show off Sydney's natural charms. There were excursions to Middle Harbour, with the afternoon on the water, a smoke night, social, trips to the theatre, and a visit to the Hawkesbury River and Newport, by motor car from Manly. On several harbour trips, on bright, glittering days with just a teasing wind, Bruce Sloss conducted a musical chorus that featured Hughie James, with his deep, rich voice on bass, and Jack Cooper, among others. Bruce lent his tenor voice to some of the tunes too, reminding everyone that there was more to this group of men than just the game they played.

Victoria went through the carnival undefeated, winning five games and beating South Australia in the final, watched by 15,000 spectators. George Heinz, a rover with Geelong, was named the player of the carnival by the *Referee* newspaper. Heinz would change his name to Haines to avoid the anti-German sentiment that became prevalent at the onset of war. And then he enlisted for the Australian Imperial Force (AIF).

But overall, the carnival was a financial and strategic disaster. Poor attendance at some matches meant expenses were not covered. Losses were estimated to be £1000. Gate receipts were well down on takings from the Melbourne and Adelaide carnivals. If this was Sydney embracing Australian Rules, it was a hug without warmth or intent. The war's arrival had shifted the nation's – and Sydney's – focus to heavier matters than sport and interstate rivalries. If the Sydney carnival was the Australasian Football Council's best attempt to make football a national game, it too was a casualty of the Sarajevo assassination. One Melbourne correspondent put the international situation and the Sydney mindset together to explain the carnival's lack of success: '[W]ith the notification that war had been declared there was no spirit in Sydney people for sport today and especially for a sport of which they knew little and for which they cared less.' The footballers dispersed at the end of the carnival to return to their state-based leagues.

Some of them would be reunited two years later in London, where once again they would pull on their boots and put on an exhibition of Australian football's finest skills. They were brought together by the game they played, connected to a football fraternity that was a unique and binding network. It didn't matter which club they played for, or which state they represented; football marked them apart, as men who understood a certain language, initiated into the mysteries of the bouncing oval ball, adherents to a game that demanded a brand of athleticism that few other games did. And it was Australia's game. There was nothing quite like it anywhere else.

These players weren't best mates. Some had gone to school together but their lives had taken different routes before they found themselves back playing football. By 1916, they would be wearing the colours of their country, not their clubs. And, for a number of them, it would be the last game of football they would play. For the moment, though, as the nation mobilised in support of the Mother Country, such grim consequence was a half-formed and distant thought. But to those wise enough to recognise it, the message of the war's impact on sport was clear: the simple joy of kicking a football was about to be challenged by the expectation of young, fit men doing their national duty. Nothing – least of all football – would be the same again.

1

Where it Began

Each of the men who made up the teams that played Australian Rules football in London in 1916 had their own story. Some of the stories were hidden, parts were shared and the rest was just the routine of daily life. Only two things connected the men: their khaki uniform and a love of football. And such limited coincidences guaranteed that no two men shared the same history or circumstance. Often, their tales began in strange and unusual ways.

There was a pub called the Robert Burns within walking distance of Arthur Trotter's home in Melbourne's Fitzroy where he occasionally stopped, after he had a good day. And, as Arthur later admitted to a relative, Monday, 6 January 1913 was probably his best ever day. Trotter was a salesman for MacRobertson's, the confectionery company, and business was good. He had just returned from a fortnight's holiday over the Christmas and New Year. His first day back at work was always going to be lucrative, as he criss-crossed Melbourne, from Carlton and North Melbourne to Footscray and Yarraville, to pick up shops' Christmas takings. Trotter's driver brought him home to his pleasant six-room house, with a neat front garden and red-tiled roof, in George Street, around 8.30 pm. Trotter's wife, Beatrice, and five-year-old son Harry were waiting for him. They shared a late supper, and when Mrs Trotter went to bed, her husband stayed up to count the day's takings. As was his practice, Arthur Trotter would deliver the takings to his office the next morning. It was an arrangement that suited MacRobertson's and Trotter. Then Trotter joined his brother-in-law Albert Myers for a drink at the Robert Burns.

Trotter was in good spirits, and he exchanged a couple of pounds of silver for gold with the licensee's daughter. The men parted company after two drinks and Trotter walked back home. At around 11.30 pm, Arthur Trotter finally went to bed. His wife and son, tucked up in his cot in the same bedroom, were asleep. Trotter put the day's takings in a leather bag under his mattress before he climbed into bed.

Two hours later, the bedroom burst into light. Beatrice Trotter's eyes jerked open and she saw two men in the room, each of them holding revolvers, their faces masked. Her husband shouted, 'What's your game?' One of the burglars, tall, lean, menacing, said, 'Get up; we want your money.' Arthur Trotter denied there was any money but the burglars knew better. Trotter was defiant. 'I have only got my boss's money, and you won't get that,' he told them. Stirred by the din, Harry woke up and urged the men not to shoot his father. Beatrice pleaded with her husband to give the burglars the money. 'Don't shoot!' she shouted. One of them, shorter and quieter than the one holding the gun on Trotter, tried to reassure her she would not be harmed. Trotter weighed up the situation. One of the burglars was standing near his side of the bed, the other with a gun levelled at Beatrice. Arthur made a desperate decision and rushed at the burglar next to him. He flailed at the intruder, who took a calm step back and shot Trotter in the head. The bullet went through his left eye. He staggered to the wall, and then collapsed. The burglars lifted up the mattress on Trotter's side of the bed and took the £200 Trotter had stashed there. And while Mrs Trotter screamed, the pair ran off. Arthur Trotter was rushed to St Vincent's Hospital but the bullet had penetrated his brain. He died at 8.30 am on Tuesday, 7 January 1913.

Police were initially baffled at the crime. Mrs Trotter tried to help with identification but, because of their masks, she had little but their gruff voices to go on. She recalled the taller one wore a dark suit – perhaps navy or green – and a felt hat. But a description of the shorter one eluded her. The newspapers carried lurid speculation and no clues, until police got a breakthrough and charged Harold Thompson, a notorious low-level crook.

The case hinged on the emerging science of fingerprints. A print was found on a windowsill at the Trotters' house and it was sent around every state in search of a match. Police in Adelaide identified it as Thompson's print. Thompson vehemently denied he was a murderer. He wasn't even there, he claimed. The chief justice, Sir John Madden, presided over the trial and did his own inspection of the fingerprints, with a magnifying glass and his associate standing behind him, holding a candle. Despite the fingerprint experts' evidence, the jury didn't believe that the print on the windowsill and Thompson's print were identical. And, during the trial, Beatrice Trotter could not be sure it was the voice she had heard several months earlier. The jury took only four hours to find Thompson not guilty.

Thompson walked away and was greeted by a group of cheering supporters. His accomplice was never identified. But police were almost certain who else was there on the night and was probably the brains behind the burglary, a short, young hoodlum called Joseph Leslie Theodore Taylor – or Squizzy Taylor, as he was known around Melbourne's underworld. Taylor was only 24 when Trotter was murdered. In time, there would be plenty of other gruesome assaults, scams and murders that would be laid at Taylor's neat little feet before his criminal career ended with a bullet.

Arthur Trotter had lived with his brother's family for several years before he was married. Arthur's brother George was also a salesman, whose home was in Middle Park with his wife and five children, including their eldest son, Percy George Trotter. Percy was a footballer with Fitzroy, but not just any footballer: he was, by 1905, considered by some judges to be the finest player in the Victorian Football League (VFL). Percy Trotter played with Fitzroy in its golden era, when it strode across the League landscape with a swagger, and dashing Trotter was the quicksilver in its veins. The coaching guru Jack Worrall saw something explosive in Trotter's football: 'At a big circus show a performer is placed inside a cannon, and at a given signal is actually shot out of it. When I see Trotter roving for Fitzroy my thoughts turn to that fellow being shot out of the gun, for that's how Trotter comes out of the pack.'

Rod McGregor, a Carlton legend who became one of the first players to cross into the new radio medium, labelled Trotter the best player he saw during his career. To the Fitzroy fans, he was simply 'Beautiful Percy'. What made Trotter so good? He was quick and balanced. And, at a time when the game was still ponderous, prone to stopping and starting, Trotter kept the game flowing, with speed and skill. He also had the rare ability of being able to kick with both feet.

But perhaps his best asset was a football intelligence: he was a shrewd thinker with a sound instinct, so he avoided trouble for himself and created opportunities for others. He was a crowd favourite too, because he always played wearing Fitzroy's maroon cap. Everyone could spot him. And he believed in keeping the game simple. 'The one system that tells is unselfish play, judicious and fair use of weight, and a determination to get the ball and kick it again as far as often down the central as possible,' he explained.

Fitzroy won two flags in 1904–05 with Trotter, and only missed a third by two points in 1903 and again in 1906, this time by 49 points. Trotter played 109 games with Fitzroy and then crossed to Essendon, in the Association, for what was described as 'private business reasons'. What that meant was never clear. By then, however, the Trotter family was starting to struggle. In 1909, another uncle – William – died when he broke his neck after being thrown from a horse and cart. And then Trotter's father, George, became unwell.

The cause of his illness was not clear but his wife, Mary, had the awful task of having him committed to the Kew Asylum. George Trotter was 51, a desiccated figure with white hair and a drooping moustache that framed a mouth etched with unhappiness. George had lost an eye years earlier and his general health was poor. He was beset by business worries and was suicidal when he arrived at the asylum. 'Dejected. Delusion that he is unclean. Thinks he is lost. Suspicious about his food. Visceral melancholic,' the asylum admission report read. The conclusion was as categorical as it was hopeless: 'Diagnosis: senile dementia. Prognosis: Incurable.'

Three months after he was admitted, George was allowed home on trial leave but he was really no better. There was some concern about his heart but the overwhelming diagnosis was that he was mentally 'enfeebled'. 'Insane', the asylum supervisor, Walter Barker, declared. George Trotter lingered in this terrible limbo for another three months. Then, at 2.30 am on 14 September 1910, his heart gave up and he died. His wife remarried the next year, to Charles Schneider, who changed his name to Taylor after the war started.

Percy had already left Melbourne, ostensibly to play football with East Fremantle in Western Australia. But because he had never actually received a clearance from Fitzroy to play with Essendon, the VFL could not allow him to play for East Fremantle. It was a stand-off that East Fremantle blithely tried to ignore by playing Trotter anyway. That was until the other Western Australian clubs protested. It meant that Trotter stood out of football for a year, until the clearance came through and he could officially play for East Fremantle.

In the meantime, he had found work on the Fremantle docks as a 'lumper' or stevedore. He was there when he was told of his uncle Arthur's shocking murder and burglary. There was no secret about where his uncle kept his takings – even Percy knew. '[I]t was his custom to count at night the money he had received during the day, and to place it underneath the mattress of his bed. The bedroom stands back from the road, perhaps 35 feet, and between it and the footpath is a garden where a man might conceal himself,' Trotter explained. But for all of that, the murder remained unsolved.

George Foster Pearce was an abstemious man. He didn't like the carousing that he had seen in the South Australian farm belt where he had grown up. It turned him off alcohol for life. And Pearce only took up smoking when a doctor recommended it to help him deal with the stresses of being Australia's longest-serving Defence minister. 'My wife and I had always lived carefully and had never wasted our money on pleasure,' Pearce wrote, with a monkish self-discipline. Pearce's world view was founded on a deep loyalty to certain core ideas: the power of Labor MPs to improve the conditions of the working man and that Australia was its own man but an indivisible part of the British Empire family. What this meant in practice was an enduring commitment to the Labor cause and an unshakeable sense that Australia's achievements were also Britain's successes.

Pearce's Labor credentials were unmistakeable and bound up in his working life. He was a blacksmith's son, one of 11 children. He started work at just 11 and became a carpenter in Perth and then a prospector in the Western Australian goldfields. When he returned to Perth, he helped revive the Trades and Labour Council before entering parliament in 1901 at the same election as the future wartime prime minister Billy Hughes. Pearce's attitudes were formed early. And there were some things he saw that just didn't sit right with him. Watching out of the window of his home in the genteel Melbourne suburb of Windsor one Saturday afternoon in 1907, Pearce was struck by the number of young men making their way to watch St Kilda play football. Amid the large numbers of football fans, Pearce spotted a solitary figure walking against the tide. He was a man in khaki, a military uniform.

'He was buffeted from side to side of the footpath and had at last to take the road,' Pearce explained later. 'There was one of our defenders, endeavouring to do his duty to the country, and scarcely able to move along because of the number of citizens who were anxiously rushing to spend their leisure in a different occupation.' Pearce couldn't contain his aversion to what he had seen. As far as he was concerned, there wasn't a choice between defending your country and a devotion to sport. Your country came first. Always. That was where a man's loyalty should be. It was a choice in 1907 that seemed irrelevant or elusive to many, but it would grow more pressing, more intense, and finally more bitter each year for the next decade as war arrived and Australia's role in the conflict grew.

The epiphany for Pearce was the Japanese war with Russia in 1905. Up until then, he had shown scant interest in defence. But after Japan's victory, he pondered the Asian military threat to Australia and came to believe the nation needed to be prepared. Disdaining the charge of 'jingoist', Pearce went to some lengths to explain in 1907 that Australia was perfectly safe from a European threat but Asia was a different matter. 'Our White Australia legislation is so much waste paper unless we have rifles behind it and are prepared to back it up by force if necessary.'

Pearce's solution was compulsory military training for Australian males aged from 14 to 25. Pearce was still in Opposition when he raised the idea but he knew that the time young Australians spent training had to be at the expense of other activities. They had to give up something in the national interest, and if that was sport, particularly football, then so be it. It was just after 9 pm on Thursday, 7 November 1907, when Pearce rose to his feet in the federal parliament in Spring Street, Melbourne, to put his views to the country: '[W]hat a travesty it is on the name of sport to designate as sport the actions of those 30,000 or 40,000 people who stood around the football arena hooting and yelling all the afternoon! That is of no use to them, except, perhaps to exercise their lungs . . . Apparently, the only exercise he gets at football matches is that which enables him to extend his vocabulary and his lung capacity.'

Some of Pearce's Senate colleagues were supportive but there was no urgency to act on it. Pearce, though, had found his cause, and there was no turning back. In all his years in public life, he would never resile from the view that spectator sport was all well and good as long as it did not interfere with a man's duty to his country. And football, because of the masses who went, was the centrepiece of his argument: 'For every hundred youths who play football today, a hundred thousand look at them and "barrack", talk football, yell football, but never by any means kick a football . . . In putting in to force these compulsory [military training] provisions, we shall not be taking away from the youth of Australia anything that is worth anything to them. I do not say take every Saturday but to haul them off by force for a few Saturdays, if necessary from the football grounds and give them a few manly exercises on the military field, where they could be taught to square their shoulders and carry out military evolutions.'

Pearce's 'military evolutions' would take time before becoming law. It might have been the desire to establish a national defence that determined the adoption of compulsory military training, but it was forced on a community with a fervent commitment, especially in Victoria, to Australian Rules. Once most workers were given Saturday afternoons off from the late 1880s, the game's popularity grew. Suburban rivalries flourished. Other winter sports lost their influence. Football playing – and watching – crossed the divides of wealth, religion, education and gender. In 1910, Britain's Lord Kitchener was invited to provide a defence blueprint for Australia, and he rubber-stamped Pearce's plans for compulsory military service. There were many young men who had already booked their Saturday afternoon, and it wasn't for compulsory military training.

Pearce's program consisted of three grades of training: 12-year-olds joined the junior cadets; senior cadets were for the 14–18-year-olds; and those aged 18–26 became part of the Citizens Military Forces (CMF). Junior cadets were trained for a total of 90 hours a year at school. For senior cadets, the requirement was 64 hours a year, and for the 18–20-year-olds 16 all-day drills a year. Once they had reached the age of 20, the requirement was only an annual parade. There was also a punitive measure, for those who didn't observe their obligations. Absentees were fined, and serial offenders could, in Victoria, be sent to the lock-up at Fort Queenscliff.

Absentee numbers were often large – 120 were assembled in one hearing at the Essendon court in Melbourne in June 1914. There were some notable instances of footballers becoming caught up in the dilemma between training and playing on Saturday afternoons. Some even involved Pearce's Cabinet colleague, Frank Tudor, who was also Richmond Football Club president. Pearce was resolute and rebuffed Tudor's approach for a player's dispensation, and even those from then Attorney-General Billy Hughes. One Richmond player with family military connections, Percy Ellingsen, was a perennial no-show at training. He went to court four times, was fined, and even then failed to attend defaulters' parades. It was all too much for his relatives. His uncle George had to withdraw from a court of inquiry that he presided over when he learnt his nephew was facing a serious charge. Another former trainee was sentenced to 14 days' detention at Fort Queenscliff after admitting it was 'hard to pass the Collingwood football ground'.

The newspapers found the hard line difficult to stomach. 'It does not follow that because a boy dislikes drill he is lazy. On the contrary, he is probably a most energetic footballer. Still less is it an indication of dishonesty,' one paper pointed out. But Pearce was fortified by personal experience when he was a child, labouring on a South Australian farm. Given the choice between military training and toiling in the heat and dust, Pearce knew which way he would jump. 'I would have looked upon [training] as a God-send if, for one Saturday in the month, I could have been taken away from the eternal cow or the plough handle and given a chance on the parade ground,' he said. Pearce thought the criticism of the military training was 'puny and insignificant' but there were still murmurings of dissent, in peacetime.

Within five years, some of the same debates would be played out against the more devastating consequences of a world war. By then, Pearce was at Prime Minister Billy Hughes's right hand, as Australia's Defence minister. He not only drove a Defence bureaucracy that supported Australia's war effort, but he was also integral to the public urging for sportsmen around the nation to give up their games and enlist for the national good. By late 1914, Pearce was in no doubt that Australia must back the Empire with every available resource, especially manpower. There was no turning back once Australia committed to war. The nation owed it to the Empire.

George Barry's first appearance in court occurred in Perth on 29 September 1913. He was just 22, well dressed, described as a typist and quite certain that he had not defrauded anyone by passing off a cheque as a legitimate document. When the case came to trial 16 days later, police claimed Barry tried to obtain money under false pretences. There were four charges, but for the total amount of just five pounds and two shillings. The list of charges arose from Barry visiting a storekeeper, and then a butcher and another store (run by the butcher's son) trying to pass off a cheque in exchange for goods. What added a level of premeditation to it all was that Barry turned up at one shop wearing a railway uniform and told the shopkeeper he was a guard on the government railway who had recently been transferred from Fremantle to Perth. It was at this third shop where the cheque was accepted and some change returned to Barry. Perhaps the success convinced Barry to keep trying, and he successfully tried the same ploy to buy pickled pork and a bottle of pickles at a ham and beef shop. But a further attempt to spend a cheque with a milkman failed when the milkman didn't have any change. Police were called, and the young man with the dark brown hair and wild blue eyes was charged. Barry was put on remand for eight days and continued to protest his innocence. He said he didn't know much about the law but he did have witnesses to support his side of the story.

Barry's connection with football was not conventional. He was born in Croydon, Queensland, and came to football after the family moved to Western Australia. But Barry became an umpire, not a player, at a time when only the brave took on the official's role. And it is entirely feasible that George Barry was temperamentally unsuited to the job. Umpires across the country were finding themselves firmly in the eye line of angry fans, many of whom were keen to get some physical redress for the umpire's perceived failings and biases.

The thorny issue of player payments potentially tilting the motivations for winning and losing for some less than honourable players only compounded the pressure on umpires. Were umpires involved in the scams? Was it possible that umpires were actually part of sinister schemes to fix games? Inevitably, fans thought the worst. Whistle work had rarely been so contentious. The violence directed towards umpires reached a low point when an inexperienced umpire was hit on the head by a stone hurled from the crowd at a VFL match in 1914. Not surprisingly, the umpire lost control of the match and it soon became a gruesome brawl.

The umpires were not even safe from the players. Two Victorian Junior Football Association players assaulted experienced umpire Edward Watt in separate games in 1915. In one instance, the Williamstown player was suspended until the end of 1916. But these outbreaks did not silence the public criticism levelled against umpires. Instead, the post-match debate about umpiring standards became an integral part of the press commentary on matches. 'It is being pointed out that there are several field umpires under the auspices of the VJFA not quite competent to take [charge] of the games,' one Melbourne journalist noted, in one of the more restrained critiques. Players got off lightly in comparison.

The criticism was symptomatic of the wider struggle umpires had in order to maintain any authority, especially when players would often exact a malicious toll on their opponents in a manner that provoked the crowds and drew some hostile criticism. 'No one objects to a strenuous game, but tripping, punching, elbowing, jumping on to a man's back are becoming the leading features of what should be a fine, manly sport,' one newspaper noted. The umpiring task was already difficult: the ground was larger than that used for other games, there were more players on the field at any one time, each game lasted a long time and, unlike soccer, there was no offside rule.

Despite all of that, Barry embarked on the role with youthful enthusiasm. He started as a 20-year-old in Geraldton, when he was a clerk in the local council. The local league decided to give him a trial in a scratch match in May 1911, and although it was ostensibly to test him against another candidate to become the league's umpire, Barry and the other candidate both finished up being appointed. Barry claimed that he learnt the rules from a man who was considered the pre-eminent umpire in the country, Ivo Crapp.

The title 'Prince of Umpires' was conferred on Crapp after 25 years' umpiring in every state. Crapp played a season with Carlton before he started his umpiring career. Even after he settled in Western Australia in 1906, he was frequently called to umpire interstate finals or at the 1914 carnival. Crapp was a tall man, and his height gave him some presence on the field, but he admitted years later to struggling with his own problems when he began:

> Umpiring my first few games according to the letter of the book, I made an unholy mess of things. Pals and critics told me my display was rotten. Disappointed and worried, I ripped the rule book to pieces and scattered its pages to the wind. I decided to handle matches, taking common sense views and not caring for the consequences. I was never interfered with by officials, nor would I have tolerated it.

It would have been wise advice to another novice umpire but it seems George Barry either failed to heed it or was never given such insights. Barry's umpiring career was blighted by trying to impose too much control on his matches. And the public scrutiny was relentless.

One letter-writer to *The Geraldton Guardian*, going by the nom de plume of 'Looker On', was outraged at the abuse Barry endured in one match:

> Why? Simply because some of the barrackers never had a rule book in their hands all their life, and some of them have never studied the points of the game. Now, I think it is not

fair for an umpire of Barry's class to have to submit to such abuse. To my mind, he is one of the best umpires that has ever umpired a match in this town.

Such support was not enough to keep Barry at Geraldton. He looked for other opportunities, and found them in the Goomalling Football Association, a three-team competition south-west of Perth. The Association was only eight years old and was keen on finding players, and an official umpire. Barry made a favourable impression, especially on his strict interpretations of the rules, but that soon became a problem because his judgements were considered too legalistic and too frequent. Consequently, the matches lacked flow and momentum. He was whistle-happy, although the early reports were good. 'There is no doubt about his impartiality,' the local paper said. 'He did not please everyone, but it is the general opinion that the Goomalling Association are to be congratulated on securing his services for the season 1912.'

Within a month, there were signs that all was not well. He turned up ten minutes late for a match, and the teams started without him, trying to umpire themselves. Once Barry arrived, his decisions were erratic, although his performance improved as the game wore on. Barry appeared to be feeling the pressure. He approached a local reporter to explain the problem he was having with players abusing him. The reporter backed Barry and reminded the players in his football column that 'for the sake of football they [players] should refrain from using bad language'. The column also urged that a report should be made to the Association about the poor behaviour towards the umpire.

Barry followed the advice and complained about the abuse immediately after the next game, when the situation had not improved. But the Association executive was not particularly keen on hearing about his problems, unless he could identify his abusers. Barry knew who some of them were. One prominent local resident had called him over during one match and offered him a pair of binoculars, but such droll witticisms were the least of Barry's problems. It was the scathing assessments from people he didn't know that were the problem. Barry continued to complain, telling the Association that he didn't feel comfortable about spectators encroaching onto the ground. By September, it was clear that whatever goodwill Barry had from the Association and fans was gone. The local paper had turned against him, with a snide assessment of his latest performance: 'If Barry wishes a recommendation as an inconsistent umpire, let him apply to the Goomalling Football Association. This is voicing the opinion of friends and opponents alike.'

Barry was already exploring other options. He appeared as the umpire in a Perth junior football match, but the criticisms followed him, as he was once again ticked off for his overuse of his whistle. And then came the arrest.

There is no way of being sure what happened next. It seems, however, that Barry collapsed under the combined strain of his criminal charges and perhaps the constant criticisms of his umpiring. Barry read the newspapers; he expressed his distaste at abuse to reporters and he might even have posed as 'Looker On', the letter-writer in Geraldton. Barry developed an unstable state of mind. On 29 October 1913, he was moved from Fremantle Prison, where he was on remand, to the Claremont Mental Asylum. The facility was only ten years old, and quickly acquiring a retinue of long-stay patients. It was built on a hilltop, with an impressive vista that included sights of Perth and the Indian Ocean, but it soon became clear that the new hospital was not much better than its predecessor, the crumbling and horrific Fremantle Lunatic Asylum.

Barry was in a terrible, frail state. Despite his umpiring, he had little physical conditioning. He looked stunned, his bearded face dominated by a fixed stare that suggested a man struggling to keep control. But it was his mental condition that was most alarming. He was wild and erratic, unable to hold a conversation. Barry's doctors noted that he lacked an understanding of what had happened to him and the circumstances he was in. He had tried to commit suicide in Fremantle Prison by stripping himself in his cell and burning his clothes. When doctors asked him what happened, he couldn't remember. He gave evasive answers, and all the time there was a restlessness to him, a fathomless confusion and aimless wandering. He was put under special observation. Barry remained in this awful condition for almost two months. His treatment is not documented, but, by Christmas 1913, he was improving, becoming more lucid and seemingly physically stronger. His improvement continued into the New Year, and he was discharged from Claremont on 7 February 1914 and returned to prison. A month later, he was back in court to finally face the fraud charges.

Barry's defence was spirited, and his lawyer applied for a dismissal of the case because there was no evidence that Barry knew the cheques were fraudulent. The judge disagreed. When Barry gave evidence, he recounted a tale of a young man struggling to cope with the pressure of studying to become a council health inspector, juggling all the required reading with a passion for astronomy. He had suffered sunstroke and its effects had lasted several weeks. He couldn't sleep and was stricken with headaches. It was true that he had worked for the railways but he couldn't explain why he was wearing the railway uniform when he passed one of the cheques. He even umpired the day after passing a cheque. Barry also revealed he was engaged before he became unwell. A doctor Barry consulted about his sleeplessness and headaches admitted there had been something 'strange' in Barry's manner and he didn't seem mentally acute. However, there was a hole in the middle of the case, and it was Barry's apparent lack of knowledge about the events surrounding the cheques. The witnesses he claimed to have didn't eventuate.

'Did the actions of the accused on the day of the alleged offence suggest insanity?' Mr Justice Burnside asked the jury in his summing up. 'It was to be regretted that it had not been possible to give [the jury] a greater degree of assistance to enable them to say with more certainty what was the state of the accused's mind in July.' One doctor had added that if Barry's state of mind in July when he was umpiring was anywhere near what it was when he had diagnosed him in October, he could not have been in control of a football match. It went some way perhaps towards explaining Barry's on-field performances.

The jury did not deliberate for long and acquitted Barry on the grounds of insanity. But the drama did not end there; Justice Burnside could not, by law, allow Barry back into the community if he was acquitted because of insanity. Burnside noted the legislation was appropriate for those who remained 'insane' after their trial but Barry had apparently suffered a bout of temporary insanity. Barry's case showed the legislation was out of date. The only way to deal with it was to send Barry back to remand until he could secure a dispensation that would enable him to walk free.

It was only a matter of days before Barry was released. Yet liberty had its own problems and Barry found himself back in court two weeks later. This time, it was for stealing a hat and a tie from a gentleman's outfitters. Barry tried to explain that since he left the asylum his mind had wandered and he had a bicycle accident that compounded the problem. The magistrate, Mr A.S. Roe, took an unforgiving line. 'You are no more mad than I am!' he told Barry and promptly sentenced him to six months in jail. Barry pleaded for a lighter sentence but Roe was not to be moved.

Then the matter started to get complicated. A furious fortnight of lobbying ensued – letters were sent to the attorney-general, the magistrate on the case, the head of the prison and the speaker of the Western Australian Parliament to try to get

Barry an early release. Barry wrote in his own cause, to the attorney-general, Mr Thomas Walker, a rambling, four-page submission that revealed some of the young man's past and difficult circumstances. In handwriting that became progressively smaller and less legible, Barry explained he had six years of education at a Christian Brothers school, knew how to use shorthand and was a trained lifeguard. He had been hit on the head in an accident some years earlier and was in hospital for some months, which Barry implied was perhaps responsible for his inability to remember what he had done. He did, however, remember after his release the first time being at his family's farm, near Sandstone, when his only brother was fatally kicked in the head by a horse. The grief of the loss – and the responsibility he had to undertake to run a property with 220 sheep and 150 pigs – had conspired to prevent him behaving appropriately and, according to Barry's argument, helped land him back in jail a second time. '[I] am only 23 and the youngest prisoner here and I feel my position very much, especially as I lie in my cell, thinking of my good old parents,' Barry wrote.

His mother had been writing assiduously to the authorities too, in the hope that there would be some mercy for the young man. The flint-hearted magistrate Roe remained unshakeable. 'He made no mention whatever of the farm or death of his brother or indeed of any of the facts related in his letter [to the Attorney-General],' Roe said. 'His whole actions at the time of the stealing showed that he knows perfectly well what he was doing.'

But Roe was in the minority. The speaker of the Western Australian Parliament, Labor's Frank Troy, wrote on behalf of Barry's parents asking for Mr Walker to remit Barry's sentence: '. . . I do not think [he] has criminal inclinations but whom I feel is somewhat weak in decision and character'. The safety net for Troy's plea was that Mrs Barry had arranged for George to move to Sydney, where he was going to stay with his brother.

The apparent contradiction between George Barry's claim that he had seen his only brother die at the family farm and the existence of a brother in Sydney offering refuge did not trouble the attorney-general. He approved the remission and sent George Barry on his way.

But there was one final wrinkle: George Barry, after all of that, did not want to go. A prison official wrote to the attorney-general's office, 'It is a great pity we were not consulted, the prisoner flatly and absolutely refused to be shipped out of the state and wished his mother and others would mind their own business.' George Barry was clearly an unpredictable man because he managed to make it onto the ship to Sydney. Perhaps he realised then that there was something appealing about leaving his complicated past behind. With one exception – umpiring. George Barry rather fancied a return to the whistle.

Although Lady Helen Munro Ferguson initially stayed in Sydney while her husband conducted the Empire's wartime business in Melbourne, she was quick to communicate her thoughts to the new Australian recruits who were gathering at the Broadmeadows training camp on Melbourne's outskirts, preparing to join the Allied army in Europe. 'A warm welcome awaits you in England, where a strong committee has been formed to look after the interests and supply the needs of the Australian soldiers of the King,' she told the troops in a message in September 1914. 'You are playing the game. Australia is proud of you, and is confident that by your conduct at the front you will do your part in upholding the just cause, the honour of the Empire, and the reputation of the Australian Imperial Forces.'

'Playing the game' was an innocent shorthand for what was ahead. It was a familiar phrase that resonated with thousands of young men who had enlisted with good intentions but a naive understanding of the nature of the looming conflict. Many of them were sportsmen who implicitly understood the idea of 'playing the game'. The slogan set out to not only connect all those men with a familiar idea but also diminish the personal threat of war. It could only resonate with a nation that had yet to experience the wholesale carnage of a world conflict. It was, in its way, a casually brutal way of selling an idea to an audience who felt an instant connection to its spirit.

And yet there was a subtle truth to it. The official Australian war correspondent, Charles Bean, spent the war up close with his countrymen and concluded some years later, 'All the adventurous roving natures that could not stay away, whatever their duties and their ties; all those who plunged heads down in to war, reckless of anything else, because it was a game to be played and they were players by nature . . .' Australia was indeed a nation of players. It had hundreds of players and thousands of spectators. They had an understanding of the random nature of a contest, and all its risks and rewards. There were practical reasons for this sporting bounty: the climate suited outdoor activities; there were large open spaces; transport was effective; leisure time was growing; and the facilities, by and large, were suitable for the athletes and comfortable for the spectators.

There was also, by the outbreak of war, an emerging view that sport prepared men for war. Their training and playing not only laid the groundwork for the physical rigours of battle, it also helped them understand what was required of them during a conflict. That, at least, was the theory, already taking on the power of Holy Writ. 'What is the good of games if they do not provide a training ground for the sterner battles in our lives,' one newspaper asked. 'If they do not give us men whose hands they have taught to war and the fingers to fight, then it would be better that we blotted them out from [our] daily lives altogether . . .'

The companion view to this, from an overseas perspective, was that the Australian soldier's exposure to sport, a sunny climate and a robust diet from the nation's rich agricultural bounty turned him into a remarkable physical specimen that was the ideal for some kind of fighting machine. Perhaps the Digger was actually healthier than the Tommy. He might well have been a tougher fighter than Johnny Turk or any Fritz who emerged from some waterlogged trench, but it was, mostly, a myth. And over the years it would take on a kind of nationalistic shorthand that was as resilient as it was wrong-headed. The first Australian troops were anything but professionally trained and conflict-ready. They were amateurs, enthusiasts and adventurers in the main, some of whom just happened to be among the best sportsmen in the country.

There were, however, class differences about the purpose of sport. The middle class, with the smell of the Empire still in their nostrils, saw sport as an instrument to impart the important values of life. To be a 'good sport' had meaning. You were fair, loyal and considerate. Sport taught you how to endure defeat graciously and accept victory with humility. It was also an activity best done for free. Amateur sport was the bastion of virtue. Professional sport was all well and good, but it was open to corruption, especially in a moral sense, because money was involved. How could you trust a footballer who was paid? If he accepted money to play, he could, in theory, accept money to help determine the result. More importantly, being paid to play meant it was harder for men to give it up and do their national duty. Money was the chain that tied sportsmen to their game. Without it, they were free to abandon recreation for higher purposes.

But the working class saw sport in its most fundamental form, as a physical contest, a piece of raw entertainment, an opportunity – through gambling or being paid to play – to escape the working-class travails. How else would a labourer find some respite from the drudgery of his life? This was escapism, pure and simple, but valuable nonetheless. Football on Saturday afternoons was an ideal way to let go of the working week, especially supporting what was an entirely 'local' game.

Elements of this class division were reinforced in the public school system. Sports lessons for character development were integral to several schools with strong links to the English public school model, such as Wesley in Melbourne and Sydney Grammar, where sport also helped drive enrolments.

As the war progressed, the divisions in sport – and particularly in football – came to exemplify the community divisions about the war itself, and how best to do one's duty. The amateurs – the athletes, the rugby and tennis players – fancied themselves as the true patriots and disdained professional sportsmen, who, by continuing to play for a wage, placed money above their country. The professionals, understandably, claimed that they were fulfilling a need for entertainment in the community. The polarities of the argument were regularly paraded in a range of newspapers and in public meetings across the country, but it was less of a problem among sportsmen themselves.

The collegiality of sport, and indeed the extensive football network that branched across Victoria, South Australia, Western Australia and Tasmania, overrode any lingering misgivings about who played for money, who stayed and who went. They were, after all, sportsmen together. Enlisting didn't change that happy bond. For most sportsmen, it wasn't a choice between playing sport and doing their national duty, as Senator Pearce had tried to frame it seven years earlier when arguing for compulsory military service. They hoped – and then saw the evidence to confirm their optimism – they could enlist and still play sport while they were in uniform.

The army was happy to enable them to continue to play sport because it recognised its value to the military effort, not just from a morale and physical point of view but also as a means of filling in time between some of the dull routines of soldiering. It was true in the British Army, where sport was an integral part of the military culture by 1914, and it held true for Australian troops too. The one element that bridged sport and the military was that they were both about men. Sport was, in 1914, a largely male pursuit. And the army was an institution completely and uncompromisingly designed for men. It was no surprise that sport and the male networks that went with it translated seamlessly into the AIF.

The Martins, of Dunolly, Creswick and St Kilda, were a well-connected family whose network of influence extended from the Victorian government deep into Melbourne's medical fraternity. Patriarch Irvin Martin was sheriff of Victoria, after entering the public service at 19. He spent his career with the Crown Law department, which included a long stint as court clerk at Bendigo. He was a stern and assured figure. When Martin was given the sheriff's job in 1905, he was described as an 'officer of the first class'. His salary was an exceptional £540 a year.

This skein of service ran through the Martin family tapestry. Irvin's brother David was secretary of the Board of Public Works, while their sister Annie was married to a state government member of legislative council George Godfrey. The Godfreys had four children – one of whom was the government medical officer, two were Melbourne solicitors and one, a daughter, was married to a local GP. It was an environment where the family members were, in due course, expected to take up a privileged place, either in medicine, the law or public service. Irvin and his wife, Mary, had four sons and a daughter. Stanley Carlton, the youngest son, had been set for a medical career like his cousins. To prepare him for the opportunities his family anticipated would come his way, Stan Martin was sent to Wesley College in 1902. Martin rubbed shoulders with the sons of families with similar pedigrees, but the early signs for Stan's academic career were not promising. The young Martin seemed more interested in sport than study. He was an enthusiastic swimmer and diver at Wesley, but his finest school achievement was on the football field.

Stan Martin won his colours for football in 1905 and three years later was the First XVIII's vice captain. Wesley's long-serving football coach Harold Stewart gushed in the *Wesley College Chronicle* that Martin was 'a brilliant footballer . . . plenty of resource; fine long kick and mark; turns quickly and dodges cleverly. Has supported his Captain (H. Carter) well, being very assiduous in training.' This was not some passing recreational adjunct to the scholar's life; Wesley placed a high value on sport, and the senior football team took part in a vigorous public schools sports competition. Some of the finest athletes of the time were in those public school teams, so Martin's football achievements went some way to covering his less than stellar academic performance.

The Wesley football team was the benchmark for three years, winning the public schools championships in 1907, 1908 and 1909, defeating Scotch, Geelong, Melbourne Grammar, Xavier and Geelong College during the five-game season. At the school's 1908 champion team dinner, Martin heard the former Wesley president and missionary Rev. Dr E.I. Watkin claim that the work of 'a great Public School was not complete unless due attention was given to manly sport, and to the lessons which might be derived therefrom'. In a commentary that was prescient – and testament to the school's deep connections to the notions of Empire and sacrifice – Dr Watkin continued, 'As they strode on the football field or the river, so it might be that in their future they would have to fight for the motherland, their King and the Commonwealth.' Dr Watkin added that he felt the spirit of rivalry and competition would stand them in good stead and that 'whenever Australia needed them the old boys of the Australian Public Schools, and especially those who had taken their part in the games, would be side by side upholding the honour of those schools and of their land'. Cheers rang out through the school dining hall.

The words were steeped in the English public school model, packaged up for an Antipodean audience; the boys of Wesley would do their duty on the playing fields and, as it turned out, on the Turkish beaches and Western Front trenches in the years to come. This was the notion of muscular Christianity at its finest – the notion that physical effort enhanced a man's moral fibre and Christian commitment. The playing fields would develop the robust qualities of self-sacrifice, national duty, teamwork, loyalty and courage that were the hallmarks of the decent modern man. For those in the audience, there was no doubt where their duty lay.

Yet it all seemed a long way from the carefree nature of schoolboy football, where Stan Martin displayed his skills. Here was a loose-limbed young man, blessed with dash and poise on the football field, and ideally suited to be a winger, that outside runner, with his running drop kick that sent the football on a flawless, rotating arc into the forward line. Football was where Martin could best express himself. His talent was rewarded in his final year at Wesley, when the college made him captain of the school team. Wesley won the public school championship again, without losing a match.

The Martins lived in St Kilda, and it had made sense for Stan to apply to join the local team when he opted to continue his football after leaving Wesley. He had sent off his paperwork before the start of the 1909 season and played with St Kilda in several practice matches. But some of Martin's football mates from Wesley had gone on to University and lined up for the University football team. Martin liked the idea and turned up at the Uni club, keen to play. It sparked a minor kerfuffle when the club lodged its papers with the VFL, because Martin was still registered with St Kilda. The issue could only be resolved if St Kilda withdrew its own registration. If not, Martin would have to stand aside for the season, while University applied for him to play in 1910. In the end, the Saints acceded to the University request and Martin made his senior debut in 1909 for the Students against South Melbourne. University lost by 20 points but Martin earned some positive reviews for keeping his opponent on the wing quiet, while displaying some of his skills in bad conditions.

Stan Martin's footy career was up and running. He would play more than 60 games with the Students before he enlisted. His first season with University coincided with the club's second season of VFL. It joined the expanded competition – along with Richmond – in 1908 after a series of dominant seasons in the Metropolitan Junior Football Association (MJFA, later the Victorian Amateur Football Association). The Juniors were an amateur league, and University remained an amateur club, which made it something of a novelty in the VFL. Melbourne, which was under the administration of the Melbourne Cricket Club (MCC), shared University's abhorrence of player payments after the VFL formally approved the arrangements in 1911.

Martin was happy enough to give up being paid to play football, as long as he could play with University. But being a student was part of the deal, so Martin enrolled in medicine at the University of Melbourne. It proved to be an ill-starred attempt. He was a reluctant scholar, a teenager more likely to stare out the window at the nearby oval than grapple with a biology text. In December 1910, Martin sat examinations in the requisite medicine subjects natural philosophy, chemistry and biology, and failed all of them. He sat them again in 1911 and failed again. And in 1912. And again in 1913, all of them failures. In 1914, Martin changed tack and enrolled in dentistry. The result was different but really no better; he was absent in his four subjects and no mark was recorded. It was, by any account, a dreadful record. It points to a man carrying the burden of family expectation but having neither the inclination nor the ability to achieve it. Who could blame him? Stan Martin was having a fine time playing football with many of his mates. Football, not medicine, dentistry or the public service, offered Stan Martin what he was looking for.

The allure was partly driven by the familiarity of the young men around him, because many public schoolboys moved seamlessly on to University for their professional training and qualifications. Martin's academic record never came close to many of those young men he played alongside and he would never return to medicine or dentistry, or indeed university.

2

The Believers

The footballers returned to their state leagues after the Sydney carnival in August 1914 to resume the competition for local honours. But no matter how much they might have wanted their sporting life to be normal, the war was starting to shift how the game was seen and what role the players would take in the looming conflict.

Just four weeks after war was officially declared, most football competitions started their finals series to establish which team would claim the 1914 premiership. Bruce Sloss was in the South Melbourne team contending for the flag. Carlton, one of the strongest teams of the era, finished on top of the VFL ladder and had a right to be considered flag favourites. But South Melbourne, which finished second after the home and away season, had beaten Carlton in a wet preliminary final, setting up an intriguing contest between them for the following week.

A light shower of rain ushered in the start of the grand final before more than 30,000 spectators at the Melbourne Cricket Ground (MCG). Sloss was named on a half-forward flank and within the first minute kicked the opening goal from an acute angle to set South on its way. The match was a prickly affair to begin with, and the players traded bumps in a fierce contest.

Carlton, though, seemed more assured in their ball-handling and created more opportunities for scoring. But it was South who scored again, and once more it was Sloss, with an expert place kick, who kicked his team's second goal to give them a two-point lead going into quarter-time.

South had the wind in the first quarter, so Carlton took full advantage when its turn came, kicking three goals and five behinds in the second term while keeping South scoreless. It proved to be the decisive quarter. Beaten in the centre and under constant pressure in defence, South could not make any inroads into its forward line, and its key players started to fumble under pressure. At half-time, Carlton led by 21 points and South looked 'hopelessly beaten', one observer wrote.

South emerged transformed after the long break and started to show the finesse and drive that distinguished its best football. But once again their forwards, including Sloss, sprayed the ball in front of goal and squandered their momentum by kicking a solitary goal and six careless behinds. Carlton was held scoreless but, for all South's effort, it was still nine points behind going into the final quarter. Carlton had the wind and looked to have its nose in front. Once again, it was Sloss who helped create opportunities – winning the ball and finding teammates or doing it himself – but South, again, could not convert. Instead, Carlton scored a goal, before South managed to reply. With ten minutes left, there was still only seven points between the two teams. The match ebbed and flowed in the final minutes, neither side able to score as error-prone forwards struggled to penetrate grim defence. In the final scramble for a score, South managed a point, which turned out to be the last score of the match. Carlton was premiers for the fourth time, by a solitary kick. In the final quarter, Sloss did the work 'of three men', the South Melbourne paper noted, but it was not enough to lift his team to the flag.

Sloss's grand final performance surprised no one. He was one of the outstanding players in the competition. But he didn't acquire that reputation from blasé displays of his extensive skills. Bruce Sloss attached a value to hard training and believed it made him a better footballer. This was not a man cosseted by privilege and entitlement. Bruce Moses Farquhar Sloss worked hard for everything, because he was focused on building something lasting from the ashes of poverty and tragedy that beset his family. Together, the Slosses were a mixture of the brave and the eccentric, good-hearted and religious, and devoted to one another. There were eight children – five boys and three girls – all with family pet names, and some of them even having separate names for each other as well. It could have been confusing but somehow it all made sense. It was a unity forged in hardship and continually tested by life's circumstance. Some families would have fractured under the strain, but the Slosses held firm.

James and Christina Sloss started their family in a hamlet called Naringalingalook, between Numurkah and Shepparton in Victoria. James Sloss ran a farm with a collection of stray animals, including a hen with a broken leg called Limpy, a pig and a selection of horses. Their firstborn, a girl, carried her mother's name Christina, but was known within the family as Tullie. She had the boldness of the eldest, the willingness to take risks and the determination to chart her own path. Tullie never settled, always a restless wanderer with a zest for adventure and the exotic. She was lean, often stern, but when she smiled, her serious demeanour disappeared. Bruce enjoyed Tullie's no-nonsense approach. Her astringent worldliness was a contrast to his more generous approach, and he looked to Tullie for guidance and, on occasions, for her approval.

Tullie found herself in unique situations but these weren't the fancies of a teenage girl. Her life was a compelling saga, with enough drama for two lifetimes. It started in the paddocks at home when Tullie was a girl. She suspected bushranger Ned Kelly had taken one of her father's horses when a strange thoroughbred, on the verge of exhaustion, was found on the Sloss farm. Tullie reasoned that the Kellys were active nearby and had exchanged their tired horse for a fresh one in the Slosses' care. Ned's mother, Ellen, even turned up at Tullie's school, looking for money. 'I opened the door to her. All I can remember now is that she was very old, wrinkled and dirty and the papers telling of her arrest called her "an old hag",' Tullie wrote in her diary, compiled years after the event.

Tullie's place in the family became more important after the Slosses decided to move to Melbourne. Tullie didn't like leaving the country; it tore at her love for nature, her pets and the trees that surrounded their home. 'I have wandered over many parts of the earth and have seen many, many kinds of trees since but still think the lonely gums rising like sentinels on the Australian hills are the most wonderful in the world,' she wrote, some years later. The Slosses rented out their farm but, in what Tullie believed was the first of a series of bad omens, they missed their morning train that was to take them all to Melbourne and had to wait until the afternoon for the next one. Christina was heavily pregnant, and the next morning Roy was born in a hotel in Flinders Street.

The next few years saw the Slosses living at a series of addresses, until they finally settled in a house with an adjoining stable in Carlisle Street, Balaclava, in 1890. Bruce was still a baby, his older brother Roy still a toddler. It was a brisk autumn night, and all the children were asleep when a fire started that rushed through the house. Just after midnight, Tullie, aged 15, felt the flames licking at her bed and woke to see the room full of billowing smoke. Firemen were already there, trying to get all the children out. Tullie struggled her way through the burning house to the street, where her mother was holding Bruce. But Roy was nowhere to be found. Tullie decided to go back for her baby brother. She found Roy, still in his bed, and grabbed him just as a fireman shouted for her to run for it. One of the walls was falling. Tullie dashed for the street and jumped clear just as the wall collapsed. She had only singed her hair. Roy was safe.

The loss of the property was a brutal blow but worse was to come. The house was rebuilt for the family and then, near dawn on 9 June 1890, James Sloss told his wife that he smelt gas in the parlour. James went to investigate and decided to light a match to find out where the gas leak came from. The explosion lifted the roof off, and the brick wall that separated the house from the shop at the front of the street collapsed on Sloss. The blast knocked down three of the children, sheltering in the hall. Tullie was lifted off her bed and onto the floor. Sloss struggled to his feet from under a pile of bricks and in the chaos managed to put out the flames that had sparked into life. Bystanders came to lend a hand. Sloss was taken over the road to the chemist and given some treatment for his injuries, but they were more severe than anyone thought. He died a few weeks later.

The move to Melbourne had been a disaster. Tullie believed her father always regretted it. James was not a worldly man and found the city full of sharp practices. 'When tired and weary how many times have I heard Daddy say how he longed to be back at Naringalingalook,' Tullie wrote. 'He soon learned that city men were not to be trusted as were his simple country companions . . . So he lost everything . . .'

The rebuilt house wasn't insured, and Christina moved the family on. Tullie left school and got a job away from home as a live-in governess. Her mother and sister Biddy tried to support the rest of the family by sewing, but it was hard work with small returns. Tullie came back home for Christmas to a house barely able to celebrate the festivities. She was distraught at how hard her family's life had become. 'Home to Christmas – minus its spirit – no tree – no gifts – any stockings except those with holes in. Home to a Christmas with small children crying to have their stockings hung up, and the tired voice of the mother saying there was nothing to put in them, not a penny even,'

Tullie wrote. The younger children, including Bruce, found it hardest. '"But Father Christmas will put something in them [stockings]," Bruce calls back, sobbing to [his mother].' Tullie vowed she would help:

> So that they should go to bed quietly I told them I would hang their stockings for them. I did and went to bed leaving over-tired Mother at midnight still sewing . . . this was the only time in my life that I doubted in God. Where was He that night when the widowed Mother needed not only toys but food for the stocking?

To question her faith was a profound moment in Tullie's life. The Slosses had been regular churchgoers in the country and joined the Malvern Presbyterian Church in Melbourne, presided over by the Scotsman Donald Macrae Stewart, who would later become an army chaplain. Bruce was an active member of the church, where he taught in the Young Men's Bible Class and was part of the church's cricket team. The church provided the family with some comfort in moments of despair, but even Tullie felt its limits.

Bruce started his football career with Essendon in 1907 but managed only three games before moving to Brighton the following season. He was a stand-out recruit and was selected to represent the Victorian Football Association (VFA) team against its South Australian counterparts in Adelaide in 1909. Tullie was living with a family in Mount Pleasant, South Australia, at the time and went to Adelaide to see him. She was impressed that he played with a damaged toe, after he lost a nail kicking a goal. 'The grit of the boy!' she said. South Australia won by 19 points but Sloss was named as one of Victoria's best players.

Tullie's real message to her brother was delivered on the Sunday after the game. Bruce and his teammates were to be entertained by several Adelaide families later in the day. Tullie reminded him that he should try to get to church later that evening. 'You freak!' Bruce said. 'How can I get away from all the boys? Can't possibly do it tonight.' Bruce started to leave, but Tullie had one more card to play. 'Mr Stewart [the Malvern reverend] would like to think of you being there, Bruce,' she said. Sloss left and called at his sister's hotel later that day. They went off to church together. 'I shall always remember him as he stood beside me and hear his lovely voice singing the hymn "Christ will hold me fast". Church over, he again rejoined his mates,' Tullie wrote.

Bruce might have taken life seriously but he was not without humour. Despite the grinding difficulties of his upbringing, he was remarkably genial and often playful. There were family photographs in the Slosses' home of a young Bruce in a series of mannered comic poses, including one image where he stood in a group, holding an alarm clock, wearing a cap at a rakish angle, in front of a tent carrying a sign saying 'Babes in the Woods'. His family revelled in his sense of fun, relying on Sloss's comic turns at family events and dinners to keep them entertained. If he wasn't doing some kind of act, he was singing.

And he had a long-time girlfriend, Gladys Hamilton, who became his fiancée. To Bruce, she was always 'Glad'. They met at church when they were teenagers and romance flourished. Gladys was a striking looking woman, and Bruce, with his fair hair and blue eyes, helped complete a handsome couple. Gladys's father, Arthur, was a builder and the couple had asked him to build their home on a block they had bought in Malvern. Bruce and Gladys agreed that they would be married and then move in to the completed house. It was the kind of plan thousands of young couples made every day.

Bruce's arrival at South Melbourne was not without its hiccups. He applied for a clearance from Brighton to join South in 1910, but it was revealed he had left Essendon without a clearance. What's more, when Sloss belatedly asked for a clearance, Essendon said it wanted to pick Sloss if the League allowed it. A couple of Essendon officials tried to lure Sloss back after he left, but Sloss told a League hearing that he didn't believe he was good enough for the team in 1907 or 1908. He went off and played a couple of matches with a church team and then arrived at Brighton. But now he wanted to try his luck at South Melbourne and was appealing Essendon's decision to refuse his clearance. The League upheld Bruce's appeal and he made his debut for South in its win against Richmond on 2 July.

On the same evening as hearing the Sloss case, the VFL again rejected an appeal from the Western Australian Football League to allow Percy Trotter to play in Perth. The League decided that Trotter had left Fitzroy without a clearance and, as a result, he couldn't be given a permit. It would be another year before the impasse was resolved.

The Melbourne Cricket Club awarded teenager Carl Willis one of its prestigious prizes for promising cricketers from private schools in 1910. Willis was one of several Wesley College boys who were given the opportunity to develop their cricket skills at Melbourne's premier cricket club. Willis was also a gifted footballer, blessed with an enviable sporting talent that crossed the seasons. But more than that, Carl Willis had personality, an easy charm, that was summed up by his nickname, 'Smiler'. In the photographs of the day, Willis is invariably grinning, looking just pleased to be where he was and doing what he was doing. It was all a bit of fun, really, for Willis, whether he was playing football at University or honing his cricket skills at the MCC. Or so it seemed. And that was why a moment towards the end of University's game against St Kilda in 1912, when Willis lashed out at his opponent, Fred Hansen, and hit him several times in the face, seemed so out of character. When

Hansen started to get up, Willis challenged him, 'If you want any more you can have it.' Willis claimed that Hansen had caught him around the throat during a tackle and he was only retaliating. The incident coincided with the VFL's introduction of a new procedure for reporting such on-field episodes: the adoption of a steward system to help reduce behind-the-scenes incidents. The steward had no doubt what he saw and Willis was suspended for four weeks. It became a notorious precedent. Willis was the first person suspended by a steward and he became the only University player ever suspended.

The dubious honour rankled Willis. He was not that kind of young man. He was studying dentistry at the University of Melbourne. He was member of that bastion of sporting privilege, the MCC. His father, Rupert, was a doctor and had been one of the founders of the University's student medical society. He too was a Wesley old boy, and he was working as a GP at Daylesford when Carl, the middle of three sons, was born. The boys were all destined for a professional life. The eldest, Jack, was the navy surgeon on the Australian supply ship *Aorangi* during Australia's first foray into war, in German New Guinea. Coincidentally, the youngest Willis son, Alan, went to work in Papua New Guinea years later. In 1897, the Willis family moved from Daylesford to Malvern, where Dr Willis set up a practice. Over time, he became vice president of the Old Wesley Collegians Association and then mayor of Malvern. It was, in every respect, a privileged upbringing for the Willis boys. But Carl was not one for being too predictable.

Willis's representative at the hearing into the St Kilda incident was the former Fitzroy premiership captain and Willis's University coach Gerald Brosnan. He tried to mitigate on the grounds that Carl was just retaliating, but there was no sympathy for that line. Brosnan was forced to concede that if the League admitted it was natural for a player who was struck to retaliate, there would be trouble every week. But, for all of that, Brosnan's explanation was a fair reflection of what occurred. In an era where on-field violence was all too common at the football, Carl Willis was far from a serial offender. The provocation, in this case, had been too much to resist. Willis copped his penalty and never reoffended. Two years later, Willis was playing with South Melbourne when a Melbourne player hit him on the neck during a series of violent exchanges that triggered a melee and a crowd invasion lasting 15 minutes. Willis wasn't reported but a Melbourne player was, and he too claimed provocation. That player was suspended for eight weeks.

Willis was not a sportsman hewn from the classic mould, either in cricket or in football. At the batting crease, the young Willis was considered to be talented but prone to impulsive moments that might have been explained by lapses of concentration. As a footballer with University, he lacked some of the grace and speed of his teammates, but he was sure-footed and creative, and had a knack for being where the ball was. One of the important consequences of his time with the Students football club was getting to know Brosnan, a wise mentor, who saw something special in the young man. Brosnan was a talented writer, who had years of sporting experience to draw on and shape into a career in sports journalism. He believed Willis had a similar gift, although the young man had a lighter touch and lacked the gravitas of his mentor.

Then the war came. In an act of perversity, Willis declared on his enlistment papers – in a bold, strong hand – that he was agnostic. One might have wondered just what effect Wesley's religious instruction had on Willis, if any. He was 22 years and seven months old, and very certain of himself. A declaration of agnosticism might have looked like a brave intention to shock a jaundiced recruiting officer, but it was entirely in keeping with Willis's nature. He wanted to make it clear that he was his own man.

★

The early preparations for Australia's entry to the war were a challenge to a nation that had only been formally established 13 years earlier at Federation. Outside the official arms of government and defence, there was a growing number of organisations that wanted to take a role in the conflict, including the YMCA, or Young Men's Christian Association. The organisation became an integral part of the war effort, establishing a presence at the training camps in each state and supplying designated 'officers' to travel with the troops and provide sport and recreation. Troops in training could also use YMCA-branded paper to write letters home – 250,000 sheets of it printed by 18 August 1914 – while also being exposed to the Association's determinedly Christian notions of heroism and sacrifice. 'To help the sturdy sons of Britain hurried the hardy stock of Canada, the brown warriors of India, the keen-eyed marksmen of the veldt, and alert, lithe men from Australia and New Zealand,' the YMCA's local publication, *Melbourne's Manhood*, noted. How lucky was the Empire to deploy such shining examples of masculine skill and power in its urgent defence! But the YMCA's goals in all of this were simple: 'the opportunity of linking men up in activities for mutual advantages, whereby the highest and noblest qualities of the man and soldier are developed'. Here was war providing the opportunity for troops to develop into men of honour. This was muscular Christianity at its finest.

In the first convoy of troopships that left Australia on 1 November 1914, the YMCA had supplied multiple sets of sports and recreational equipment that included 40 packs of cards, 20 sets of draughts, 20 sets of dominoes, ten skipping ropes, a pair of punching mittens, two medicine balls, 20 mouth organs, 20 whistles, a blackboard and a map of the world. There was a gramophone for every 500 men, and, on ships carrying over 500 soldiers a piano, an organ and a library.

But the YMCA's commitment to the physical – and spiritual – health of the troops went beyond mere equipment. It extended to providing personnel who could help to organise the competition that, in its view, nourished the spiritual and physical dimension of the soldier and the man.

One key YMCA recruit was ideally suited to this task, although he came to the role by accident and, given a choice, would have preferred to have seen real action, rather than the sport he organised. Frank Beaurepaire was already a well-known swimmer in Australia when war broke out. In the 1908 London Olympics, aged just 17, he won a silver medal in the 400-metre freestyle and a bronze in the 1500-metre. Beaurepaire's success was built on a fierce determination and no little skill. He was only four when his father tossed him into the tidal water at Stubbs Baths in South Melbourne, with just a rope around his middle to help him. The boy quickly learnt how to 'dog paddle', and from there he started to build a lifelong devotion to physical fitness. Even a debilitating bout of rheumatic fever when he was ten couldn't stop Beaurepaire, although the effects stayed with him.

After his Olympics success, Beaurepaire was approached by the principal of Wesley College, Dickie Adamson, and offered a half-scholarship. The Olympic Games was the pinnacle of amateurism, which made Beaurepaire's appearance in Wesley colours instantly appealing to Adamson's highly developed faith in amateur sport. The headmaster also understood the power of having a teenager who exemplified such an ideal in the school.

Beaurepaire was at Albert Park State School, with a teenage boy's passing interest in the academic life but a passion for sport and the outdoors. The Wesley opportunity seemed ideal. He passed the Wesley examination, which guaranteed the half-scholarship, and for nearly two years he was a 'Wesley boy'. Family friends keen to see the talented teenager take advantage of every opportunity met the costs that the scholarship didn't cover.

Although Beaurepaire's sporting prowess was in the water, he was also a good footballer who was in the running for the state school player of the year in 1906. 'If Frank had time to follow football as he did swimming he would have made as great a name as he did as a swimmer,' one of Beaurepaire's schoolmates remarked years later. So it was perhaps not surprising that Beaurepaire played in the Wesley First XVIII that became the Victorian public schools champion, alongside Carl Willis. As a footballer, Beaurepaire was solid and uncompromising, using his muscular frame to good effect. But, in such talented company, the Wesley sportsmaster, Harold Stewart, could not give Beaurepaire the highest accolades. '[He] has plenty of football in him but holds the ball far too much; fair mark and kick,' he observed.

Swimming opportunities lured Beaurepaire overseas again, and in 1910 he embarked on a fierce timetable of competition across England and Europe that created his reputation as one of the world's best swimmers. It was not a tour replete with the comforts of first-class travel. Instead, the journey was a catalogue of difficulties, including a 17½-hour train journey from Berlin to Budapest, sitting up all the way. But Beaurepaire was a resilient and profoundly competitive individual. He carried all before him, winning titles such as the British half-mile championship, broke records, easily bested the French champion over 500 metres and even took on five Finnish swimmers working in a relay over 500 metres and won by 12 yards.

On the eve of war, Beaurepaire contemplated his options, best among them an offer to go to Springfield University in the United States to become a swimming coach and study medicine. He had given up his amateur status in 1911 when he'd become a swimming and physical education teacher for three pounds a week with the Victorian Education Department, which meant he was barred from being an amateur for three years. There is no evidence to suggest that his eventual decision about his future was motivated by the change in status.

Beaurepaire had served with the 56th Infantry Battalion, known as The Yarra Borderers, and military service emerged as an appealing option. He felt the patriotic pull and decided against going to Springfield. He enlisted, and was commissioned as a second lieutenant in the 7th Battalion, which was largely made up of Victorians. But a serious attack of appendicitis rendered Beaurepaire so debilitated that he was not fit for service. He found it intolerable. Beaurepaire's infirmity meant he had to resign his commission, and it would have taken some months before he was fit enough to re-enlist. He was an active member of the Presbyterian Church in Middle Park, had joined the YMCA years before, and had helped the Association's swimming club. So Beaurepaire decided to become one of the YMCA's overseas officers. The Association was smart enough to know that Beaurepaire was an ideal recruit for its cause.

There weren't too many football fans who thought that Charles Julius Perry had much of a future with the Norwood Football Club in South Australia from his first few matches. He was reed-thin and looked out of his depth among the stronger, older bodies. 'I remember him playing his first game for Norwoods [*sic*] last season and was absolutely the biggest mug that ever went on the football field,' an observer noted. 'I think he got two kicks during the afternoon – one before the match and another in the shins during a rough-up.' But Perry was no mug; he was vice captain of the Prince Alfred College senior football team and won the school's football prize in 1909. He was the mobile ruckman and one of the best players in the school team that was narrowly defeated by the Melbourne Grammar First XVIII in July 1909.

While he was still at school, Perry was selected in Norwood's second team. The local experts were positive too, pointing out his long reach and ability to out-mark his opponents.

Most telling, though, was his calm temperament and hard work around the ground. The missing elements in this impressive package were size and strength. Between 1909 and 1911, Perry filled out and put on muscle. His larger physique transformed his potential into eye-catching performances for Norwood and, from there, to representing South Australia against Victoria in August 1912.

Charles was a young man with a well-developed sense of civic virtue. He was pious but not sanctimonious, earnest without being humourless, and he instinctively understood the allure of sport and its power to bring people together. Charles's older brother, Frank, became an industrialist and politician, who would later be knighted. The boys' father, Isaiah, was a Wesleyan cleric. He was born in Shropshire and migrated to Adelaide in 1880. He moved around the state, ministering in a number of parishes, and had four sons and a daughter with his South Australian-born wife, Caroline. Reverend Perry died on 30 November 1911. Charles was already working in the church that nourished his father by then.

Charles and Frank shared the hand–eye coordination that made them stand-out competitors in most ball sports. Frank, two years older, liked tennis and golf too. Charles was keener on football, and played the game on the Mount Lofty oval with men while he was still at primary school. For young sportsmen in winter, football was the premier sport in South Australia. A football association was established in Adelaide in 1877, and in the early years Norwood was the competition giant, finishing on top of the ladder ten out of the first 14 seasons. The club played its first game wearing red stockings and, inevitably, was known as the Redlegs from then on.

Norwood's biggest rivals were Port Adelaide and South Adelaide, but the competition struggled to draw a crowd until Norwood's own, W.B. Griffiths, proposed a district-based competition that injected new life into local football. By the time the Perrys appeared together in Norwood's navy blue and red in 1909, the club was integral to a competitive league. In such company, Norwood was seen as an 'establishment' club, which had history and tradition as its foundation. Norwood won the premiership at its first attempt in 1878, ushering in a period of such dominance that it won the next five flags.

The early success generated a profile – and financial rewards – that underpinned the club's dominance. In 1888, Norwood defeated South Melbourne for the 'premiership of Australia' and then defeated a team of English footballers, organised by a trio of English cricket entrepreneurs. The club was so success-ful it became a benefactor to struggling football clubs – West Adelaide and North Adelaide – and provided relief funding to the Adelaide Rowing Club, badly affected by floods. The public impression was of a club at the centre of the football community, magnanimous in success, sure of its place in the Adelaide scheme of things.

There was a downturn, when the club's dominance slipped away in an inevitable cycle of renewal. But the Redlegs were reinvigorated in the early years of the new century and embarked on a stunning period of dominance, including defeating Port Adelaide for the 1907 state championship in a match played at such a frenetic pace the umpire had to be replaced after suffering a minor heart attack. The highpoint was then defeating the 1907 VFL premiers, Carlton, in what was a de facto national championship.

By the time Charles Perry made his senior debut for Norwood against North Adelaide on 8 May 1909, the club was on a gradual but ignominious slide that plunged it into the uncharted wooden spoon territory. Frank played only six games with Norwood but Charles stayed with the Redlegs through the club's thin years. His two stand-out positions were at centre half-back or the ruck, and in a Norwood team that lacked finesse and star power, the red-haired Perry's dash proved to be eye-catching. But if there was an obvious manner to the way he played the game, it was the air of a man doing serious business. Perry's efforts were characterised as 'grim courage and perseverance', a badge of sorts that underlined his commitment to the club.

There was one other element that drew appreciative commentary – his 'gentlemanly' conduct in an age when spite, on-field violence and abuse were common. It comes as no surprise that a man with his eyes on a career in the church showed such humanity, but even the most devout of football fans would probably have forgiven Perry the odd outburst in the midst of a fierce contest. It never happened. He told a congregation of sportsmen at a special service in the middle of the 1912 season, 'If anyone has any reason to get wild in the football field, maybe I have . . . I have been blue almost head to foot – some of you know that. On Saturday afternoons I have gone out with the determination that come what may, I would not lose my temper.' Niggling and confrontation could be found on either side of the field's fence; one female fan became notorious for stabbing an umpire with her hatpin during a match at Norwood.

Perry's determination not to respond to the on-field physical taunts was an impressive feat of self-discipline, an example of the Biblical entreaty to 'turn the other cheek' played out on a football ground. He had some other messages for the men in his congregation too: refrain from swearing and rein in one's physical passions. When in doubt, the reverend urged, adopt the simple precept of saying nothing that would offend their mothers or sisters. There was something radical in talking to footballers about such sensitive social topics but Perry was not your average cleric. Playing football gave him the key to the inner circle at Norwood. Playing as well as he did delivered the respect of his teammates and an opportunity for him to persuade them of the moral and spiritual aspects of the game. Perry's views were so accepted and his influence so profound at Norwood that the team sang a hymn, 'Lead, Kindly Light', on its way home from away games. Perry's achievements were more remarkable when the team was getting regularly beaten.

All of which made Charlie Perry's nickname of Red Wing seem all the more mischievous. It sprang from Perry's crop of rich red hair and was inspired by a popular song of the time, 'Red Wing', originally written in 1907, about a Native American girl and her lover:

She loved a warrior bold,
This shy little maid of old,
But brave and gay he rode one day,
To battle far away.

Now the moon shines tonight on pretty Red Wing,
The breeze is sighing, the night bird's crying.
For afar 'neath his star her brave is sleeping,
While Red Wing's weeping her heart away.

Gentle chiacking extended to other nicknames, such as The Sky Pilot and the Footballing Padre. Perry took all of it in good humour and with a predictable dash of forbearance.

After Perry entered the Methodist ministry in 1911, he began the itinerant life of the probationary cleric. He was, though, considered something of a spiritual balm to Norwood, and the club encouraged him to deliver services across all sports when he was available. The services regularly drew more than 300 people, including many of Perry's Norwood teammates. If they couldn't attend, they would send telegrams wishing him well and apologising for their absence. Perry's sermons frequently referred to sport as a testing ground, and he believed that the discipline required on the football field was 'equal to, if not better' than that required to train soldiers. If sport was 'clean', Perry urged, it was good for the individual and the community.

In one such moment when the spiritual followed the recreational, Perry played with Norwood against Broken Hill in two matches in July 1913 and then delivered the Sunday evening service to a congregation of footballers in the mining town. The church was packed, and many of Perry's teammates joined the 80-voice choir for stout renditions of the hymns. Perry, still only 24, delivered a sermon that spoke loudly about his own outlook:

> When a man failed in life he made as an excuse, 'I am what God made me.' That was not correct. When he succeeded, he said: 'I am a self-made man.' That statement was also incorrect . . . man was the only animal capable of moral struggle or a moral conquest and yet while endowed with that divine intelligence, he was the only creature that willingly disobeyed God's will.

He left a strong impression on local churchgoers. 'Why, that young minister must be the two ends of a magnetic pole to be able to carry a crowd of young hot bloods like that,' one local observed. It was indeed a remarkable feat to placate noisy and robust footballers with a spiritual message, but Perry managed it.

After establishing himself in the Norwood team, Red Wing Perry's obligations to the church meant that he had to miss the 1914 season while he carried out his pastoral duties at Waikerie. The Murray River township was established with only 280 settlers in 1894, and it took another 20 years and pioneering irrigation to make fruit-growing the area's main earner. The hinterland was tough and inaccessible. Men of the cloth were expected to travel across the district to provide guidance to their disparate congregation. The trips were often fraught, across harsh countryside on rutted and rough paths. Perry was visiting a remote part of the parish and jumped off his buggy to close a gate when his two ponies bolted for the river.

Despite some desperate attempts to save the horses, it proved futile and the pair drowned. But such was Norwood's respect for the young pastor, it raised 23 sovereigns to help him replace the ponies.

Perry returned the favour by joining the Norwood team on its trip to Western Australia, where the Redlegs played two games against Fremantle and one against a combined Western Australian team in August 1914. The standard of the contests was debatable, with the West's best players in Sydney for the 1914 carnival. But Norwood made the best of it, sending a squad of 39 players and officials across for the matches.

The trip started in a festive air. En route on the SS *Katoomba*, the footballers were done out like they were off on a holiday – suits, ties and straw boaters – and were treated to light entertainment from the ship's orchestra on the deck. The frivolity was short-lived. War was declared while Perry and the Redlegs made their way to Perth. And there was no doubt, for many of the Norwood footballers, where their duty lay. Norwood secretary John Woods promptly made the connection between the physical specimens who charged around every week in pursuit of the ball and the require-ments of war service. 'The military authorities recognised that football was of great importance from the military point of view in producing men of nerve and courage,' he said in the week after war was declared. When the time came, the Norwood men would be signing up in numbers, including the Reverend Charles Red Wing Perry.

By the time Carlton was celebrating its 1914 premiership, University had announced that it would take no further part in the VFL. It was, in many ways, a sensible decision. The club – not surprisingly given its student base – had a high turnover of players in its seven seasons. The drain of trying to fill teams with students taking examinations and not being able to train or play regularly meant that the club quickly became non-competitive.

From 1911 to 1914, the Students won just two matches and lost 51 games in a row.

And there was another reason why the club was getting thrashed week in, week out, which underlay all the others: professionalism. Every other team in the League had paid players. Money bought good players – and kept them too. 'It is understood that the authorities of the Alma Mater have a strong distaste to the Students participating in a professional game, which is only natural for the University in other parts of the world is looked upon as the genesis of amateur sport,' one newspaper noted. But how could an avowedly amateur club keep up with its professional rivals?

Professionalism was indeed a problem for the VFL. There was no doubt that, by war's outbreak, player payments and clubs touting for recruits were common. It helped to drain the player reserves in other competitions, such as the Metropolitan Amateur Football Association, which years later became the Victorian Amateur Football Association. No wonder then that, ethically and practically, University was not competitive. At a time when other League clubs were dealing with the vexed issue of player payments in the years immediately before the war, University increasingly looked like an anomaly. Some purists saw the club as a moral bulwark against the onset of professionalism, but there was no avoiding the commercial – or playing – reality that the club was not sustainable.

University's initial success was based on the quality of its players – students at the University of Melbourne who would become the next generation of doctors, lawyers, dentists and engineers. Once the club withdrew from the VFL to the Metropolitan Junior Football League, it seemed inevitable that the sons of the city's privileged classes would continue their football with Melbourne Football Club, also an amateur stronghold. In April 1915, Melbourne approached its namesake University to pick some of the best students to join it, on the condition they remain amateurs. Nine University players finished up being approached and offered complimentary or honorary memberships. Jack Brake, already an MCC member, went across from the Students, along with Leo Little but Carl Willis decided to take his chances elsewhere, His decision caused ructions with the University and he was hauled before the Sports Committee to explain his decision. Willis's transgression was that he had not applied to University for permission to play for another club. Willis, in what was entirely in character, pointed out to the Sports Committee that he thought asking a club that had already left the League for permission to play with another League club was unnecessary. The committee huffed and puffed, and asked Willis to formally apply for the required permission. But there is no record of Willis fulfilling the request. What did happen was that Carl Willis joined South Melbourne and there the matter ended.

Jack Brake was studying agricultural science, and was arguably University's finest footballer. He played 81 times for the Students and represented Victoria on eight occasions, a remarkable performance in a success-starved club. He was born in Horsham in the Victorian Wimmera and won a triple blue at University for athletics, football and rifle shooting. His athletics achievements were remarkable; he was the national amateur pole vault champion in 1911, launching himself ten feet nine inches and reaching 11 feet three years later. He was a square-shouldered young man with a serious demeanour. And his physical resilience was a feature of his football.

Leo Little came from a large Catholic family in Bacchus Marsh. He and his four brothers all boarded at St Patricks College in Ballarat. Little was not only a talented footballer at University but also a Victorian handball champion. He went to the other perceived 'amateur' club, Melbourne, when University left the VFL. Throughout the debate about professionalism in football, the Melbourne Football Club set itself apart, like University, believing in the nobility of playing for nothing other than the thrill of the contest. This too was a public school rubric, which many of the Melbourne establishment carried with them into the Melbourne Football Club. As the custodians of this ethos, the burghers of 'old' Melbourne disdained the lure of the pound and shilling for the higher purpose of untainted competition. But, unlike University, Melbourne had establishment money and support to ensure it survived.

Melbourne was the football sibling of the MCC, the cricket club that saw itself as the 'home' of Australian cricket. It was based at the Jolimont ground, which by 1914 was becoming an important locale in the city's community. The club secretary was the former Australian Test cricketer Hugh Trumble, a beanstalk of a man, with an imposing physique but a quiet and engaging manner. His role at the MCC became increasingly important in the early days of the war when he was urging the club's members to do their duty. The MCC responded to the call throughout the war, with 1088 of its 5449 members enlisting.

The MCC's alacrity exemplified the surge in volunteers in the war's early days. Australia promised Britain 20,000 men, which turned out to be an easy promise to keep. The enthusiasm and support for the Empire and its war was clear. Within two weeks, there were 7000 Victorian men on the books, and more than 10,000 had applied in Sydney. There was a few discordant voices but, in the early days of the conflict, scant attention was paid to such views.

Inevitably, the war had an instant impact on sport. Suburban sporting competitions of all kinds were struck by the exodus of men enlisting. Eight days after war was declared, the South Australian Amateur Athletic Association indefinitely postponed its five-mile cross-country championship 'in consequence of the mobilisation of the troops interfering with the personnel of some of the teams'. Ten days later, lacrosse — a popular game of the era — announced it had to draw on its reserves to fill teams because of the numbers it had lost to enlistments. Hockey put its hand up too. 'Some well-known figures were absent from the field and among the busy tents at Broadmeadows [camp],' it was reported. The mainstream sports announced similar issues. Queensland cricket sources said enlistment was 'cleaving big holes through the ranks of cricketers', and Melbourne's local football suffered, with one suburban club losing three players to the AIF.

The sporting groups of the time that were most directly prepared for the advent of war were the rifle clubs dotted across the country. 'Silently, automatically, without preliminary warning in the short space of time intervening between one Saturday afternoon's sport and the next, the declaration of war by England has transformed a body of sportsmen in to an army of potential soldiers, ready and willing to take the fighting chance,' one dramatic report in Sydney stated ten days after the war started.

All of these sports, however, were played by amateurs. No wonder their enthusiasm for the cause was exemplary – they only had their recreation to give up. While the rifle clubs and others welcomed the war as an opportunity to put their sport to the test, the Australian Rules football clubs were far more reluctant about the war's impact on their players.

The big clubs in Melbourne now had to accept they were going to lose some of their players. Alan Cordner, a footballer who promised so much at Collingwood, enlisted early. So too did Fen McDonald, who started his VFL career at Carlton and then moved to Melbourne. And also there was Claude Crowl, who started at Carlton before joining St Kilda, Charlie Fincher, who was at South Melbourne, former University player Rupert Balfe and the Melbourne stalwart Joe Pearce. All of them were at Gallipoli on 25 April 1915. None of them survived that first day of confusion and mayhem. It was a sombre reminder that, despite all the mock-heroic sentiments, sportsmen were not invincible creatures who could outrun bullets and survive shrapnel.

The war's impact was felt in other ways too. St Kilda's jumper, by grim coincidence, was the same red, black and white tricolour as the flag of the German Empire. It was replaced by the Belgian colours – black, yellow and red – for the start of the 1915 season, in what was described as 'admirable admiration for the pluck of Belgium'. The VFL went some way towards making its position clear. It voted £250 to the Lord Mayor's Patriotic Fund once war was declared and increased ticket prices by sixpence. The surcharge had a swift impact on attendances. Football fans working in factories and other businesses were already making contributions to patriotic funds. Now, they were expected to pay more for their recreation too, and the reaction was obvious and measurable. In 1913, there were 54,846 at the MCG for the grand final. A year later, with the war underway, there were only 30,495 to see Carlton's win over Sloss's men. R.W.E. Wilmot, the avowed supporter of amateurism in sport who wrote as 'Old Boy' in *The Argus*, was unhappy at the suggestion that the increased charge had an impact on attendances. 'The football public,' he sniffed, 'however, enjoying the sport, which had grown so prosperous in the times of peace and under the conditions which prevail under British rule, ought well be expected to show their loyalty by a small contribution to the patriotic cause.'

The outbreak of war coincided with the tail end of the football season, and it guaranteed the debate about the morality of playing a game at a time of national emergency would only build in volume through the spring and summer. The consequence was that the prelude to the 1915 football season was heated and divisive. There was also an initial expectation that the war would not last long. That soon proved to be a chimera. Yet there was no misunderstanding about the importance of sport to the men who enlisted. At every training camp around the country, there were regular sporting contests to not only keep the men fit but also help the troops get to know each other. There were days devoted to contests that ranged from 100-yard sprints to high jumps, relays, tug of war and novelty events.

The competition was strong; there were professional foot runners in the Australian battalions, as well as men with impressive junior athletic records. Lester Kelly, another old Wesleyan – who held the national high jump record and was the Victorian 440-yard champion – won the individual championship in the sports day at Broadmeadows on 6 October 1914. Kelly won the high jump, tied for first in the 100 yards and came second in the 440 yards.

The competitions were a reminder of the athletic calibre of the men Australia was sending to war. This not only heightened the potential sense of loss should any of these men be wounded or die, but it also increased the pressure on those athletes – footballers, cricketers, runners, swimmers – to join up. At the heart of the issue was the simple question posed for sportsmen and spectators: could you do your national duty by continuing to be a player or a fan? The answer would prove more vexed than anyone could have forecast.

3

Taking the Shilling

Before the 1914 football carnival was over, New South Wales captain Ralph Robertson had enlisted. His keenness surprised no one who knew him. Robertson was one of life's enthusiasts, keen for new experiences and always willing to do what was required. He was only a tick over 18 when St Kilda decided to select him in its senior squad, and he stayed there, playing 14 senior games, despite his youth. And then, on moving to Sydney in 1900, he took up rugby union when the city could not support an Australian Rules football competition. But when football started to establish itself, Robertson returned to the game and captained New South Wales in three national carnivals.

Robertson turned 32 on the day war was declared. When word came for Australia to take a role in knocking out the wireless station in what was then German New Guinea, he joined up. He might have been an older recruit but there was no disguising his excitement. He looked the part too, with his strong build and hint of a grin under his generous moustache. Off he went to war, fit, robust and keen to be part of what became the first Australian action of the conflict.

The Australian Naval and Military Expeditionary Force achieved its goal of silencing the German wireless station but lost six men doing it. They were the first Australian fatalities of the war. Robertson struggled with the heat in the days that followed the mission's completion. To counter the tropical torpor, the soldiers – all of them from New South Wales – turned to rugby for entertainment. 'We had sports at Rabaul recently,' he wrote. 'Started at 8am, knocked off at 11, and resumed at 2pm. Wound up with a football [rugby] match at 4.30.' Robertson and another footballer took part in a football kicking competition, but they lost – much to their disappointment, as well as that of their friends, who had backed them at good odds. 'You should try drop-kicking in military boots,' Robertson offered in his defence.

It was a good piece of advice for every footballer who donned a uniform. Robertson experienced the first of what would become a regular feature of Australian activities overseas during the war: the sporting competition, usually accompanied by the football match. It happened everywhere, from Cairo to the Greek island of Lemnos, from the training camps in England to the Western Front. There would be all forms of football – rugby union, league, soccer and Australian Rules – plus boxing and cricket. The military top brass knew that sport was the ideal way to keep idle men occupied. But whatever sporting wisdom Robertson wanted to impart was soon swamped by the mobilisation of Australian troops for the European war. This was the first real opportunity for Australians to show their commitment to the Empire's cause. The first convoy of troops that left Albany on 1 November 1914 was initially destined for Europe, but military planning in London changed all that.

While anticipation was building for the 1915 football season, the Australian troops were preparing for the Dardanelles campaign – a plan that Lord of the Admiralty Winston Churchill devised to provide the Allies with the opportunity to cleave Turkey from its partnership with Germany and open the path to Constantinople. It was – depending on your point of view – a bold strategic move or a folly that could only have one ending.

Either way, as the Australians undertook their preparations in Egypt and then Lemnos in the Mediterranean, the lobbying for sportsmen to enlist had taken a more insistent turn.

On the evening of Monday, 8 February 1915, a group of men filed into a room at Nicholson Chambers in Swanston Street, Melbourne, directly opposite the Town Hall. Leading them was a state MP who was about to embark on one of the most challenging roles in the country. He was Donald Mackinnon, a lawyer and pastoralist from Boorcan, south-west of Melbourne, and he was, at the time, president of the Victorian Cricket Association (VCA). At the tail end of the summer but at the looming first sharp point of the war, the VCA convened a meeting to decide what its position would be and who it would send to a public meeting the following night to discuss Victorian sports' approach to war and recruitment. Mackinnon knew what he was going to tell the VCA delegates. And when the time came, he was going to trust his passion to carry his position.

Mackinnon's public-speaking skills had taken some time to acquire. In his first political meeting as the MP for Prahran, he was so nervous he gulped down a mouthful of water after every pained statement, prompting a heckler to warn him that he might fall over if he didn't stop. He steadily became more assured as his parliamentary career took him from the backbench to the ministry as attorney-general and minister of railways. Mackinnon's connection with cricket dated back to Oxford University, where he had been a round-arm bowler, but – perhaps because the skill was quickly becoming obsolete – he didn't make the University cricket team. Nonetheless, he had an enduring commitment to the game, and if anything his time in England reminded him again of Australia's place in the Empire. When he spoke to the VCA delegates, it was with the Mother Country in mind.

'Very little reflection will make us see that there is no earthly reason why we should allow English sportsmen to bear the brunt of the fight,' he said. 'We know well that the Australian does not lack physical courage. But an aspect that has not been laid before them is that there is a certain meanness in our young fellows not taking the share that the young Englishman has to take.'

A certain meanness? It seemed a harsh assessment of the perceived lack of enthusiasm for enlistment. The remarks were an indication of Mackinnon's inability to understand the reasons why young men might not volunteer to join the AIF. What could possibly keep them at home? 'This is a real opportunity for young men: an opportunity of seeing the world and of taking part in the greatest fight humanity has ever had to contest,' he wrote some months later. 'It should make their hearts tingle and lead them to participate in the great war.'

Thousands of other men and women across the country shared his view. For Mackinnon, the war offered not only adventure but also the chance for a young man to prove himself. He later wrote to his son Brice, who had joined the Black Watch regiment in England, 'Forty years ago when I was your age I had an easier time than you are having but your luck's to be able to play a true man's part.' There is a hint of wistful regret in Mackinnon's letter that he never had the same opportunity to serve the nation and the Empire. Mackinnon felt the challenge of war should work so powerfully on young men that they would need no compulsion to get there.

It was a position that would pose some distinct challenges of its own in the years ahead. Mackinnon's speech at the VCA meeting was one of his preliminary forays into the public debate on sport and war, and it would not be his last. The VCA committee applauded Mackinnon and appointed him and VCA secretary John Healy to represent it at the following evening's meeting. Nine months later, Mackinnon resigned from government to become chairman of the Victorian recruiting committee, and in November 1916 he was given the national recruiting job.

The night following the VCA delegates' meeting, 2000 people, including 100 men from the governing bodies of the city's sporting organisations, met at the Town Hall. The MCC had organised the meeting, in its self-appointed role as the leading sporting organisation in Victoria, to start the debate on sportsmen and recruitment. The first step was to get sporting organisations to surrender their grounds for training troops. Another was to establish a volunteer unit of sportsmen so that 'fellow sportsmen shall be able to play the game side by side among greater and grander fields'. The meeting established a committee that represented cricket, football, British football (soccer), tennis, bowling, yachting, baseball and athletics. Frank Beaurepaire was added to the committee along with Dickie Adamson, the Wesley headmaster. Mackinnon moved the key motion 'that in the opinion of this meeting immediate action should be taken to impress on the sportsmen of Victoria that it is their duty to at once respond to the Empire's call by enlisting, and if that be not practicable, by actively participating in training, drill and rifle shooting'. The motion was passed.

Mackinnon added that, after 40 years of sporting rivalry with England, sympathy and kinship should make Australian sportsmen do their share towards defending the Empire. Here was another line of argument – that the fraternity of sport generated through a longstanding competitiveness with the Mother Country created an obligation to enlist.

George Foster Pearce told the Town Hall meeting it was sportsmen's 'turn to go in': '[T]he captain had called and it remained to be seen whether they would skulk in the dressing room, or go out in the field and take the chances and risks like the sportsmen they professed to be.'

One of the few measured responses came from the commandant of Victorian military forces, Colonel Robert Wallace. He told the meeting it wasn't necessary to start a recruiting drive. It would be enough to say, 'Come along, be a man, take the bob;

do it now.' Colonel Wallace was articulating a wider view that Australians' basic decency would be enough to meet recruitment needs. It might have done if the war hadn't lasted so long, or if Australian involvement had been limited. But the situation was about to become dire and the demand for men would go beyond an optimistic faith that they would do the right thing in a brief conflict.

Despite the unanimity of the support for Mackinnon's views among the sporting fraternity, the committee established after the Town Hall meeting did not reconvene. The motion passed at the Town Hall was only ever a formally decorated call to action, no more compelling than a public notice nailed to a door. There was no legal, political or commercial imperative for sportsmen to enlist. However, a sportsmen's battalion was another matter entirely.

The idea of such a battalion grew out of Lord Kitchener's extraordinary recruitment drive that generated thousands of British volunteers. There were a number of special interest battalions in the British Army, such as public schools and sportsmen's battalions, and then, even more specialised, with the creation in December 1914 of a footballers' battalion. Mackinnon, with Hugh Trumble, worked in earnest on establishing a sportsmen's battalion in the summer of 1915. If sportsmen could not be lured to join general battalions, perhaps the incentive of sharing their national duty with like-minded sporting souls would make a difference. There was, on the face of it, good reason to convert a sporting camaraderie into a military one, as 'the esprit de corps . . . would be very keen'. But the downside was equally clear. 'At the same time, there is an old and very true saying about packing all your eggs in one basket, and if disaster met the sportsmen it would be a serious blow to sport,' one anxious sports reporter noted.

Although there appeared to be widespread enthusiasm for the idea, it stopped well short of being strong enough to create a battalion. Pearce wasn't keen on a sportsmen's battalion and offered instead to keep those men who played sport together in the same military unit. In Adelaide on 4 March 1915, a meeting of the state's leading sporting administrators finished up with a version of the Melbourne declaration with one addition: '[T]he players of field games have first to realise their value as fighting units, and then to submit themselves for training.' The message was clear that sporting administrators thought sportsmen had to be *told* their physical prowess was a weapon of war. According to that notion, it was only some kind of blind spot shared among those with superior sporting skills that prevented them enlisting. Once the penny dropped, they'd be off. All of which justified sustained discussion in the newspapers of why sportsmen needed to enlist.

But it wasn't every sportsman who was subjected to the press clamour. Sports involving payment – football, boxing, racing and cricket – were the main targets of the commentary and the pressure that went with it. Many of the amateur sports across the country were showing no signs of tardiness and were therefore excused from such debate. A fifth of Melbourne's registered yachtsmen had enlisted by February 1915. Soccer's strong links to England helped account for the strength of the game's response in Australia to the war. There were estimates of 241 enlistments among Western Australian soccer players by October 1915 and a further 143 from Victorian clubs by April the same year. And the Victorian Amateur Swimming Association recorded 81 swimmers who had volunteered by the start of 1915. Small sporting clubs were particularly vulnerable to the exodus of talent. The East Sydney athletics club had a healthy list of 80 members in 1910 but by 1916 there were only 13.

The sportsmen's battalion idea, potent as it seemed at the fag end of the 1915 summer, dropped off the public agenda for six months, before Sydney recruiting authorities tried to revive it. By the end of September, 1100 men had joined the New South

Wales Sportsmen's Battalion. But organisational problems meant the recruits were distributed to different units, rather than kept together under the Sportsmen's banner. Instead of discussions about sportsmen having their own battalions, the debate became more focused on getting sportsmen, any sportsmen, into uniform and away from paid sport. The reasoning went that if the best sportsmen weren't on view, then the fans too would stay away. That in turn would help shut down sport at a time of national emergency and force the remaining sportsmen into uniform. The chief agitator in all of this was Adamson, of Wesley, and he propounded the view with the rhetoric and passion usually heard from the pulpit on Sunday mornings.

Adamson was a somewhat severe-looking man, as befitted a headmaster and a person sure of his opinions. He was educated at England's Rugby School and absorbed its notions of amateurism, muscular Christianity and the pre-eminence of the Empire with the unquestioning devotion of the acolyte. He excluded cricket from his critique of sport, believing it defied the evils of professionalism, but had no qualms about criticising Australian football's perceived failings. In this, he was a remarkably successful polemicist, with a peerless gift for moral self-assurance.

Adamson's particular problem with professionalism was that playing for money inevitably tainted the nobility of sport. At wartime, it made it easy for the paid player to compromise his obligation of patriotic duty. The consequence of offering sporting entertainment was that it drew spectators away from the contemplation of weightier issues, such as the war effort. No one could be in any doubt about Adamson's commitment to amateurism – he was president of the amateur Metropolitan Junior Football Association from 1896 to 1932. His views were long-held and often expressed. Three years before the outbreak of war, he urged 'the better class' of player to resist playing football – despite his regard for it – because of the game's problems. His rationale was that any game was useless 'unless it is regarded also as a moral training in controlling the temper, in unselfishness and in the virtues of hardihood, chivalry and how to lose decently' and 'that where considerations of money and its advantages enter in to the playing of the game, that game can scarcely provide the moral side of the game . . .' Certainly, there were problems with football, on and off the ground. Football was a game still in search of itself. But Adamson insisted that its failings were moral, and therefore football could not be the best use of anyone's time, either on the ground or in the crowd.

It came as no surprise when, on Tuesday, 20 April 1915 – just four days before the opening of the football season – Adamson launched into a speech in front of the boys at Wesley that reiterated his position on paid sport. This time, the message was delivered to the drumbeat of war. 'Does a game or competition offer any inducement to men to abstain from enlisting? If so, then it should cease during the war; if it does not, then by all means let it go on,' he said. Adamson documented 18 League footballers who had enlisted, including two who were professional soldiers and six from the amateur club University. Carlton, the 1914 premiers, provided one player, he said. South Yarra, an amateur club, had lost 18 players to the khaki.

'All that patriotic Germans need to do is to subscribe to the funds of our professional football clubs, and so support our paid gladiators to perform in the League or Association Circus, instead of joining the colours,' Adamson said. 'Why not Iron Crosses for the premiers instead of medals?'

It was a powerful speech, which worked at a public level and on the boys in front of him because he reminded them that the sixpence they paid at the gate to see their team play was just another inducement for the footballers not to enlist. Adamson explained, '[A]s public school people, who have always, I hope, held the game out as a means towards an end. As Wesley boys, who have over 180 of your own school-fellows engaged in this war, you must sacrifice your inclinations in this matter, if your inclinations bid you help the non-enlisters' payroll.' It was a speech driven by an emotional imperative. As a piece of rhetoric, it was vehement and extraordinarily effective. Of course, Adamson had ascended to the moral high ground with the sure-footedness of a mountain goat. He stayed up there, surveying the next four years with a gimlet eye for backsliders, slackers and shirkers.

One Wesley old boy characterised his headmaster as a general, not only in charge of the boys, but leading public opinion too. 'He was our wartime leader ahead of his troops and the five hundred of us at Wesley were his Household Brigade following close behind him . . . I think that as an individual he did more to shape pro-war opinion than anyone else in the state.' Adamson did, however, have some facts on his side – by 2 February 1915, only 18 VFL footballers had enlisted. When combined with the VFA, there were 51 footballers who had enlisted, or 13 per cent of the competitions' number. The general enlistment rate for men aged 18 to 44 at the time was almost three times that: 38.7 per cent. The evidence was all running Adamson's way.

War crystallised the professional sportsman's dilemma. In simple terms, footballers were paid 25 shillings a match and the Aussie soldier six shillings a day. It wasn't a bad incentive to stay home and play football. Adamson's argument was put in sharp relief when, three days after his speech was published, Australian troops landed at Gallipoli. It would be several weeks before some of the worst details of the failed invasion would appear in Australian newspapers. But putting aside the propaganda and hyperbole that was part of the stories, no one denied the loss of life that occurred on those twisted hills and broken ravines. Here then was evidence of something deeper and more profound than a game. This was no adventure; it was a drawn-out conflict in all its vile manifestations, from loss of limbs to fractured sanity, to debilitating wounds and death.

The longer it went, the harder it became for sportsmen across the country to ignore the pressure. The VFL debated a proposal to suspend the 1915 season but it was defeated by 13 votes to four. The VFA wanted to talk about reducing player payments but was rebuffed by the League and then continued with its own season on the basis that soccer was still being played in England.

Bruce Sloss was a footballer who also had a career to consider. He was foreman engineer at Marks Brothers in South Melbourne, a firm that had employed him since 1910. He had been a fitter and turner with a business that made farming equipment, and he'd then moved to another company that made steel windmills. Marks Brothers, however, gave him the chance to develop his own ideas. It was proof of the distance Bruce had travelled from his straitened family circumstances. And while it looked like he was a self-made man, there was more to him than diligence, focus and commitment. There was a creative spark too.

Sloss was given to tinkering with machines and wondering how they worked. Ever curious, he started to experiment with developing and patenting a unique slicing implement for melons, replacing the fixed knives in the existing factory tool with revolving circular wheels that turned out perfect cubes every time. He was particularly proud of the machine and gently chided Tullie in New York for not keeping up with the tool's development. 'I thought I gave you to understand that I have got a machine in working order that will cut just on eight tins a day of eight hours,' he wrote, each word underlined. And he was proud of its success after the Australian Jam Company trialled it for its melon jam. '[T]he cutting that when it was made in to jam, the manager said, it was the best jam that they ever made,' Sloss told his sister. The Sloss machine was apparently 'the only machine on the market we know of that do[es] this work satisfactorily'.

After some delays, the Jam Company's managing director, Acheton Palfreyman, told Sloss it was interested in buying one machine for £200, and if it worked as well as they expected, the company would order another 14 machines at £150 each. It was a lucrative proposal; no wonder Bruce wanted to share the news with his sister. But Palfreyman was fighting some battles of his own, initially with a Royal Commission into fruit and vegetables and then criminal charges that he sold 500 tons of sugar at a higher price than declared under the *Price of Food Act*. He was found not guilty on the sugar charges, but by then the company was working on providing jam for the troops. There was just no opportunity for the Australian Jam Company to push ahead with the Sloss melon cutter.

The first round of the 1915 football season in Melbourne started on 24 April, on the eve of the Gallipoli landings. It took another 12 days before the first eyewitness account of the landings appeared in Australian newspapers. The reports came from British war correspondent Ellis Ashmead-Bartlett, whose cabled dispatch appeared on the back page of the late-afternoon edition of *The Herald* in Melbourne on 7 May and then in the nation's morning papers the next day. The account would take on an enduring, emblematic significance, as the first draft of the Anzac legend. And within Ashmead-Bartlett's colourful prose was his certainty that Australian soldiers were somehow giants, robust and cheerful, remorseless and reckless as they went about climbing the jagged hills that confronted them at the landing:

Here was a tough proposition to tackle in the darkness, but these Colonials are practical above all else, and went about it in a practical way. They stopped for a few minutes to pull themselves together, got rid of their packs and charged the magazines of their rifles. Then this race of athletes proceeded to scale the cliffs, without responding to the enemy's fire. They lost some men, but did not worry. In less than a quarter of an hour the Turks had been hurled out of their second position, all either bayoneted or fled.

And: 'The courage displayed by those wounded Australians will never be forgotten . . . In fact, I have never seen anything like these wounded Australians in war before.'

There were plenty more examples, but the 'race of athletes' was a powerful enough observation to send a vibration through the national spine. There was no doubt that the Fleet Street journalist, the outsider, had spotted something that was warmly reassuring and inspiring to an Australian audience. Recruitment figures jumped in May, by 50 per cent on the April numbers, and by 100 per cent in June. The Anzac landings were tragic but inspiring, and such recruiting peaks would never be assailed again.

Adamson's colleague at the Metropolitan Junior Football Association, R.W.E. Wilmot, writing in *The Argus*, inevitably used the landings as an opportunity to make the point again about sportsmen and those who watched them. 'Who is the hero, the man who followed for four quarters or the soldier, who leaping into the sea from the boat, dashed for the Turkish shore and stormed the foothills of Gallipoli?' *The Australasian* expressed its overall agreement in somewhat less incendiary terms:

[Y]et at a time when more men were required the [football] clubs had decided to continue to play and payment, and the players had determined, in the spirit of the cynical old Persian poet, to 'take the cash and let the credit go' . . . We need only keep our eyes and ears open in places where youth assemble, to realize that unhappy fact that the professional footballer – the player of the spectacular senior game, and not the patriotic and gallant Australian soldier lavishing his life on Turkish ridges is still their idol, professional football their daily theme.

Here then was the moral bind – while football continued, young male spectators remained in thrall to their heroes, rather than elevating the soldier's sacrifice above such entertainments. It was not quite that morally clear, though, despite what the papers said.

There were signs that some players felt they couldn't ignore the call to enlist any longer. They had started to lose interest in football. Jack Worrall, who coached four VFL premierships (three at Essendon and one at Carlton), was still involved with the game through his journalism for *The Australasian*. Two months after the news of the Gallipoli landings, Worrall wrote about a footballer who confessed to him that he 'found the call of the blood too strong'. 'I tried to finish the season out,' the player told Worrall, 'but my heart is not in the job and I am off to fill one of the gaps and take my chance.'

Worrall discerned a change in the mood among the players as the season stretched into winter; the war was making its mark. 'The atmosphere in the dressing rooms is very different from what it was a month ago. The men are more serious and the usual light-hearted gaiety has practically disappeared. In common with the rest of the country, footballers will fill gaps, and prove worthy sons of Empire.' Worrall also pointed out that there were plenty of sportsmen who were able athletes and wanted to enlist but who carried some ailment – 'a hammer toe or some bad teeth' – that ruled them out on medical grounds. Even Donald Mackinnon agreed with him: more than half of those who volunteered were rejected, he lamented.

Sometimes it wasn't the external pressures that galvanised recruitment. Sometimes it was a mate's testimony. A few months after Gallipoli, Richmond footballer Arthur Beethoven Danks – known to his teammates by the more prosaic nickname of 'Darko' – received a letter from George Gibson, with whom he had played at Richmond. Gibson was one of the first to enlist, joining up on 17 August 1914 and getting in the thick of it at Gallipoli. He was shot and evacuated to Alexandria, where he wrote to his old mate:

> I am in a convalescent home now after being six weeks in hospital. It was good, Darko, up at the fight. We were all enjoying it. I was beginning to think they could not kill me, as I had got two flesh wounds in the leg and a bit of a cut on my face. I thought my luck was in because they were going down one by one all around me, and my wounds were only slight up until then but one through the left lung finished me. They brought me to the boat and the doctor gave me ten minutes to live, they say. I was out for two days and I am still kicking, although the bullet is still in my stomach and they reckon it is dangerous to shift it . . . tell them [all the Richmond players] that this is the most exciting match ever a fellow was likely to play in. It is the most exciting I have ever been in, and I have seen some close finishes. I can tell you, Darko that there was some playing to the centre and wings when we first landed and many a good straight left given. It was all in, boots, fists and bayonets, for a start, and our side won by points. It was good, Darko, but there was no umpire and the sides got mixed up. The game is still going on.

Gibson's melange of sporting metaphors was powerful propaganda for the footballers – and other sportsmen – who were wavering about enlisting. It certainly worked on Darko. The day after he received the letter, he gave up his job with the railways and enlisted. (Gibson was discharged on 31 August 1916 and Danks served out the war overseas as a driver before he was discharged on 2 August 1919.)

But it wasn't always easy to enlist, even if you wanted to. Ted Derrick, a Richmond footballer, was rejected six times because of a hammer toe. Eventually, a doctor who saw Derrick take some tough knocks on the field passed him fit. Carlton champion George Challis had a similar ailment – one toe curled over another – and was rejected in 1914, much to the amusement of the columnist in *Punch*. 'What irony! What a reply to the croaker who deplores [the] brutal roughness of football that a footballer such as Challis is not considered fit to stand a campaign of war!' It was a fair point. After Gallipoli, though, Challis was accepted. Australian men didn't always measure up to the lofty ideals of the classic physical specimens Ashmead-Bartlett envisaged. The basic requirements for recruits at the outbreak of war were to be at least five feet six inches tall, 34 inches across the chest (fully expanded) and able to eat without false teeth, for those who wore them. In the first year of the war, a third of volunteers were rejected.

As casualties mounted, standards dropped. When the Army Medical Services were alerted in July 1915 that some League footballers had been rejected 'for trivial defects' when they tried to enlist at Melbourne Town Hall, there was an instant response. The acting head of the Army Medical Services, Colonel Fetherstone, told medical officers across the country that if volunteers were obviously fit enough to put up with a campaign, they should not be rejected for minor ailments. But it didn't seem to make any difference to the numbers signing up. Other reasons were holding back sportsmen.

Across the nation, the football codes were confronting the same challenges. Before Gallipoli, the League claimed it would be a mistake if the season was suspended, largely on the grounds that people needed somewhere to go on a Saturday after-noon. After 25 April, the situation became more complicated, as the League tried to deal with the vexed issue of how much the clubs should donate to the Patriotic Funds. More generous clubs might save themselves from the opprobrium of still being in the competition. VFL chairman Alexander McCracken was wary of charging more to see football, but the debate within the League was becoming more willing. 'People who go to football also contribute in other ways,' McCracken explained to the League executive. 'They cannot be asked to give up too much.' To which the Essendon delegate responded, 'None of them have given up as much as the Belgians.'

The VFA took the players' point of view, and sounded defensive doing it. 'Some of the footballers are unable to go and they admit it,' a VFA official explained. 'Most of the players were working men living from hand to mouth. No player received anything from the association that could be counted to professional payment . . . In the five months of the football season a player got 15 pounds or 17 pounds and 10 shillings. If he got injured he received only a pound a week.' The Association chairman, J.G. Aikman, continued the theme. 'No doubt many people want to see footballers go to war. They have plenty of dash and staying power and would be sure to do well. The payment the footballer got was not keeping him away from the front.'

In the country, the situation was less clear-cut. Prominent community members in Rochester forced the town's football club to withdraw from the Bendigo League because football was interfering with local recruiting. But the players didn't want any part of it and went back to the League to be readmitted. The League dismissed the players' request with 'contempt', and League officials described the players as unpatriotic and the club unsportsmanlike for even tolerating the idea.

In South Australia, football went on as before, but it too struggled to reconcile the notion of serving your country and serving your football club. Norwood, in particular, felt the sadness of losing Phil Robin, one of its finest and most popular players, who was killed at Gallipoli on 28 April. His body was never found. Robin was one of 18 Norwood players who were at Gallipoli. Several of them had written to the club about a series of football matches they organised against other battalions while they were training in Egypt. Robin was the captain and the first match was played only 400 metres from the Cheops Pyramid. Robin was the first South Australian Football League player to fall. It cast a pall over the club that not even Red Wing Perry's return could remove.

Perry was vice captain for the 1915 season, but the club won only three of its 12 games. Perry did everything he could, roaming across half-back to prop up a weak defence and working tirelessly around the ground in the ruck. He was selected in the League's carnival matches that raised £150 for the Wounded Soldiers' Fund, albeit in front of modest crowds of about 4000 spectators. At season end, Perry finished in a three-way tie for the League's best and fairest award, the Magarey Medal, with South Adelaide rover Frank Barry and Port Adelaide's Shine Hosking. When the umpires were asked to vote to break the deadlock, Barry was the unanimous winner. Three weeks after winning the medal, Barry was on his way to war.

In Perth, football in the West Australian League continued, although 1915 would be North Fremantle's final season in the competition, when lack of success and an exodus of players to the war forced it to close. The Goldfields, which provided many volunteers, still had its league in 1915, although the loss of talent meant the standard of competition started to deteriorate.

Other sports around the country responded differently. In New South Wales, the middle-class amateur rugby union was immediately behind the war effort and cancelled competition in 1914. It was estimated that 90 per cent of the New South Wales Rugby Union players enlisted. Clubs disbanded. The game's supporters claimed it was the sport that equipped men better than any other for the stern struggle of war. 'The Rugby Union footballers seem specifically adapted and inclined for the work in the front,' one fan wrote. It was a total commitment to the cause, and 115 players died for it in 1915 alone.

But rugby league, still developing its hold on the working classes in New South Wales and Queensland, continued despite uncompromising criticism from New South Wales Premier Holman. 'Your comrades are calling you. This is not a time for football or tennis matches, it is serious,' he thundered. Rugby league, though, was actually in a battle for its own survival, and its presence throughout the war years helped establish its hold in the two northern states. Its official justification echoed the VFL's view about the need for harmless entertainment at such a distressing time.

The grim news from the Dardanelles was also starting to have an impact on the public appetite for entertainment. Crowds were down wherever football was played. Attendances in Melbourne fell. Flags flew at half-mast in country matches, and black armbands became a constant sad accessory to players' guernseys. The VFA cut short its 1915 season by five weeks. Momentum was building for the players to do the 'honourable' thing.

The campaign for sportsmen to enlist was not the reason why Bruce Sloss was undecided about playing for South Melbourne in 1915. Sloss's brother James enlisted in April, and, soon after, Bruce decided to withdraw from South Melbourne out of respect for his brother's service. Les Charge, who had rucked in the losing South premiership side with Sloss the previous year, made the same decision because he had a brother serving overseas. Bruce's predicament was a simple one that hundreds of other men were confronting: was it fair that he continued to play football while his brother was in uniform and in danger half a world away? The complicating factor for Bruce was that he was on the verge of consolidating his standing as one of the VFL's elite players. Another season like 1914 would polish his reputation. But then again, what kind of standard would the League offer, what kind of test would it be for Bruce, when some of its best players were already overseas or forever lost to the game?

James McKenzie Sloss was 36 and single when he enlisted. He had already seen something of the world, after working for eight years fixing engines and boilers at James Moore & Sons, a timber merchant in South Melbourne. He also worked on the Western Australian goldfields as an engineer before joining Bruce in business. Once James enlisted, he was dispatched to the Australian Flying Corps, a fledgling group of aviators who were sent to India as part of what became known as the 'Half Flight'. Along with four pilots and 40 other support crew, James Sloss became part of what was a remote frontier of the war and an enduring source of stress for the family left at home.

Bruce felt the pressure of competing obligations to Christina and the family, to Glad, to South Melbourne and to his national duty. But James's enlistment started a trend: before 12 months had elapsed, Bruce, John Stewart (known as Jock) and Roy were all in khaki. Tullie was working as a governess in New York when she received word that the Sloss boys were about to enlist. Desperate to see them before they left Australia, Tullie booked train tickets, packed her trunks and booked her passage from San Francisco to arrive in Melbourne on 26 May 1915.

Tullie arrived back home to find a city gripped by an excitement that betrayed a lack of knowledge about what was really going on in Europe. The sadness would come, but not just yet. She stayed almost six weeks and had a farewell party just before she left. It was midnight and most of the guests had left the Sloss house. Someone started playing the piano, a tune called 'The End of a Perfect Day'. Bruce was out on the verandah and started to sing. 'Standing there with his lovely voice he sang it to the end. I never hear that song now but I see him there, tall and straight, leaning against the post,' Tullie wrote in her diary.

Bruce and the family went to the train the next morning to see Tullie on her way. Bruce was in good spirits. 'He was his usual funny self on the platform and had everyone around him in peals of laughter,' Tullie said. As the train pulled away from the platform, she shouted to Bruce that she would see him in France. 'Whenever in [my] imagination I see him now, he is still smiling and happy as he was on yon day.'

Days after Bruce enlisted, the Victorian Parliamentary Recruiting Committee released a huge two-by-two-metre poster carrying the message 'Will They Never Come?'. The slogan was borrowed from a British recruiting poster and the artwork localised by Melbourne artist Jim Hannam. It contained the image of a wounded Australian soldier standing over a dead mate, and in the top right-hand corner was the MCG, packed with football fans. To top it off was the plaintive headline 'An appeal from the Dardanelles'. It was quite a statement for Australia's first recruiting poster to make.

It was circulated to every town and shire council in Victoria. Another 250 were allocated to railway stations and a further 400 were attached to hoardings across Melbourne. Within days, the poster had been sent far and wide, to Toowoomba in the north and Hobart in the south. In case anyone missed the message behind the football crowd in the poster, the *Mercury* spelt it out: '[T]his is intended as a reproof of the "slackers" who were wasting time over sports, when their help is needed to save the Empire from disaster.' There was no doubt that the pressure on sportsmen and those who watched what they did was building. It would take the best possible reasons or a thick hide to avoid its impact.

More demands were to follow. The War Census asked Australian men aged between 18 and 60 to fill out a survey on their potential for military service. The census identified 600,000 fit Australians below the age of 45, but there was no way of knowing how many of them were going to sign up, no matter how many men Pearce promised the British Army Council to reinforce Australian divisions in the field. The census results even gave some football administrators comfort, when they analysed some of the answers. 'There was not any justification for abandoning football. The fact of football being played or not being played did not matter at all to those who were not enlisting,' a Carlton official told the VFL executive.

The impasse with football was devolving to the solid working-class clubs in Melbourne – Collingwood, Richmond, Fitzroy and Carlton. Fitzroy captain Harold McLennan took the unusual step of putting the players' case to the public, through the columns of *The Argus*. He explained that each Fitzroy player was on a flat rate of 25 shillings a match:

> All the players are men who work at regular occupations, and no one should begrudge them the solatium they receive for the hard training they undergo and the many little sacrifices they endure in order to keep themselves fit and to give the public the amusement derived from the best exposition of football ... are paid footballers any more laggard than amateur footballers, or baseballers, or cricketers, or racegoers or any other sports, or, in fact, the public in general? I think not.

McLennan was peeved at the level of abuse footballers were receiving for continuing to play, especially in the newspapers' letters columns. 'Would any of your correspondents be patriotic enough to supply each football club with a set of recruiting posters to be in the training rooms, and so bring home frequently to every footballer the reality of the war and the call for volunteers?' he asked, with an unsportsmanlike rhetorical flourish and more than a hint of naivety. 'If sport is interfering seriously with recruiting, I agree that it should cease. But what is the good of stopping football unless other sports are stopped?' McLennan had a point. His other key observation was that professionals were less likely to enlist because many of them were married men. In contrast, amateur footballers were single. 'Of the eighteen players representing Fitzroy in the last three matches nine are married, and of the other nine, some at least have family ties almost as binding,' McLennan said. As for his own circumstances, McLennan admitted to never having been paid to play but for the 1915 season he was going to accept his 25 shillings and donate it to 'our gallant little allies – the Serbs'.

Carlton's rationale for continuing to be involved avoided the professional question altogether. 'It was felt that the playing of football on Saturday afternoons had no adverse effect on recruiting, was a relaxation for the public from the serious problems of business and war, and that it would be unwise to deprive thousands of people of that source of recreation,' the club resolved. And cutting staff and player salaries twice during the 1915 season 'had no effect whatsoever on their training or their zeal to win the Premiership', the club reported, in a statement that some amateur-minded types might have interpreted as an argument against paying players at all.

Richmond remained confident that it was doing all it could to support the war effort. At a club event to farewell seven footballers who had enlisted, club president and federal Labor MP Frank Tudor claimed the club had sent more men to the Front than any of its rivals. Others on the committee spoke about the need to keep football going during 'natural gloom surrounding war conditions'. 'Footballers were not unmindful of their duties, something like 1,500 of them having enlisted,' one committeeman told the crowd. In some circles, it might have been a powerful argument. But there was a contrary view that footballers shy of enlisting were just waiting to see how long the war would last.

Bruce Sloss's well-developed sense of responsibility made him a natural fit for officer training. It meant that the months ahead would be more onerous than just the drilling and marching that would be the staple of the non-commissioned officers' (NCO) existence at Broadmeadows, or the alternative camp at the Melbourne Showgrounds in Ascot Vale. Sloss arrived at Broad-meadows on Monday, 6 September and wrote to his mother and family at the end of the week that he was 'treated very well . . . [and] the meals are as good as a one and threepenny meal in town'. But he was there for three weeks without leave, so he couldn't see Glad, his fiancée, as he'd planned. He kept writing home, describing the training he did – 'sham fights' and 'march covering a few miles', 'lectures' – and his wish to go to the theatre on his weekend back in Armadale. It was a strange half-existence – in the army but not overseas, able to have a sporadic social life when time off was allowed, or, in some instances, dispensation to play football after the League allowed clubs to select enlisted players until they left the country.

By September 1915, the consequences of Australia's involve-ment in the war were becoming clearer at home. The papers were carrying daily casualty lists. The August offensive at Gallipoli was a renewed push to break the Turkish defences by outflank-ing them, with five British divisions of reinforcements to boost the AIF surge. It was launched from the Anzac position. But the ground the Allies gained during the offensive came at great cost and was always precariously held. Lone Pine was a gruesome Australian tale all of its own; brutal hand-to-hand combat, extraordinary courage and a victory that was soon lost amid the aggressive Turkish counterattacks. The initiative was snatched away from the Allied troops. The last best gamble had failed.

Already, many of the Gallipoli wounded were home. By the end of 1915, 6000 veterans had returned, a third to Victoria. Many of them were football fans, and the League wanted to do the right thing by giving them free entry to the finals. But the consequences of the act of charity were unpredictable. Some of the soldiers tried to force their way through the turnstiles at the MCG for the semi-final between Collingwood and Fitzroy, and when they were rebuffed they started to sing 'Australia We Will Be There' before forcing open another gate, opening the way for 'hundreds [who] streamed into the members' reserve, laughing and shouting'.

While this might have appeared as some good-natured fun, it was indicative of a trend that would become more prevalent – the unpredictability of returned men. There were increasing examples of erratic behaviour in Melbourne. One returned man attacked a pieman; another bit the leg of a military policeman; others assaulted a grocer. There were reports of returned soldiers begging on the streets. Drinking and abusive language were other problems. 'When soldiers are misbehaving themselves no matter what the details of the case are, the general public are inclined to side with the men . . . with the result that the men are regarding themselves as beyond the reach of law and order,' one unnamed military official said.

Here was the first evidence of the brutal psychological impact of the war, which would become a terrible burden for a generation. Local authorities in the aftermath of Australia's first sustained engagement of the war had no understanding of such things; all they wanted was some form of order to be restored. There was a hope that football, in its way, might offer a balm to the horror the soldiers brought home. So for a time the game that had been reviled for its negative effect on recruitment came to be seen as a distraction to the damaged soldiers who came home. Yet there was another niggling truth behind the new development. If this was what happened to the men who signed up, why would you do it? Who would willingly enlist after seeing the human cost?

Two of Collingwood's best players, Malcolm 'Doc' Seddon and Paddy Rowan, joined up on 14 July, making it clear that, despite the club's strong showing that season, they wanted to be part of the war effort. The club, officially at least, was supportive, stating the pair 'unselfishly made their desires and ambitions subservient to the national needs'. But before the pair went overseas, they were in great form, getting exemptions from their training to help Collingwood finish on top of the ladder, two points and a healthy percentage clear of Carlton.

It was inevitable that Seddon and Rowan would be part of the Collingwood finals campaign, but a meningitis outbreak in camp led to strict quarantine conditions that prevented them from playing the final home and away match. But it was not the exercise of public-health discipline that kept the pair away from the MCG on grand final day; it was a ten-mile march that morning, followed by a bowl of thick Irish stew. An alarmed Magpie coach, Jock McHale, sent a car to pick up his two players from camp in time to get them to the match, but the damage was done. As Carlton surged in the final quarter to establish what became a match-winning lead, Seddon and Rowe had no energy. They were spent.

Seddon recalled years later that the adjutant who ordered the march must have been a Carlton supporter. If so, it was a stunningly successful tactic, as Carlton charged to a 33-point win and its fifth flag. Not that the crusty old *Bulletin* magazine's version of what happened left anyone in doubt about what it thought of the fuss:

> The [Collingwood] club secretary whirled out to camp in a motor-car. What he said is not known but the military potentate, who had failed to bow down to King Football relaxed his iron hand . . . Over in Gallipoli tired soldiers . . . settled anew to repel a charge of ignorant heathens who had never heard of Collingwood, and would probably burn it to the ground if they were given a chance to enter it.

For all of that – and a crowd of 39,343 (almost 9000 more than the 1914 final) – the League and military authorities believed there was still a taste for football, especially if it could be turned into a source of patriotic funds. In what looked like a tacit acknowledgement that footballers were finally getting the message, the VFL and the Victorian Amateur Football Association started sending old guernseys to the camps to promote intra-camp competitions. The most high-profile example of this determination to keep footballers inside and outside of the camp playing the game was to stage a match after the grand final between the premiers and a team drawn from the training camp.

It was a good idea, on paper. The entrepreneur and sports fanatic John Wren – Collingwood Football Club philanthropist, creator of the infamous Tote, and racecourse owner – thought so too. When he enlisted and was sent to Royal Park for his training, he promptly arranged for a football match between a team from his camp and the one at the Showgrounds. Wren understood the lure of sport, both as an entertainment and as a money-spinner. Not surprisingly, he was appointed secretary of the camp's sports and entertainment committee, which put him in an ideal place to organise such games. He donated £50 towards a fund that would support a stadium for boxing and other shows. Private Wren only lasted until December, when he was medically discharged from the army, but the power of the sporting competition in the camps remained potent, regardless of his presence.

The Camp team was a strong outfit, including Sloss, Geelong's George Heinz and Bill Orchard, and Melbourne's Charlie Lilley. Perhaps unsurprisingly, Seddon and Rowan were not available, this time because of injury. Blues captain Alf Baud, George Challis and Herb Burleigh, who were part of the grand final victory the previous week, were named in the Camp team to play against their own club. The strange selection summarised the odd nature of the contest. It turned out to be a lacklustre affair, which drew 6000 fans to the MCG and raised £248 for the Wounded Soldiers Fund. According to one commentator, the most attractive feature of the match was the Broadmeadows Military Band.

The atmosphere of a home and away match was missing, despite the intent of some of the players. It was also not helped by the Camp team wearing donated Collingwood jumpers and being hard to identify. Yet the Camp team stuck with Carlton for the first half, only falling behind when Carlton rammed on six goals in the third quarter. The burst of scoring set up Carlton for a 21-point victory. Sloss, seemingly already to have lost some match fitness after four months without football, had a quiet match, and Heinz was named the soldiers' best player. It was the final game of major football in Victoria for the season, but football's closure only pushed another sport into the recruiting limelight.

Donald Mackinnon was proud of his role as VCA president, especially when Victoria won the 1914–15 Sheffield Shield. But when Mackinnon presented the team its Sheffield Shield winners' medals at the VCA meeting in September, he had his recruiting hat on. He told the players that cricket helped build armies, and although cricketers were thinking about the game, their feelings naturally would go to those who were fighting for the Empire, and to the families left at home, mourning lost relatives. The mood was similar in Sydney, where the New South Wales Cricket Association (NSWCA) official Syd Smith said in September 1915 it would not be right 'for the association to do anything in the way of sport that might cause the younger players to play cricket instead of doing their duty to their country'.

This was mild in comparison to what happened next. Cricket, with its strong middle-class connections, had not been subjected to the same level of debate as football about its players enlisting. But all of that changed when a small journal launched a withering condemnation of the nation's cricketers. On 7 October 1915, the weekly publication *The Australian Statesman and Mining Standard* published an editorial entitled 'Cricket and Shirking'. The newspaper's attack was the most pointed of all the press reactions towards the playing sportsmen and was most likely written by its editor, a journalist and Elizabethan scholar, Ernest Oliphant.

The editorial pointed out that, despite the unpatriotic behaviour of Victorian footballers, it did not compare with the example of the nation's cricketers. It went on to claim that only 11 Sheffield Shield cricketers from New South Wales had enlisted, seven from South Australia and only one from Victoria, Tommy Matthews. The list of 20 Victorians who had not enlisted was published. Most of them were senior players and professionals, such as Warwick Armstrong, 'Dainty' Ironmonger, Wesley old boy Dr Roy Park, Collingwood Cricket Club champion Jack Ryder, Fred Baring, and Fitzroy footballer and cricketer Ted McDonald.

In some cases, there were extenuating circumstances. Armstrong, for example, was 35 and suffered from malaria. He also had elderly parents and two younger brothers who had enlisted. These reasons might have been sufficient for him to feel that he could not enlist or that he was medically unfit for service. Ryder's reasons for not enlisting were never disclosed and he did not even tell his family why he did not join up. Park did enlist later in the war. McDonald's eldest son, Allan, believed for years that his father, who also played football with Fitzroy during the war, had seen action. It was one of the reasons Allan McDonald joined the air force in the Second World War, but it was an illusion. Ted McDonald, who became one of Australia's finest fast bowlers before he threw it in to pursue the lure of the pound in English league cricket, never enlisted.

In December 1915, the NSWCA wrote to the VCA that it would not allow New South Wales cricketers to take part in a proposed Patriotic match between the two states 'because it did not want to do anything to impede recruitment'. Mackinnon took the contrary view and maintained the match would act as a spur to young men to enlist, by reminding them of the need to do the right thing. Mackinnon, as always, had faith that once decent men were presented with good reasons or compelling evidence to enlist, they would sign up. Here was an illustration, if anyone needed any better example, that there were two compelling sides to the argument about sport's role in wartime.

The match went ahead at the MCG over Christmas 1915 between the Victorian XI and the so-called Next Fifteen. But, in much the same way as the Camp team contest against Carlton, it was a bloodless affair. Oliphant's rage in the columns of *The Australian Statesman and Mining Standard* might have been mollified by the decision to suspend first-class cricket in Australia during the war. An Ashes tour of England was also cancelled. The consequences were that grade cricket became the only meaningful cricket contest, and Victorian grade cricket the most competitive because of the number of Sheffield Shield players who did not enlist. There was, however, no grand final or pennant.

4

The Larrikins

Frank Beaurepaire's role at the YMCA meant he was busy making sure the troops were being given sufficient physical activity to keep them fit and in good shape. A week before Christmas 1915, Beaurepaire got the MCC onside to host a sports program at the MCG to raise funds for the soldiers at Gallipoli. Little did anyone in Melbourne know that the plans for evacuation from the Dardanelles were so far advanced that Australian troops were only days away from leaving Anzac Cove. And, although the MCG attendances were modest, the donations were generous and the interest was keen.

One event in particular captured the public's interest. It was called the Military Marathon, which meant that, rather than mirror the original marathon distance of 26 miles and 385 yards, it would be only 11½ miles, starting at the Broadmeadows camp and finishing at the MCG. Although the Victorian Athletic Association had suspended all meetings in July 1915 because of the war, there was still strong residual interest in running, in particular. The Military Marathon took on a different dimension when Private H.W. Davis, who had only been at Gallipoli for 15 hours before he was wounded and invalided home, was one of the 23-man field. It was a remarkable feat that he was fit enough to undertake the event at all, let alone finish it in an hour and a half. One other runner was particularly noteworthy – Thomas Sinton Hewitt. Hewitt was in the leading pack of runners for most of the race, moving into a strong position when they hit Sydney Road and headed towards the MCG. He defied a strong headwind to take the lead as the pack charged into Victoria Street. Hewitt maintained his lead as he entered the MCG for the final half-mile, and crossed the line first in just over 75 minutes. How Hewitt came to be in the field is a story of a young man's persistence to carve out a niche for himself. His choices were unconventional, even unpredictable, but never less than interesting.

Hewitt was already 28 when he ran the Military Marathon and had crammed in a fair bit of living. His father had, in the language of the day, deserted his wife and five children, to head off on an adventure to places more exotic than suburban Melbourne – just exactly where, though, was never certain. Thomas, at the tender age of 12, decided to join the Boer War and be the drummer for Colonel Tom Price, who was on his way to the Veldt, but his mother made it clear he was going nowhere. She had less success in preventing him embarking on a financially perilous acting career.

Hewitt worked two jobs – one with famed milliner Mrs Huntsman, in Chapel Street, Prahran, and the second acting, when and where he could. Thomas Sinton Hewitt was not in acting because of any matinee idol good looks: he had a pugnacious countenance, was short and solid, and this rugged appearance was topped off by a receding hairline. He looked old before his time. Yet he exuded a charming optimism. He was up for anything, and thought everything was possible. He wanted to dive off every bridge from Burnley to the city. It was a boast that was never realised, although he managed the Heyington Railway Bridge, over the Yarra at Toorak, with his cousin Laurie. And he even won a high-diving competition in Sydney.

His acting started with one of Melbourne's finest acting troupes, the Bland Holt company, before he took over managing the Star Picture Company, which toured movies across Victoria. On occasions, Hewitt would revert to his own performances; his relatives would play piano and Hewitt would recite Kipling's poem 'Gunga Din'. There were similar performances at the South Yarra Baptist Church, where Hewitt, impeccably attired in tails, would do imitations of prominent figures, including British MP Austen Chamberlain (the half-brother of England's future prime minister Neville), while accompanied on the Edison-Bell phonograph. It was an unconventional introduction to middle-distance running, to say the least.

But it was probably Hewitt's untrammelled enthusiasm that led him to the Malvern Harriers, an amateur athletics club near his home. The Malvern club was established in 1892 and, unlike some of its rivals – Melbourne Harriers and Collegians – it offered a touch of the greasepaint that Hewitt loved. The athletes exercised to music, worked on parallel bars and gave public exhibitions of boxing and wrestling. Hewitt was soon a selector and club handicapper. And his performances started to attract attention, including a 15th in the Victorian ten-mile cross-country championship. But the athlete who would become best known at Malvern was Percy Cerutty, who brought some athletes from his first club, Ennismore, to Malvern in June 1914.

For a short time, Cerutty and Hewitt were clubmates. Hewitt went to war and Cerutty stayed at home to build the framework that became the basis of his unique athletic coaching career, which would help make John Landy and Herb Elliott champions. Hewitt was fit and single when he tried to enlist after Gallipoli but was rejected in what seems like another recruitment anomaly. When he tried again on 9 September 1915, he was accepted. Hewitt married Ida Jennings on 4 January 1916 and remained in Melbourne until he left for England in May. It would be there that one of his most productive associations would begin.

Bruce Sloss completed and passed his first training require-ments in Melbourne on 7 October 1915. He was a sergeant but the next stage of his training – 26 full days – would elevate him to a second lieutenant before he left. He completed his course on elementary tactics a week before Christmas 1915. Two weeks earlier, on the other side of the world, Bruce's brother James became part of the Siege of Kut, a bleak episode in the Allied battle with the Turks. Details of the siege were scarce. In truth, the Sloss family knew very little of James's mission. He sailed under sealed orders, and Christina and May, his sister, tried to say goodbye to 'Son' before his ship left Port Melbourne. 'We waited at the pier all afternoon hoping they would let us on. When we were eventually let on it was so dark we could not see a thing. We looked and called Son but he did not hear us and neither were we sure now that he was on this ship,' May wrote to Tullie.

Eventually, they thought they spotted James on board, illu-minated by the flame of a match near his face. The Sloss family would know little about the strange events that had led James to the siege and its aftermath, and Bruce would be in England before he knew the worst of it. But there was a growing aware-ness that the war was touching more families, ensnaring brothers, husbands, fiancés and sometimes fathers in its trap.

No matter where Australian soldiers went, there was always a game of football in the offing. It wasn't just Phil Robin's team that played under the Pyramids' shadow. Three months after Victor Laidlaw, a South Melbourne tailor, left home, he saw his 2nd Field Ambulance take on the 4th Light Horse in Cairo. Laidlaw was disappointed in the result. He wrote in his diary, 'We were leading up until a few minutes to go when a Light Horse [soldier] received a free kick which ended it.' The free kick gave the Light Horse the chance to seal the match, and it won by three points.

One of the players in the 2nd Field Ambulance team, Clyde Donaldson, would go on playing football, at every opportunity he was in khaki. Donaldson played with the Brunswick juniors before he joined Essendon. He had two seasons for Essendon before he enlisted in the first batch of volunteers. '[He] would have developed in to a champion as he had speed, resolution and kicking power,' one newspaper observed, with a fatalistic sense that Donaldson's budding career was already over. 'But he is playing at higher stakes, and may his dash remain undiminished.'

Richmond was a working-class inner-city Melbourne suburb, crammed with knitting mills, bootmakers, textile manufacturers, tanneries and engineering firms. Not surprisingly, its football club was a staunchly working-class outfit, in outlook and spirit, although not always in composition. But the Richmond locals were happy to accept outsiders, especially if they played for their beloved football team. Hughie James hailed from the other side of town, in Ascot Vale, not necessarily well-heeled but not as overrun with industry as Richmond. But that didn't mean James got ahead of himself: he was a skilled labourer, the oldest of three sons, all of them bricklayers, all of them former students of the Moonee Ponds West State School. Hughie was also something else – a footballer with the compelling combination of a touch of larrikin and the gift of leadership.

After a few appearances with the Essendon Association club, where he seemed particularly unsuited to football, James took himself off to Richmond in 1909, where he became a ruckman who insinuated himself into the very fabric of the club by dint of his performances and loyalty to the yellow and black. Before long, it was hard for Richmond supporters to think of the Tigers before Hughie came along. The game suddenly made sense to him, and he was able to dominate it. Hughie was a clean mark but more importantly he had the ability to be where the ball was. Coupled with his bullocking work around the ground, Hughie James not only made a big contribution to the team but also stood out, even when some of his kicks for goal floated or tumbled off target. He was hard to forget. Physically imposing, with a firm jaw and even gaze, he generated a sense of calm and purpose. It was a temperament that engendered confidence in those around him – a valuable attribute in troubled times.

After the 1915 season wound up, seven Richmond players enlisted, including legendary rover Frank 'Checker' Hughes. Hughie James had persevered during the 1915 season but didn't want to do it again. Just like Bruce Sloss, he felt the pull of family. Hughie's two younger brothers had already left. Arthur signed up early, aged 21, and was on the first ship to leave Melbourne in October 1914. His other brother, Laurie, just 19, followed in January 1915. Hugh was 25, had a wife, Ethel, and baby daughter, Sylvia, in Ascot Vale, but he felt the pull of doing his duty, even if he did his best to create the impression of someone just heading out for a Sunday drive.

He regaled onlookers with the story of how he had initially been rejected because of poor eyesight. 'But it seems they mixed me up with another chap. Anyhow, I objected and told them I would submit to a test on the other side of the street. The doctor was very nice when he found out how matters were. It was all over in a moment or two,' James explained. 'I thought it was up to me to do my share. You see, I'm young and in good condition. And who knows? I might be on the ball again in a season or two.' James's enlistment at the start of 1916 was just the kind of propaganda the recruiters were looking for.

Richmond was also the football home of Leslie Edward Lee, a clean-cut, boyish young man with rich auburn hair, who went by the nickname 'Leggo'. Lee played with the Richmond junior side and was set to have a long career as a ruckman with the senior team. He debuted late in 1913, played the next game, which was the final match of the season, and then went back to local Richmond district club Balmain in 1914. From there, he went across town to Williamstown, in the VFA.

The reasons for his departure from Richmond are unclear but perhaps fitting, given that Lee's life was anything but straightforward. He was born in Parkside, a suburb of Adelaide, on 21 November 1894 and given the names Edward Leslie Barnes Cooper. His father was Edward Cooper and his mother Isabella Barnes. The couple wasn't married and Isabella returned to Richmond, where she had been born and where most of her extended family still lived, with her baby. There was no allowance or pension for a woman in her position, and work that fitted in with the demands of motherhood was rare. Isabella's best option was to have her family look after her baby. So she gave her son to her eldest sister, Eliza, who was married to George Lee. The couple already had a son (George Bedford) who was around the same age as Isabella's boy.

Isabella's decision was more than just handing over her son to her sister for care. Edward would take the family name and for all intents and purposes be a Lee. So Edward Leslie Barnes Cooper became Leslie Edward Lee. But what was better than having one mother was having three. Isabella and Eliza's other sister, Ann, who also lived in Richmond, were keenly involved in raising young Leslie too. Despite Isabella's closeness and contact, Les Lee grew up thinking that Isabella was his aunt, not his mother. It led to a poignant consequence that none of them could have foreseen.

But, for the time being, Lee, a labourer, decided that he too would do his duty, and he enlisted in March 1916. He was one of the reinforcements for the 10th Machine Gun Company, where Bruce Sloss was the lieutenant. Lee left Melbourne just two months after he signed up and did some cursory training.

There was no doubt about *The Winner*'s intended audience when it launched a week before the outbreak of war. The weekly broadsheet based in *The Herald* and *Weekly Times* stable was going to report on every sport possible for readers who wanted to follow results, analysis and commentary from experts.

There would be racing, boxing, wrestling, football, golf, bowls, cycling, coursing, lacrosse, athletics, rowing and quoits. There would be rifle-shooting, gymnastics, croquet, tennis, hunting, fishing and hockey. Frank Beaurepaire was hired to be the paper's swimming writer and Carl Willis would write cricket.

Willis's appointment was a surprise because it seemed based only on his impressive potential, which featured a stunning and chanceless 168 he made for the Victorian Colts against their New South Wales counterparts in January 1913. But the paper's football writer – and Willis's former football coach at University – Gerald Brosnan was the likely reason for Willis's appearance in the paper's columns. Willis played 14 games for his new club, South Melbourne, in 1915, but even before the club decided to withdraw from the 1916 season, he had enlisted.

Willis, as was his way, had quickly made friends at the paper, and when he signed on there was a farewell for him at a St Kilda cafe, presided over by the paper's editor-in-chief James Davidson. He told the staff and contributors that 30 per cent of the paper's journalists had already enlisted. One had died and two were badly wounded. Davidson went on to praise Willis's 'qualities of heart, head and muscle' that made him a popular figure. There were poems read and a range of speakers, including Brosnan, who wished Willis well. When Willis responded, he reached for Sir Henry Newbolt's classic poem of the era: 'To set the cause above renown/To love the game beyond the prize/To honor, while you strike him down/The foe that comes with fearless eyes'. Willis's principal at Wesley, Dickie Adamson, would have nodded his approval. Willis explained that his every effort would be to model his actions on the poem. There was applause and vocal agreement with the sentiments. Willis was given an inscribed silver cigarette case and match box.

Willis started a trend at the paper by writing about his military experiences from a sportsman's perspective. Brosnan was keen to encourage such material, and correspondence from a range of sportsmen at the Front increased the longer the war went. Brosnan was a natural mentor, who had been well schooled in the basics of mathematics, writing and poetry at Miss Clancy's private school in Geelong. He was prone to quoting the poets Tennyson and Browning, and believed in fostering writing talent such as Carl Willis.

Once in camp, Willis was quick to provide a droll summary of what life in khaki was like. He had the knack for delivering sharp insights wrapped in self-deprecation, which he extended to others who, like him, found sport an easy task but military training a different beast altogether. Willis found the perfect example with the camp's firearms training:

When the shoot commences there are many humorous remarks and scenes. It is a remarkable fact that men who are champions at one form of sport cannot imagine how they are not champions at shooting at practically their first attempt, and get quite annoyed when the target is not hit . . . In common with many others not accustomed to rifle shooting I had the idea that all you did was to lie down, point the rifle straight and pull the trigger: but it is not so, as I found out.

Brosnan brought an extensive contact book to his role at the paper – he had captained Fitzroy to two flags, led Victoria against Western Australia in 1904 and played 131 games with Fitzroy. He had also coached University, which brought him into contact with young and intelligent men who gravitated towards the erudite older man who saw how sport could complement their lives. Although Brosnan struggled for success at University, it did not reflect on his skill as an astute and measured judge of footballers. Just as important was his capacity to assume the role of a mentor to the young men around him. Their regard for him was palpable, not just in the breadth and frequency of their correspondence with him, but also in the respectful tone that characterised the letters. At the core of these missives was an understanding of the shared connections sport gave them – a group of friends and acquaintances, once opponents on the sporting field, now united in a confrontation with the highest stakes of all. No wonder some of the letters Brosnan received had a nostalgic, wistful tone. To men at the Front, these more innocent moments and the pleasures of football in particular were a pleasant reminder of home and an antidote to the grim events that confronted them.

The start of 1916 did not promise less discussion about what football would do about the war. The December evacuation of Gallipoli was, in the true sense of the word, miraculous – not one Australian life was lost as the AIF left the Mediterranean boneyard under cover of darkness, without alerting the Turks. But while the AIF waited to join its allies in Europe for the next stage of the war, the line of convalescent soldiers coming home grew longer. The demand for men to replace them on the front line did not diminish. And the football codes' decisions about continuing in the face of the war remained a hot topic.

The South Australians made the call first. On Tuesday, 18 January 1916, the South Australian Football League decided 'to arrange no football program for 1916 unless the war should terminate before or during the football season'. There was an attempt to create a breakaway league, under the leadership of the resolutely working-class Port Adelaide. The new league even had a name – the Patriotic Football Association – but securing grounds without the support of the South Australian Football League or the South Australian Cricket Association made it difficult to create a regular round of matches. But the working-class clubs played anyway, whenever they could find a ground.

The Adelaide moves, inevitably, put the heat back on Victorian football, but there was no expectation the VFL would shut down its competition. The VFA confirmed it would not be holding a competition in 1916, but it was a different beast to the League – it didn't draw large attendances, and revenue would have been hard to sustain during the war.

As for paying VFL players, that was a responsibility the clubs had to bear, and was therefore not strictly a League issue. Yet there was no doubt that players from a range of clubs were finding it hard to resist the call of their mates at the Front. South Melbourne made its position clear in February when a player meeting resulted in seven players stating they would abstain from playing under any circumstances in 1916. In an echo of Bruce Sloss's sentiment almost a year earlier, the players said they had relatives at the Front. The club was quick to support its players.

The pressure was mounting on the VFL. A week later, a Gallipoli veteran penned a letter to *The Argus* that carried the weight of someone who knew what the war was actually like. The VFL, not for the first time, was the clear target:

> To view the execrable football-as-usual decision of the Victorian Football League from the vantage point of a returned soldier who has lost some of the best friends imaginable on the blood-stained Gallipoli Peninsula, is to be filled with an intense hatred for a body which can be so callously indifferent to the finer feelings of those men who are making all manner of sacrifice and enduring unutterable hell that these sport as usual fanatics who deny themselves nothing, may enjoy the freedom of British rule.

It was not an uncommon view, but the VFL was not ready to capitulate completely. The League started 1916 determined to hold a competition and initially offered up only 10 per cent of the total takings to the patriotic funds, while the clubs kept 90 per cent. The proposal was widely ridiculed, revealing the League to be out of touch with the public mood, and it quickly abandoned it for a commitment to give everything to the funds, bar 'legitimate expenses'. But Melbourne pulled out and then, at a special meeting in March, a deadlock occurred between the four clubs that wanted to continue – Collingwood, Carlton, Fitzroy and Richmond – and the remaining clubs that wanted the 1916 competition abandoned: Geelong, South Melbourne, St Kilda and Essendon.

In the end, the four inner–city – and largely working-class – clubs made up the season. Player payments, other than out-of-pocket expenses, were abolished. It might have given Adamson, Wilmot, Mackinnon and his team of recruiters some comfort but it failed to satisfy those supporters who wanted the game to continue. 'Their matches, after the first one or two, would not arouse much interest, and they would probably do more harm than good to the game,' Brosnan forecast. He was proved correct. Each club played the other four times. Technically, a club could finish at the bottom of the ladder and still make the grand final. It was farcical.

But the fans' publication *The Football Record* was in no mood to decry the arrival of another season. 'A yell was raised by the morning papers that there should not be any football . . . they opened out like Maxim guns on the game of the people. Not a word against racing, not a word against the pleasure-seekers who go to boxing matches or theatres,' it thundered. 'If conscription comes along it will put an end to all the wrangling and bickering, and there will be very few left to play or look on at football. We shall all be drilling.' And furthermore, 'Far better that the tens of thousands of Melbourne's old men, youths, women and children should have the opportunity of enjoying the poor man's recreation for two hours a week at last.'

The remaining clubs at least tried to sound the right note. 'We are going to play the game up to the hilt and will make it as interesting as possible for the public, so as to attract the crowds,' Collingwood secretary Ernie Copeland promised.

But it was a bit hard when your best players were leaving for the Front.

Dan Minogue captained Collingwood in the 1915 losing grand final and was considered one of the highest profile players in the competition. Minogue didn't need to have great foresight to predict that a four-team competition was not going to test him. He enlisted on 16 March 1916, at the age of 24 and a half. Minogue was one of those durable and tough men who fought their way through what might be called a disadvantaged upbringing. He was raised in Bendigo, educated at the Catholic Marist Brothers College and opted to go down the mines to support his widowed mother. Even there, he showed a remarkable resilience when he fell 13 metres in an underground mine, lacerated and bruised his right arm and had to have six stitches in a head wound. That was it for Dan. Mining was too dangerous. He had seen how the dreaded miners' disease afflicted his mates and now he was lucky enough to survive a fall. 'I said to myself: You'd better get out while your luck's in, Danny my boy.'

Football was Minogue's passport out of the mines. The VFL talent scouts had already picked him out as a young man to watch, and Collingwood, Fitzroy, St Kilda, Essendon and Carlton approached him. Minogue had no strong feelings for any of the clubs, but Collingwood's offer came with a job at the South Melbourne gasworks. By 1911, he was making his debut for the Magpies, although in the final minutes of his first game he broke a collarbone and missed nine matches.

He came back in time for the finals and was selected in the grand final against Essendon. Early in the match, Minogue was jammed in a pack and broke the collarbone again. Gamely, he carried on. Collingwood's famous forward Dick Lee reinjured his troublesome knee and together the injured pair tried to keep Collingwood in the game. Neither could come off, because there were no substitutes. In pain, Minogue grimly held on to a one-handed mark and managed to kick a goal, but his courage was not enough to get the Magpies over the line.

After that, Minogue became the Collingwood 'heartbeat', the tough-as-nails competitor who inspired his mates with his leadership and drive. He was the team's ruckman, strong in the contests, powerful through the trunk and legs, and willing to deploy his solid frame to shepherd and bump. He was a good kick and mark, with a willingness to handball and an aversion to covering too much territory on foot. Coach Jock McHale saw something special in Minogue and made him captain at the tender age of 22. Together, they were a double act, coach and captain, the gruff tactician and the shrewd leader of men.

Minogue believed the advent of war stymied a plan to send two Australian Rules teams overseas, to England and the USA, to spread the message about the game. He claimed he 'was assured' of being picked for the tour. Nonetheless, he was sanguine about the war's impact on football and felt the League's decision to continue in 1915 was correct. '[A]lthough there were many who thought that with the war raging sport should cease, that was rather a drastic view, especially as healthy outdoor games were helping to develop the young manhood which the Empire needed. Moreover, sport was an outlet for the pent-up emotions of the people,' Minogue said two decades later. But at the time, he reckoned enlisting was the right thing to do.

The four remaining VFL teams decided that it was a good idea to use the football talent available in the military training camps as a source of pre-season practice matches that could raise funds for the war relief fund. At the end of April 1916, Richmond took on the Pioneer XVIII, captained by Hughie James, and won at Punt Road. Minogue played for Collingwood, in his club's match against the soldiers, a week before he went into camp. The Magpies beat the soldiers by 19 points in front of a small crowd at Victoria Park. The newspapers were flippant about the contest but they underestimated the importance of the match to the players. It might have been a social encounter, but there was no lack of energy, feeling and commitment from the players. Football was a relief from the endless drills and daily routines, but it was taken seriously by those who had played the game to a high standard only weeks or months earlier. And the standard of those in uniform was rapidly outstripping that of the players left in club jumpers.

The 'season' opened on Saturday, 6 May 1916, with Richmond against Collingwood. Minogue was already in camp, at Maribyrnong in Melbourne's western suburbs, training to be a gunner. He hoped that he had dispensation to play but was on duty that day, until 1 pm. Minogue's plan was to try to leave early, trusting that Collingwood secretary Ernie Copeland's letter to his commanding officer explaining the situation would be enough. Around midday, Minogue was summoned to the office where an adjutant had Copeland's letter. 'Well, Gunner Minogue, I was not aware that you were captain of Collingwood and what is more, I did not know that such a team existed,' he told Minogue. 'Anyone would think that you were of some importance wouldn't they?'

Minogue bit his lip, but it became clear that he wasn't going to get his dispensation. Minogue resolved to do a runner, because, he reasoned, he couldn't really get sacked from the army. '[I] was furious. To be denied the opportunity of playing a game that was now part of my life was too much for me,' he said. But before he took action, the adjutant sent for him again and this time told Minogue he could go but urged him not to hurt himself playing football. The Collingwood captain thought it was a huge joke: 'Fancy telling a man who was going in to the war, to see that he did not get hurt. It was just too rich.' Minogue made it to the match, where Hughie James also appeared. James had no such problems getting leave to play. (Collingwood won by eight points.)

Soon after the South Australian Football League made its decision to abandon the season, Charles Perry applied for a commission in the AIF. Perry had moved on quickly from his stand-out season in 1915 and had become one of the chaplains at the Mitcham training camp in South Australia. Perry's experience was unusual for chaplains who joined the AIF: many knew little about the army and had to learn quickly, often acquainting themselves with their 'flock' on the way to the Front and finding some of the troops' habits – drinking and swearing – an affront to their Christian sensibilities. Perry decided that he would share the training with the men he wanted to serve beside. It gave him a valuable perspective, and introduced him to a group of young men, especially through weekly multi-denominational services that were held at the Mitcham camp.

Applications from men of the cloth to join the AIF outnumbered the vacancies, so Perry's role at the camp probably helped him secure a spot. At his farewell, there was a great deal of celebration about the 3000 South Australian Methodists who had already joined up. Perry lauded the quality of the men he had met at Mitcham, and urged everyone to pray for them and also give them sympathetic treatment. Perry understood there would be many confronting moments for the soldiers in the months ahead. Compassion at home and some attempt to understand their burden would help make life easier for them.

The soldiers were already at the heart of Perry's approach to the looming task, and he put the troops first, regardless of whichever church they belonged to. It was an enlightened approach and not one shared with many other chaplains, especially when Perry added some stern words for the church itself, when he urged it to do better. 'Why should we withhold our hand when they are willing to give their lives?' he asked. The church 'had not yet played half the game it should'. There was already a sense of what it meant to be Australian and that meant not 'rest[ing] on their oars with the achievements of Anzac' but going on to braver deeds until the war was won. There were no denominations in the camps and all the chaplains were ambassadors of Jesus Christ, he said. Perry was given a camera and a thermos flask from a grateful congregation. On 16 March 1916, he left Adelaide on HMAT *Anchises*, bound for Suez.

As momentum for organised competitions to abandon their seasons mounted, the exodus of players continued. One trend drove the other. And as competitions were suspended, football in training camps became more important and the standard of play rose. In Tasmania, the north and north-western senior leagues stopped in 1915 and the southern league, based in Hobart, the following year.

James Pugh, the professional runner who represented Tasmania at the 1914 football carnival, captained City to the 1914 Northern Tasmanian Football Association premiership before the recess. It would be a year and a half before his next football engagement. He enlisted on 1 March 1916, prompting an unusual set of remarks on his enlistment papers – his pulse rate was a healthy 66 beats per minute and he was in 'very good' physical condition. Here was an athlete at the peak of his physical prowess. At the age of 29, Pugh's career as a sprinter and footballer had made its mark. He was just on five feet 8.5 inches tall and a lean 150 pounds, the ideal physique for a running athlete.

He took to the football field again in a match between soldiers in the Claremont camp in May 1916, providing another reminder of the skills that had earned him selection for the 1914 carnival. The military training had agreed with him, giving him the opportunity to build on his own athletic practices and routines. He looked 'as hard as a stout wire nail', according to one observer who hadn't seen him for some time.

George Barry arrived in Sydney and went about reviving his umpiring career. It took him no time at all to find himself back in charge of a football match, at a standard of game elevated well above what he was used to. By June 1915, Barry was one of the senior umpires with the New South Wales Australian Football League in Sydney. It wasn't long, however, before controversy reappeared – partly, to be fair, simply because of the umpire's role. He was criticised in one match for being too strict with a key decision.

It was probably no great surprise that Barry found himself back with the whistle. The Sydney league had done well to maintain itself through the war's first year, but it was struggling for umpires, and a last-minute attempt to patch up the shortage fell apart when the designated replacement didn't turn up to a game. Barry's timing, for perhaps the first time in his life, was impeccable. The competition was, however, haphazard, and as the season rolled on East Sydney withdrew because of lack of players, many gone off to war. Another club, Central Western, also struggled for players but managed to cobble together enough men to appear in the finals. Even the usual season-opening tradition of presenting the previous year's premiership flag to the winners did not occur until the season was three months old.

Barry found himself spending the odd weekend in the Wagga region, umpiring teams such as Cookardinia and Mangoplah in the local league. This time, he received rave reviews: 'the best umpire ever seen here'. Barry also impressed sufficiently in Sydney to be given a role in the grand final, but that honour was tainted when Paddington players abused him and then tried to stop his movement around the ground during the last quarter. Paddington accounted for Newtown to win the flag, but it was another ugly moment in football and it just happened to coincide with George Barry officiating.

When the New South Wales Football Association's annual report was released, it was clear that the war was making a significant impact on the state's football. 'When Country and Metropolitan returns are finalized it is estimated that over 1500 players have gone to take part in the greatest game the world has yet witnessed,' secretary Jim Phelan explained. This significant reduction in the playing pool dashed whatever hopes the Australian Football Council had of pushing the game into New South Wales. The loss extended beyond the players. George Barry had decided that he was up for the 'greatest game'. Who could blame him after all the abuse he had suffered while umpiring matches, whether it was in Western Australia or Sydney? Barry told friends he had been studying wireless telegraphy because he wanted to join the air force. Not the nascent Australian Flying Corps, no, he wanted to be part of England's air force. In January 1916, George Barry boarded the *Osterley*. He wanted another opportunity to start again.

Artillery training at Maribyrnong camp in Melbourne's western suburbs was not what Jack Brake expected. There were only 12 large guns and not enough horses available to practise transporting the artillery. Officers and NCOs who knew about artillery were scarce. Most of them were either at the Front or on their way. 'Altogether the period spent in Maribyrnong was not very effective, beyond preparation of embarkation papers . . .' Brake wrote in the battalion diary.

Brake was a thoughtful man, given to cool and logical analysis. He also just happened to be one of the finest junior athletes of his generation. He was one of three brothers, originally from Horsham in the Victorian wheat belt, who enlisted. Another brother ran the iron store in Hamilton. Brake was made a lieutenant and posted to the 8th Field Artillery Brigade, which started its training at Maribyrnong in April 1916. In the months ahead, the training problems Brake identified proved to be one of the big issues for the AIF's newest army division.

The war changed everything. Jimmy Foy and his teammates at the Perth Football Club thought that even after losing six of the first seven games of the 1915 season, they had a chance to play finals. So when the Western Australian Football League decided towards the end of the season that it wasn't fair to keep playing when there was such a demand for recruits, Perth didn't like it. And East Perth didn't want the season to be over either, because it believed it had a chance of playing finals. Jimmy Foy had played with East Perth for two seasons before hopping across to Perth in 1912. The club had only one flag, in 1907. Maybe, with a bit of luck, they could get another one. But not if the League had its way.

Perth and East Perth combined to lodge an appeal with the Supreme Court against the League's decision. It was a compelling precedent – two clubs with the possibility of playing finals believed the League didn't have the right to end the competition on the grounds of national interest. East Perth argued that six players had already enlisted and two had died. Boys too young to join up filled those places in the team. And the club donated to the appropriate war funds. Playing football wouldn't interfere with recruiting, it argued. Perth agreed. Before the courts could make a decision, the League rolled over, in bad humour, conceding it had made an error. Jimmy Foy got to have a crack at playing finals after all.

James Francis Foy was only 23, married and settled in Mount Lawley. When Perth fans talked about Foy, they didn't just mention how cool he was under pressure but also his ability to lift his teammates' morale. He was one of those footballers who made his teammates walk taller. How else could you explain the players' resilience in taking on the League after losing those games at the start of the season to finish up in the grand final? It was about Jimmy, the boy-man who helped them believe it was possible. Some who knew the Perth team reckoned Jimmy was a party boy, with a bit of a temper to go with it, the larrikin spirit at play. But he kept pretty much to himself on the football field, skirting and dodging, ducking and running. There was something elusive about Jimmy.

Perth met Subiaco for the flag on a damp Saturday afternoon in September 1915. The conditions were miserable and the match was a low-scoring affair. With four minutes to go, Perth was in front by four points. Then Subiaco rushed forward, the ball was marked but the kick at goal didn't make the distance. Lurking at the bottom of the pack was a goalsneak who jumped on the loose ball and kicked the winning goal. Perth had no time to reply. Jimmy Foy's dream was over. His only consolation was that he was named in Perth's best, along with 19-year-old wingman Cyril Hoft.

Foy had enlisted four weeks before the grand final, and had started his training by the time the big match rolled around. Almost four months later, Hoft, from the same suburb as Foy, enlisted too. Hoft was a footballer of great promise, beginning to be known not just for his pace and agility but also for his eye-catching ability to elude tackles and keep his feet. Foy and Hoft finished up together in D Company of the 44th Battalion, which sailed from Fremantle on 6 June 1916. In the build-up to the men's departure, a view emerged in Western Australia that the reason League footballers in khaki had not been invalided home was because of 'their hardness in withstanding the rigors of the Gallipoli campaign'. It was just a variation of the view that football created men who were a breed apart from other soldiers. Whatever residual comfort the nonsensical view afforded football fans was about to be rudely and comprehensively destroyed.

Brosnan's old club Fitzroy was also farewelling some of its better players. Jack Cooper, a tough defender who made his debut in 1907, was given a send-off at the club in February 1916. He was given a gold-mounted fountain pen and a cheque for 'a substantial amount'. An anonymous donor also gave Cooper a shaving kit, something probably more useful than the pen for where he was going. Cooper's farewell, like so many of the clubs' social events to send players on their way, celebrated his service to Fitzroy, to the footballers' cricket club, and to the local company where he worked. There were speeches and songs and wishes for Godspeed on his journey and a safe return. But the tone of these events had changed from the early months of the war. In 1914, there was a sense of optimism and adventure to the farewells. By the summer of 1916, there was an implicit recognition among the broader community that the men who signed up might not make it back. The tenor of the farewell events took on an anxious and melancholy tone, a pall cast by a shadow of awful possibilities lurking, turning the evening's testimonies of a footballer's outstanding play and all-round good character into something resembling a premature eulogy.

Four months after Cooper was farewelled, he wrote to the club's timekeeper Bob King, to let him know that he was sending a donation to the club fund. 'You really don't know how important Fitzroy is until you leave it, and come what may I don't think I'll ever smile again until I see that maroon and blue [Fitzroy] flag flying in front of those two old grandstands,' Cooper wrote.

Minogue was less sentimental, and more pragmatic. He recalled thinking, 'Goodbye to football – possibly for ever,' as he left Melbourne on 27 June 1916. It was a thought that few men gave voice to, but only the deluded or foolhardy would not have considered it as their troopships left home.

In a modest house in Pirie Street, Boulder, in the Western Australian goldfields, Daniel and Kate Scullin prepared to farewell their third son to the war. Dan Scullin, the gifted footballer from the interstate carnival in August 1914 and his parents' eldest son, enlisted in February 1916, just two weeks after his youngest brother, Patrick, had signed up. The previous

March, Jack (christened John Joseph), had left his job with the local grocer, and by 4 September he had departed Alexandria for Gallipoli. Jack was 21 and keen for the stoush. But he became ill with rheumatism while he was in Egypt and had several stints in hospital. Jack recovered and found his way to France in March 1916, just before the big Allied push. Patrick, a blacksmith, was now 21, and he too decided he had to enlist. Dan was just like many older brothers who saw their younger siblings head off: he felt a duty to look out for them. All three had played football for the Mines Rovers, and although Dan was considered the best of them, all the boys were given due regard among the local fans. Dan was a battery hand at the Golden Horseshoe mine, but there were plenty of others who could fill that role. Patrick left Fremantle on 1 April 1916 and Dan was on his way three months later. That left three children at home – Mary, Margaret and Joseph.

Bruce Sloss left Melbourne on 27 May 1916 with his brother Roy. They were both in the 10th Machine Gun Company, inseparable now. Bruce had already made an impression on the men around him. His commanding officer, Harold Ordish, met Christina on the Port Melbourne dock when she was farewelling her boys. Ordish was a seasoned soldier, who was in the Boer War and trained at Aldershot in England. He told Christina how pleased he was that Bruce was part of his unit. He knew the young man would do his job when the time came.

Bruce took it upon himself to write home and share Roy's news as well as his own. The Sloss brothers were good sailors and managed to get their sea legs despite the *Ascanius* heading into a large gale. Bruce measured how well he was feeling by how many meals he missed; ten days in, and he hadn't missed one. On 14 June 1916 came the only bad news. 'We have just got word through that Lord Kitchener is dead. What a loss. We were to have had our sports this afternoon but sure to be put off,' Bruce wrote.

Whatever view the Australians took of Kitchener's role in the Gallipoli folly, he was, to soldiers of Sloss's world view, a formidable figure of the Empire. Kitchener's death, however, proved somewhat more symbolic of the passing of a different kind of general. The times had overtaken him. Sloss was about to find out how radically different war was to the conflicts where Kitchener had forged his reputation.

The long ship journeys could be tedious for many of the troops. Men used to hard physical labour – and regular competitive sport – needed something more than just military drills to excite them. The solution for Dan Minogue, on the troopship that left Melbourne on 27 June, was boxing. Minogue was not a man given to spontaneous fisticuffs on the football field. He was, in the argot of football, 'tough but fair'. However, he wanted to maintain some condition while cooped up on board. He started boxing with the Western Australian welterweight champion Ern Hickey, and won the ship's Divisional Ammunition Column (DAC) heavyweight championship.

Minogue had the build for it – he was a solid five feet 11 inches and 180 pounds, with tree-trunk legs and broad shoulders. On the downside, his opponents could target a large head, topped with a pile of curly brown hair, and a prominent nose. But his initial success led to another bout, this time with Ike Jones, a well-credentialled boxer, for the 'championship of the boat'. Jones, in the infantry rather than Minogue's gunners, had apparently 'a record as big as Les Darcy'. A £10 side wager was attached to the bout, and Minogue found some officers and soldiers who gladly put up a tenner for him. There were to be ten two-minute rounds, starting at 3 pm on 21 August 1916.

Minogue entered the ring wearing his Collingwood guernsey, feeling calm like he did when he took a stroll before his Saturday game. He was fit and confident. He won the first two rounds and then, in the third, hit Jones in the body with a left jab, before another punch to the bridge of Jones's nose finished the bout. 'The DAC boys went mad,' Minogue said. 'I am to have a medal presented to me when we land to commemorate the event.' It was never clear whether Minogue received the medal when he docked at Plymouth in England, four days after the bout. But all of that was soon lost in the excitement of getting to the old country.

5

'These Big Chaps'

Hughie James was ideally suited to the new Pioneer Battalion. It needed tradesmen and engineers, so the brickie from Ascot Vale slotted right in when the battalion came together at Melbourne's Showgrounds camp. The Pioneers were an innovation for the Australian Army – the Indians had them, but not the British Army. It became increasingly clear that a unit of skilled and practical men would be needed for the trenches, and for forward work on the Western Front.

For all of that, though, Carl Willis, a trained dentist, found himself in the same company as James. The AIF's Dental Corps was still in its infancy, and, for the time being at least, Willis was part of the Pioneers' training, even though it was unclear what role he would play in the battalion.

The Pioneers' voyage to England had been eventful. An outbreak of meningitis had prevented James, Willis and the rest of the men getting leave in Durban. Cerebro-spinal meningitis was a curse in the training camps, and it claimed dozens of lives before the soldiers even left the country. Some, however, did not become ill until they were on their way.

The absence of time ashore sat heavily with the Pioneers. '[W]e were all down-hearted, and I had not seen the troops so sad,' one soldier grumbled. 'I do not think that sickness was the only thing that stopped our landing; in fact, we were told that the authorities would not let any more Australian troops land at Durban, owing to the previous troops causing riots and damaging property of immense value.'

Instead, they disembarked for a long route march around the coast, stopping only for the whaling stations, where oil and whalebone were extracted. Willis took plenty of photographs, feeling more like a tourist than a man off to war. But the 14-mile route march didn't do his temper any good, especially when he found out the men left behind to do fatigue work had actually been given leave to explore Durban. The soldiers' only joy was a gift of local oranges from some Durban women, who also wrote their addresses inside various magazines and newspapers they gave to the troops, accompanied by the request that the Australians write to them.

The route march was the chosen activity when the HMAT *Wandilla* moved on to Cape Town, and the troops hiked up to the Cecil Rhodes Memorial. But even then, there were a few soldiers who broke ranks when leave was again refused, and they had to be rounded up in the city before the ship left later that night. After seven weeks, and the loss of two men – buried at sea – the 3rd Pioneer Battalion arrived in England.

Few of the men knew exactly where they were going when they left Australia. It wasn't until they sighted the Eddystone Lighthouse, near Plymouth, that they realised their final destination. And as they got closer to port, Willis noted the number of war vessels, destroyers and torpedo boats anchored around them. From the ship, they moved to a ferry and then to the wharf, where a train was waiting to take them to the AIF training camps in Salisbury. '[W]e then commenced a journey that was a great eye-opener to most of us,' Willis wrote. 'For the first part of the trip you dodged in and out of cuttings and all the glimpses one got were of rows and rows of houses, narrow streets and numberless children . . . All waved and cheered us as we passed along and gave us quite a reception. It is all most beautiful and there are picturesque English trees growing along the banks. The only place I know of in Australia that you can compare to it is the little stream at Fillan's Narbethong [in Victoria].'

Willis shared a carriage with some farmers-turned-soldiers who helped shape his first impressions of England. 'It almost seems as if some one had designed the place as a huge landscape garden. The cultivation can only be described as intense. They jamb [sic] vegetable gardens into all kinds of out of the way little corners that we would not think of using. The crops grow on land we would use to graze a few horses on.' So the green and pleasant England looked instantly different. There was no doubt now, for all the soothing vistas and rich green scenery, the Australians were a long way from home.

The unit reached Salisbury late in the evening. It was a massive set of camps, snaking across 42 miles through the chalk pits of Wiltshire. 'The first morning we arrived we began to run across men we knew . . . There could be some great sporting sides selected here,' Willis forecast. Of course, he had shared the ship's journey with Hughie James, but he also ran into former Essendon footballer and cricketer Bill Sewart, Stan Martin, from Wesley and University, and South Melbourne's Bruce Sloss. And Willis also wrote about the men taking part in sporting contests, several organised by Frank Beaurepaire.

Beaurepaire was not a man to remain idle. One of the keys to his swimming success had been a determination to seize every opportunity, to train with a will and develop the stamina required to outlast his opponents. A competitive streak ran through every fibre of his taut and small frame. That was why succumbing to appendicitis had been such a burden for him. Beaurepaire's body had let him down. He hated the idea of physical frailty, his own or anyone else's. So Beaurepaire was the perfect man for the YMCA job – to get the soldiers fit, to keep them occupied and to focus their minds on the job.

Beaurepaire set about such tasks with a will. But the other key motivator for him was his disappointment about missing out on becoming an actual soldier. Beaurepaire's energy disguised a desire to be in uniform for real, not just the YMCA alternative. He left Melbourne on the *Osterley* on 15 January 1916, bound for Cairo. Within ten days on board, he had a boxing tournament up and running. Always mindful of the spiritual obligations that went hand in hand with his YMCA role, he scheduled the sanctioned fisticuffs to follow a discussion of 'Discipline and Morality'. After a lecture on the need for chaste military service, the physical demands of the boxing tournament were no doubt a great relief.

Beaurepaire was not, by anyone's measure, an easy man. He was driven to succeed, and expected the same of those around him. The soldiers who sailed with him on the *Osterley* couldn't help but send up his intolerance for those on board who couldn't deal with the ship's pitch and toss. The ship's newspaper was called *The Osterley Keystone*, and it contained a sharp piece of doggerel entitled 'Those Ossifers On Board the *Osterley*', which included the tart line, 'And how Beaurepaire loves swimmin'/But thinks swearing and seasickness should be barred.' In the years to come, there would be plenty who would talk about Beaurepaire's acerbic turn of phrase and lack of good manners. Some of it could be batted away by Beaurepaire's urgent desire to get things done quickly. And no one could criticise his capacity for hard work and his sophisticated organisational skills. The YMCA and, through them, the AIF were about to receive their own secret weapon in the guise of Frank Beaurepaire.

Beaurepaire arrived in Egypt in February and was posted to the Racecourse camp at Heliopolis, where he ran a YMCA hut that looked after the 'social, mental, physical and moral wants of the boys'. Egypt was the post-Gallipoli destination for reorganising the AIF. New battalions were created from the Gallipoli survivors combined with reinforcements from home. John Monash, who commanded the AIF's 4th Brigade at Gallipoli, was in Egypt conducting training, and then at the Suez Canal, waiting on a rumoured Turkish offensive that never came. The focus of the AIF's war was now firmly on the Western Front.

The YMCA hut was one of six dotted around the Heliopolis camp, and available most hours of every day. There was a canteen at one end of the hut and a stage with a piano and folding organ at the other end. There were reading and writing tables, spaces for games such as quoits and room for seats to be set out for concerts. Beaurepaire continued his boxing tournaments in Egypt. 'Last night I put on a boxing entertainment to show the boys that the YMCA stood for all that was manly and virile,' Beaurepaire wrote home. 'We had a model assembly of nearly 400 around a ring space cleared in the centre of the hut and suitably roped and prepared. The spectators were treated to three excellent bouts, which all went the full six, two-minute as scheduled . . . For big men it was a fine, clean, spirited contest – just what a boxing match should be.'

But for all of that interest in boxing, there was still football, which remained a constant part of the soldiers' recreation. 'Football almost each evening at dusk is highly popular. Much dust is kicked up but the boys don't mind it,' Beaurepaire wrote. Beaurepaire ended his letter with the forecast that he would be moving on soon. Such was the lot of a YMCA recreation officer. Nonetheless, there was plenty of support from home: the VFL asked football manufacturer Syd Sherrin to supply 250 footballs to the Defence department for 'the amusement' of the troops.

The war had reached a brutal stalemate. The Allies were entrenched in France, arrayed against an enemy that showed no sign of retreating. The Germans planned to put even greater pressure on the French Army with constant artillery barrages of the vital French city of Verdun. The Germans made it clear they wanted to 'bleed France white', a gruesome prediction of a battle that lasted almost all of 1916. The Australian troops, after the reorganisation and reinforcements were complete, became part of a million-strong army that the Allies had at their disposal. There was, however, no end to the growing sense of loss that was afflicting the network of sportsmen who had enlisted. The free-masonry of Australian sport was slowly being eroded. Back home, recruitment numbers surged in the first three months of 1916 to 56,000 but then plunged back to 27,000 from April to June. All the campaigns, the urging and the shaming, were having no impact. The big rush to enlist looked like it had been and gone.

In June 1916, Monash was promoted to major general and given command of the new 3rd Division that had been formally established in February and would convene for training at Salisbury in England. Monash was not a conventional career officer. Although he had been in the Garrison Artillery in Melbourne in 1887, he had also completed engineering and arts and law degrees at the University of Melbourne. He was a sharp observer of human nature, an outstanding strategic thinker and, perhaps above all, a leader of men at a time when there was an acute need for such leadership. Monash wanted the Australian soldiers to be fully prepared for the next stage of the campaign. He had been at Gallipoli and knew that what lay ahead was a different challenge to the perilous nooks and snaking ravines that criss-crossed the Gallipoli hillsides.

One of Monash's instructions after he took over the 3rd Division was to summon Beaurepaire to the YMCA operation at Salisbury. The general believed the champion swimmer was just the man to provide the level of organisational skill that he needed to establish a thriving range of recreations at camp, from sporting contests to entertainment troupes. Beaurepaire had left

Egypt and was on the edge of the action, setting up diversions for the Diggers as they waited their turn at the front in France. He tried to sound light-hearted in his letters home; the weather in May was warm, and he set up another boxing tournament. But the level of danger was far greater than in Heliopolis. The tournaments required a sentry to keep an eye out for lurking German aircraft. And as the Australians waded in to action at the Somme, Beaurepaire was there, offering support for the men coming back from the Front.

With their recreation so unpredictable, there was an added dimension to Beaurepaire's challenge to maintain the troops' well-being. Beaurepaire responded by diversifying his entertainment and creating a theatre troupe of Pierrots, soldiers in costume performing in a disused stable at the end of a village where some of the Australians were encamped. The troupe even had a very small orchestra, made up of a piano, flute, cornet and violin. The new entertainment was safer because it was less exposed. It also occupied more men than just a few boxers exchanging blows. But when Monash's call came, Beaurepaire had no second thoughts. He arrived at the 3rd Division's camp in Salisbury in August with a list of diversions, entertainments and sport he had tried and perfected elsewhere.

As the Verdun casualties mounted, the Allied command shifted their attention to a 20-mile front to the north of the River Somme, with a planned attack to draw the Germans from Verdun and break the German line with a mixture of artillery, infantry and then cavalry. It might have started out as the basis of a good plan but it underestimated the German strength. British artillery had to make deep incursions in the German lines, which it singularly failed to do. And cavalry was a relic of a different era. There was no role for men on horseback in the shifting mud and in the face of a thunderous German machine-gun barrage. The end result of what was called the Somme Offensive was unprecedented carnage.

On 1 July 1916, the first day of the offensive, 60,000 English soldiers were killed and wounded, the worst losses in English military history. Eighteen days later, it was the Australians' turn at Fromelles, a French village that was just a dot on a map that once might have been pretty, even charming, but never would be again. Four days after Fromelles came Pozières, both targets in the Allied plan. That place too would have a terrible tale to tell.

The Fromelles attack was a small element in a grand strategy. It was to stop the Germans sending reinforcements to the Somme, where the British were engaged. It was an old-fashioned feint, a dupe to force the Germans to commit troops away from the main battle. Less than a year earlier, British forces had failed in a similar tactic over the same ground. This time, the 5th Division of the AIF – all 17,800 of them – took the English Army's place. Some of them found the graves and small white crosses of the English soldiers from the year before. It was not only a grim prophecy but also a cruel reminder of the mad strategy that led them there.

The Germans occupied the elevated position at Aubers Ridge – from there, they could observe in detail how the Australian and British troops were preparing. The Germans were not taken in by any suggestion that this was a major new threat. The German command was too shrewd for that. If that didn't make the job hard enough for the Allies, their artillery barrages failed to hit their targets.

The carnage began when the Australians went over the top. Five VFL footballers died as a consequence of the harebrained assault. William 'Plugger' Landy, just 19, who had played two games for Geelong, was killed when a German bomb blew up his trench, and Richmond's Bill Nolan died of wounds four days later. A German artillery shell accounted for one of the integral members of Carlton's 1915 premiership team, George Challis. Minogue, of course, knew Challis and had played against him. 'Poor old George,' Minogue wrote after he heard the news, 'he was one of the best.' Two other footballers, Hugh Plowman – a St Kilda footballer and cricketer – and Dick Gibbs, who played with University, also perished.

Challis's skipper at Carlton, Alf Baud, somehow survived Fromelles, but the 5th Division casualty list numbered 5533. It would take months for the division to return to strength. Baud wrote home, managing to sound appalled, amazed and thrilled at the same time:

> The noise [of the shells] is terrific, sounding something like a train going over a bridge, you being underneath. Tonight I go up to the trenches with the machine gunners . . . We have to pass a corner called Suicide Road . . . A man is safer in the trenches than just outside. One German, called Parapet Joe can run the machine gun up and down the parapet all the time, and if you show up you are gone. He is the 'snifter' of the game.

Baud thought it best to leaven the sense of danger with a sardonic perspective. '[There is] plenty of excitement and danger, sometimes little sleep, plenty of hard work, never know when you are going to move, so what more does a man want?'

Days after Fromelles, the Australian 1st Division was given the task of attacking up a hill to capture the crumbling village of Pozières. The attack started on 23 July and the village was taken on 25 July, but the German artillery and machine guns exacted a high price – 5285 casualties. Then the 1st Division withdrew for the 2nd Division, ushering in a six-week period when the Australians tried to push beyond Pozières towards Mouquet Farm in an attempt to seize the ridge, which was a crucial objective of the Allied campaign. Nine separate attacks followed, and almost 2000 metres of ground was gained. It hardly seemed worth the cost. The savage and debilitating fighting across the combined Fromelles–Pozières debacle accounted for the same number of Australian casualties as the whole Gallipoli campaign.

The German defences held firm, reinforced by a superior artillery and the strategic failure of the Allied campaign to insist on narrow attacking fronts that consistently exposed their troops to German machine-gun fire. The Australians limped off to find some refuge. In weeks, they would be back at the front, confronting one of the worst winters on record, their trenches as deep as swimming pools, with cold, stinking water or sapping, cloying and suffocating mud. This was a particular kind of hell. The heat of the Dardanelles, the spirit of adventure, the grand folly were already a fable. The Western Front was supposedly a modern war but it was fought in medieval conditions.

The full cost of the war on Australia was becoming clearer by the day. Prime Minister Billy Hughes was in England, where the War Office told him that, if recruiting numbers didn't increase, Monash's new 3rd Division would be broken up to meet the demands of the divisions already at the Front. It was a message that gave Hughes pause for thought. He had succeeded Andrew Fisher in the top job in October 1915 and cast a radically different shadow to the handsome Scotsman. Hughes was a Welshman, with a long face, big ears, a gnomic appearance and a combative personality. He had a coiled energy to him that was packed into a small frame. Hughes believed there was really only one way to resolve the recruiting dilemma and that was conscription.

George Foster Pearce – acting prime minister while Hughes was in Europe – planned a massive expansion of the AIF, to include six divisions. It was a good idea, on the face of it. The problem was that there was not sufficient manpower to sustain all those divisions in the face of such losses. Britain introduced conscription in January 1916 and New Zealand followed in July. After Hughes returned to Melbourne, he told parliament at the end of August that the AIF needed 32,500 men in the next month to help cover the losses. It seemed a vain hope when there were usually only 6000 new recruits each month. 'The most recent list for eleven days shows the number of casualties to be 6,743. These figures speak for themselves,' Hughes told parliament. 'The Government considers there is but one course to pursue, namely to ask the electors for their authority to make up the deficiency by compulsion.' Hughes had made his call: there would be a referendum on conscription. Hughes set the plebiscite date for 28 October. It would be a tumultuous two months.

The challenge for the citizen-soldier John Monash was to turn the 3rd Division under his command into a resolute fighting unit. All of those men – whether it was Hughie James, Bruce Sloss, Carl Willis or Dan Minogue – had never seen action. They were part of the second bloom of enlistments, post-Gallipoli and pre-Western Front. They might have been a little more worldly than those who had enlisted in August 1914 but they had little idea about soldiering. The transformation of these men from recruits to soldiers was to take place at a series of training camps around Salisbury Plain.

The AIF had quickly created a bureaucracy around its operations that meant there was a headquarters in London's Horseferry Road and an extensive training regime. The man put in charge of coordinating camp life was the former Western Australian premier and the state's agent-general in London, Sir Newton Moore. The new man did not have a military background but Moore was a good administrator and he was very clear about what the camps would offer, both in training and recreation. There would be separate training requirements for the reinforcements, which would be based on a training battalion that mirrored an AIF battalion in France, the eventual destination for the soldier. The other training strategy was a collective one, whereby the 3rd Division would undertake all of its training at the same time and together.

Moore established army schools for special training in gunnery, machine gunnery, bombing, signalling and bayonet exercise. A library and gymnasium were added to the camps, and a gramophone, records and piano were introduced to cater for a range of recreational needs. The only element missing was organised sport, but there was, by 1916, a structure within the battalions that enabled sport to thrive, driven by battalions' sports and amusements clubs, which often worked in tandem with the YMCA. Claude McMullen, a corporal from Flemington in Melbourne, was the sports secretary of the 2nd Training Battalion and claimed that experience showed sport was the best means of keeping soldiers fit for service. '[I]t helps very much to keep them in good spirits and certainly they take more interest in their battalion if it is keen on sport. Our sports club has fostered the sporting spirit,' he wrote. Corporal McMullen would soon have a larger role to play in fostering such a spirit.

Monash was alarmed at how much work he had to do. On his first trip to Larkhill, one of the main camps near Salisbury, in July, less than a third of the division had arrived. 'All the men I have seen are very fine,' Monash wrote home, 'the best Australians I have yet seen – but almost totally untrained.' This wasn't part of the plan; initially, the new recruits were supposed to have been given a rigorous introduction in their camps back home. But lack of equipment in Australia made it hard to achieve a good result. As Jack Brake had found with the Artillery at Maribyrnong, there was not enough hardware and not enough expertise to guide the novices. And Hughie James and Carl Willis had been subjected to monotonous drilling in the Pioneers' camp.

Monash, in typical fashion, identified each of the problems he had to fix. 'The men had never met as a Division. No single Brigade had met till they reached England. Even some Battalions had never been together all in one place,' Monash wrote. 'Officers didn't know their men, and vice versa. The men had no rifles or bayonets, and have never seen a Mills bomb, or dug a trench, or seen a Vickers or Lewis machine gun, or a Stokes Mortar, or handled their transport . . . All they had learned to do was to stand up straight in rows and behave themselves. All the bayonet fighting they had been taught in Australia had to be unlearnt. It was out of date.' Whatever Monash thought of his recruits' military potential, he made no judgement about their physical capacities. Being a footballer might indicate some physical prowess but it said nothing about your ability to handle a rifle or dig a trench.

Monash was firm in his resolve that the training the recruits would get at Salisbury would transform the new division into a more professional and efficient force. He set his aim on turning out a better outfit than the inexperienced adventurers who had left Australia in November 1914. The value of training had been learnt from bitter experience, at Gallipoli, and specifically at Lone Pine, a murderous few days during the August offensive. Cyril Brudenell White, chief of staff of the I Anzac Corps at the Western Front and architect of the Gallipoli evacuation, lamented:

> [N]o recollection is more bitter than the complaints of the men themselves that they had not sufficient training to give them a fair chance. That complaint was made to me bitterly before the battle of Lone Pine, and in such few hours that remained to us efforts were made to remedy the deficiency. But time was not available, and the need of the men was great. And ever in consequence, rest upon our consciences a deep sense of the responsibility incurred.

The 3rd Division finally came together in late August 1916. The plans to have everyone trained in six weeks and off to the Front proved a vain hope. Despite the organisation put in place to drive the training, there were problems with equipment and men. The camps, with their own canteens, YMCA huts, showers and toilet blocks, struggled to offer cheap and quality food. Reliable sanitation became an issue. In August, the War Office requisitioned 2800 troops from the new division to cope with the dire losses at the Front. Within weeks, Monash was confronting a shortage of men and equipment. And that meant the division would not be leaving England any time soon. 'There is no prospect of our going to France for at least another six weeks, owing to shortage of rifles, guns and horses,' Monash grumbled in September. 'They simply haven't got them in England to give us.' And then the British summer started to turn into a bleak early autumn.

The bomb-throwing school was set up at Lyndhurst, near Southampton. Courses ranged from instructor training through to 'refresher' sessions on the administration of bombing instruction, demonstrations of a bombing attack and blowing up mines. Carl Willis was sent along and returned to Salisbury with his bomb-thrower instructor's certificate.

Bruce Sloss was sent to Grantham, about 180 miles away from Salisbury, in the Midlands, to machine-gun school. It was part of Monash's plan to ensure the NCOs and officers were given the chance to absorb specialist knowledge and then convey it to other troops. But Sloss was impatient. After lengthy stints training in Melbourne, then a long ship's journey, followed by more training, he was keen to experience some action. 'Will be glad when it's all over,' he wrote to his family about the training.

He was anxious and bored, worried about his weight, afraid it would hit 14 stone if he didn't find ways to keep it in check. His one moment of brightness was the expectation of another star for his shoulder, elevated from second lieutenant. Progressing through the ranks was a feature of the AIF. Many officers were lost in the first 18 months of the war and their replacements were often quickly promoted. Sloss's rise to lieutenant had the charming quality of the transformation of a humble, self-made man into a soldier of authority. Not that Bruce was getting carried away. In fact, the training that went with his role seemed to offer only endless tedium. Sitting behind a Lewis gun in Lincolnshire might have been safe but it wasn't keeping him fit and, more importantly, engaged. It would be early September before he was back at Salisbury.

Sloss's mood wasn't helped by the news that his brother James, the first of the boys to leave Australia, was caught up in the plan to liberate Mesopotamia from the Turks. James Sloss was a mechanic with the Australian Flying Corps, which arrived in Basra in May 1915 to give air support to an Indian force of 11,000 men, 28 guns and riverboats that set out for Baghdad. The next few months were harrowing – the aircraft were under-powered and unreliable. Six of the nine pilots who flew with what became known as Mesopotamian Half Flight were captured and two were lost, presumed dead. Support crews, including James Sloss, were caught up in the siege of the garrison town of Kut. When Kut fell at the end of April 1916, James Sloss was one of nine Australian Flying Corps mechanics who became a prisoner of war (POW). Then the news about him just stopped. It was months before the Sloss family found out what happened next.

Most of the AIF trainers were selected because of the quality of their frontline service. But others were identified – such as Jack Cooper, Stan Martin and Jimmy Foy – to undertake specialised training. Once Foy completed his training on how he would impart bayonet technique, he spent the next three months training others how to use a bayonet. There was a new approach borrowed from the British troops of attacking with a bayonet in a formation. As Monash had identified, the way Australians had previously used their bayonets – by advancing singularly, rather than in a squad – was now outdated. Foy found himself running some of the training drills, and supervising the neat lines of soldiers as they advanced towards straw dummies. There were obstacles and trenches to navigate, in daylight and at night.

Foy proved an ideal man for the job – calm, patient and direct. One of his captains, Cyril Longmore, called him an 'excellent bayonet-fighting instructor'.

The role also meant Foy came to know many men in the 44th Battalion. The training stitched the recruits together and bound them more firmly to Foy. He became a popular man in the 44th. It turned out, however, that the hard work was largely useless. The war was moving into the next stage of its mechanised evolution. Howitzers were more effective instruments on the Western Front. One Australian forecast the bayonet would have more use as a toasting fork than as a lethal weapon. It turned out be a shrewd prediction.

They were also trained in how to create positions for the Lewis gun, create dugouts – often under real fire – and dig in when they were in no-man's-land. Salisbury and the adjoining villages were full of chalk, and the new Australian recruits found the soil added a bizarre element to their days. 'Rain swept the open country and poured in to the white-chalk trenches,' one Australian soldier wrote. 'When at night several companies entered the trenches to take up their positions, men floundered through pools of whitewash and got covered with sticky white mud.' They were expected to spend a week in the trenches as part of their familiarisation with what they would encounter once they got to the Front. As Monash predicted, they didn't need to build new trenches but learn how to adapt and repair the trenches already established on the Western Front.

Brake found the artillery training far more valuable at Salisbury than at home. The 8th Field Artillery Brigade was attached to a training battery and each day was full of drills. A day a week was devoted to an exercise in which every battery had a role. A visiting Australian journalist, E.H. Brewer, could not disguise his pride in what he saw at Salisbury. 'Never has a division been so hardly tested at the furnace,' he wrote. 'They are fine, these big chaps . . . England is burnishing them not merely with the most thorough training, but also the keen air of the country is putting bloom and fat in to their lean cheeks and marrow into their bones.'

As a piece of shameless propaganda that swung wildly between a misty-eyed view of his countrymen and a soppy endorsement of the Old Country's supposed facility for nurturing its colonial offspring, it was a fine example. It was replete with a quotation from an English lawyer who organised a weekly concert for the Australians at the YMCA hut. 'My dear fellow,' the lawyer spluttered to Brewer, 'it grieves me to think that any one of those dear big fellows is going to be hurt . . . I think they are the best, cleanest-minded, biggest-hearted men I have ever met.' Perhaps the lawyer was channelling Ashmead–Bartlett.

Monash was also determined to reduce some of the discipline problems that were prevalent among the Australians in Cairo. Drunkenness, venereal disease and brawling were issues that had to be dealt with. Discipline at Salisbury was deliberately tight. Monash did not compromise on a standard of behaviour that he wanted across the division. Everyone who encountered the Diggers knew the way the Australians saw the world. '"Don't" is a word the Aussies cannot make friends with,' Captain Cyril Longmore of the Western Australian 44th Battalion observed, partly in jest, partly in pride and wholly without apology. Monash had no time for such a view. He was a stern disciplinarian, and even supported execution for deserters: 'I am writing to [Defence Minister] Pearce to urge strongly that in some clear case of cowardly desertion, the law should take its course.'

But Monash's strictures, the chilly change in the weather, the lengthy delays in getting equipment and the growing sense of homesickness made the 3rd Division a restless bunch. Rumours questioning whether the division would leave Salisbury at all started to circulate. 'All the old units are still fighting, and we have not heard a shot yet,' a soldier wrote. 'Questions such as these are asked all over the camp: When is the 3rd Division going to declare war? Who will declare first, the 3rd Division or Greece? And we are sometimes called "the Division who stayed at home".' Minogue was restless and cold. He turned, once again, to football, for respite. 'To us, from sunny Australia, it seemed as though we were near the North Pole. Between parades, many of us chased a football every chance we got to keep warm. Those who didn't, just shivered themselves in to a sweat,' he wrote.

Monash, ever alert to the shifts in mood of his men, pondered ways to boost morale and break down any residual barriers between the men in the extended time before they left for France. He assembled the officers at Larkhill and told them:

> As regards the questions of keeping men fit, mentally and morally, . . . [at] Gallipoli you will know, some of you, that people started to grouse and I regret to say, started to grouse in the hearing of their men . . . It is the first duty of every Officer, no matter how he may feel, to keep himself and [his] men cheerful, and, no matter how bad the situation, to blot it out.

Monash led by example, and his Salisbury solution was to use sport as a means of distracting the men while they waited. It was not an unheard of innovation, but it was, for Monash, a demonstration of his understanding of what was important to Australian soldiers, even if it was not something that Monash was particularly interested in or skilled at. In fact, he lacked any ball sense or hand–eye coordination. Unlike many of his troops, Monash never boxed, shot or played football as a boy. And as an adult, he was only a reasonable runner, a fair shot and a mediocre horseman. But he understood Australians' 'instinct for sport and adventure'.

One of Charles Perry's colleagues in Salisbury, Reverend George Cuttriss, wrote perceptively about Monash's understanding of his countrymen:

The Australian is unaccustomed to the rigid restrictions of inflexible military regime ... The sporting instinct is so ingrained in the average Australian that amusement and athletics have become part and parcel of his life, and his efficiency as a fighting force has been increased in consequence. His well-knit, muscular frame and cheerful, free-from-care disposition and love for clean sport, have won for him a place in the estimation of those who ... understand him ...

Monash looked around the camps, saw the YMCA huts and turned once again to the man he knew. On 2 September 1916, Monash sent out a message across the 3rd Division:

The Divisional Sports Committee, with the approval of the GOC [Monash], has asked Mr Frank Beaurepaire, YMCA officer, AIF, to become Honorary Organising Secretary of the committee, with a view to helping in the promotion of various outdoor sports among the Officers and men of different Units and Brigades, and organising a whole day's Divisional sports on Saturday, 30th instant. Would you please have this information made known to all ranks. It is hoped that all units will co-operate in this matter.

Beaurepaire set about the task with his usual sense of industry. Camp life started to get more interesting.

Bruce Sloss's mood had changed too. The delay in getting to the Front meant he had some time to travel, and, with Roy, he spent time on leave visiting relatives in London and heading back to the ancestral home in Scotland. Their other brother, Jock, had joined the 2nd Australian General Hospital and were for some time stationed near Salisbury. When there was leave in the offing, the Sloss boys did their best to get together. For three men raised in such hardship, seeing the world was a wild and heady adventure. The army gave Bruce Sloss an insight into realms he had never known, or was unlikely to have ever seen. 'It's a wonderful life,' Bruce enthused to Tullie, a seasoned traveller herself. But it was more than the faded lights of London that galvanised Bruce – it was the sense of life being lived, a range of new experiences shared with a group of men he would never have known back in Melbourne.

Perhaps, too, Sloss's appreciation of his situation was sharpened by an instinctive feel for the looming danger. He was also starting to understand the important role the machine-gun unit was going to play. The Allies believed the Germans had an advantage with their machine guns, so Monash devoted more time to firearms training. No wonder then that there was not a bung note in Bruce's letters home. 'We are both fat and jolly well,' he wrote of his and Roy's health. For once, the extra pounds were not a reason for anxiety but an indication of robust good mood. And his optimism bubbled over into reassuring his mother, and the extended family, that all was going as planned. He even had a word of comfort for Christina about his brother James's predicament as a POW. 'Johnny The Turk treats all our boys very well,' he cheerfully told his mother. It wasn't strictly true. Bruce couldn't have known how hard things were for James but he put the best face on it for Christina.

On 16 June 1916, Second Lieutenant Harold Bartram disembarked at Plymouth after having spent time in Alexandria. He was back in familiar surroundings. Bartram had been at Cambridge's Trinity Hall, where he had distinguished himself as a sportsman, especially as part of the team that won the Head of the River. He occupied the rest of his time in other sports, such as tennis, and didn't finish his degree. When war broke out, Bartram wanted to be part of it, and he joined the AIF.

Bartram was born in Melbourne but spent part of his childhood in Hobart, attending the Quaker school Friends. The family, which was English, returned to England and Harold settled in to a middle-class life in the Mother Country. In some ways, though, the die was already cast – the Bartrams ran a lucrative dairy engineering business in Melbourne and it was inevitable that, if Bartram got through the war, it was his business to run. In the interim, though, Bartram set off to Salisbury to join the 5th Battalion as it prepared for the push into the Western Front. His most under-recognised role in Australian sport was about to begin.

Beaurepaire quickly became immersed in his role as the division's sports secretary. Monash gave permission for an athletics team of between six and 12 runners to take part in a six-mile race at Epsom Downs, Surrey, on Saturday, 23 September but gave only four days' notice, despite the desire to 'send the best possible team'. The Irish Guards dominated the race, finishing in seven of the first eight places. The Australian team was fourth overall and Thomas Sinton Hewitt was 26th in the field.

Beaurepaire coordinated the team, which meant he had to work with Hewitt. It was a rare meeting between two men of radically different personalities. Beaurepaire was a lauded international swimmer who radiated drive and energy. Hewitt was a talented enthusiast, whose love of long-distance running propelled him to the top of his sport, partly because of the lack of interest from other athletes in competing in such events, and partly because he made the most of every opportunity he could find. Australian running was still in its infancy. It would take Hewitt's former Malvern Harriers colleague Percy Cerutty to put the nation's middle-distance credentials in front of the world. But Hewitt refused to be pigeonholed, and his enthusiasm extended beyond athletics to the bright lights and baubles of theatre. He was an impresario of sorts, with a passion for performance. He didn't mind whether he was running or performing – one was just a variation of the other. The one shared attribute between the focused Beaurepaire and the more gregarious Hewitt was a determination to succeed. There was more than a ripple of competition between them – that much they understood about each other.

Beaurepaire got to work on devising a massive sports-day program. It was to be a mixture of athletics and theatrics. An area – 'a fine natural amphitheatre with seating room for 20,000' – was identified near the main camp as the venue. Beaurepaire started to send out memos outlining the requirements for each event, including a fancy-dress event called 'the Midnight Stakes'. 'Officers to start with a night white dress and cap with strings in bag or haversack. First time past post to have dress and cap on and strings tied. Second time past to be carrying saddle over arm.' There would be 'championships' in the sprints, a cross-country run (three miles to Stonehenge and back – Hewitt finished third), hurdles, walking, a long jump, high jump, tug of war, wheelbarrow race, pillow fight, kicking a football, throwing a cricket ball, musical chairs on bicycles, mounted events and a padres' bicycle event, starting at Stonehenge and finishing at the main camp.

Although the program might have been designed to engage both athletic and less-than-athletic soldiers, there was no doubt what Beaurepaire wanted. 'It is to be hoped that all Units and Groups will hold Sports, or eliminating events, to secure their best representation,' he wrote in a memo. Beaurepaire only wanted excellence. There might be novelty events but the competitors had to be capable, with more than a modicum of skill. Eliminations would also create a manageable field of entrants for the sports day.

Beaurepaire set up a marquee near a YMCA hut to give intending participants the opportunity to practise and also to collect any running equipment, footballs, shorts and gymnasium gear from 4.30 pm each day. And, in case anyone was wondering, Beaurepaire announced that 'any point that seems debatable or on which a ruling or interpretation is required' should be referred to him. There was absolutely no doubt that this was Beaurepaire's event. It was no wonder that he cried off a challenge from his great swimming rival Billy Longworth, who wanted to race the Melburnian over any distance. Beaurepaire told Longworth, who was in Liverpool, that he was just too busy at Salisbury to be swimming.

While Beaurepaire was a whirl of activity, most of the soldiers were still following training routines and caught up with mates in their spare time. Minogue joined St Kilda ruckman Percy Jory and they managed to find a football. '[W]e kicked till we were tired, and then had a talk until 10 o'clock,' Minogue said. Once again, football was a catalyst for soldiers coming together.

While the sports day generated a great deal of interest among the 3rd Division, the bigger event was King George V's inspection, three days before the carnival. Sloss thought it was all good fun. He decided the event was a good way of telling Tullie how he was doing. 'We (the King and I) had quite a long talk together. He said that I was looking well, since we last met. (So I am.)' Sloss wrote. Others' observations were more formal, including the King, whose statement after the inspection had the familiar echo of Ashmead-Bartlett. 'I was particularly impressed by the soldierly appearance and physique of the men of the various units,' the King said. The commander-in-chief of the Home Forces, Field Marshall Lord French, went further: '[the King] expressed his great appreciation of the practical work performed by the troops, their appearance, physique and general bearing. He considered they would be a magnificent contribution to the Empire's forces now in the field.'

It was perhaps inevitable that the King would have been impressed by the freshly minted Australian division. They had yet to experience the rigours of battle. They looked fit and well nourished. The desiccated and devastated Allies at the Somme were just shadows of these specimens. The King could have been forgiven for wondering whether there were another 20,000 men just like them back in Australia who could be called up immediately for action.

Back home, the same notion was exercising Billy Hughes's mind in the midst of the eight-week conscription campaign. Hughes made a tactical error when he was spooked by September's poor recruiting figures into introducing an aggressive conscience call that demanded single men aged between 21 and 35, with no children, turn up to camps for training. Less than a third of the eligible men obliged, and many fit enough to enlist applied for exemptions. The campaign revealed deep divisions across the country, most profoundly on class and sectarian grounds. The working class, the trade union movement and the Catholics were opposed. The middle classes, most of the main newspapers and the Anglicans thought it was an entirely appropriate response to the Empire's troubles. Monash, not surprisingly, was in favour of conscription and didn't understand why any of his troops couldn't see its merit. '[T]here are many rumours that many of the men object to compulsion, often on very stupid and inadequate grounds,' he wrote to his wife. Hughes hoped the troops would be the ones to swing the vote to 'yes', and there were plenty of letters published from soldiers who would have reinforced his optimism. The troops' vote on the referendum was held on 16 October, 12 days before the nation voted.

There was more excitement among the soldiers at the sports carnival. It was a fine and crisp day. Sloss was a steward and took a relaxed approach to the events. Perth footballer Cyril Hoft won the long jump, with a leap of 19 feet 11 inches. Dan Minogue won the place-kick competition, but he only managed 30 yards in the drop-kick section after the football skewed off his foot. Minogue wandered around the camp and even visited the German prisoners kept nearby. They had no doubt what the future held. 'They are a fine, bright lot of men and seem quite satisfied that Germany will win,' Minogue wrote.

Word had arrived at Salisbury that Fitzroy had done what no other club had done — won the premiership from the bottom of the ladder — but the novelty was that there were only four teams in the competition. Fitzroy grabbed the flag after recording only five wins for the season. But football had finally taken the kind of back seat that Adamson, Mackinnon and Wilmot had wanted. Attendances were low: the highest attendance of the year was 20,000 at the grand final, which was well below the record crowd of almost 60,000 who attended the 1913 decider. The standard of play was also compromised. The four VFL clubs were not allowed to seek additional players from the district competitions to cover the exodus of enlisted talent, so there was a lack of 'star quality' to many of the games. Minogue wrote home that he hoped to be back at Collingwood for the 1917 season but, by anyone's estimation, it was wildly optimistic. The war was entering its next awful phase, and the 3rd Division would be there. But Minogue had one consolation: he wouldn't have to wait too long for his next game of footy.

6

The Game

It was getting cold in Salisbury and the days were getting shorter. The Pioneers had the tough task of building bridges, propping up trenches and making sure the soldiers at the training camps had something sound to sleep in, shoot out of and shelter behind. The job was to make a replica of the Front in the safe surrounds of the Salisbury villages. But, as summer evaporated and the English winter loomed, the Pioneers found their minds wandered and not all their tasks got done before dark. And the trench that ran across the plains separated not only units but some old friends too, many of them from the footy fields at home. So braziers were lit, a few drinks were shared and plans, inevitably, were hatched, across the jagged trench line.

Hughie James found himself in the circle, surrounding the fire. 'The result was that, after a few noggies around a brazier the visitors would find the cold air too much and that ditch took a lot of negotiating,' James said. 'Well it was just such an occasion as this that the idea of the football match originated.'

It was early September 1916. The AIF's football fraternity in Salisbury was getting restless. The newspapers at home regularly identified the roll call of talent, the footballers who had done what was asked of them and thrown in the game for their national duty. But the demands on sportsmen to sign up didn't stop. For those who were in England, though, nothing much was happening. They were training and waiting. Idleness was an issue. They wouldn't be going to France for a while. What if there was time to pull on boots again before they headed off? It felt like the football season – cold and wet. There was enough talent across the AIF to get two good teams on the paddock. Could they find a ground large enough? Who could do that? And, just as importantly, how could they make it happen?

Australians played football in their downtime whenever they could. It was usually played between battalions and fiercely competitive. But there were no tournaments, and, more importantly, the matches were only for the Diggers' entertainment. The idea of using sport in a wider sense across the AIF became feasible when the Diggers were in Britain, where competition could be organised against British units and other Australian battalions.

A former British Lion, John Leaper Fisher, had joined the AIF and, in his role of provost marshal at one of the Salisbury camps, took it upon himself to arrange as many sporting engagements as possible. He wrote to the British Army Service Corps' rugby union club and Marlborough College, but they didn't have sufficient troops to oblige. Fisher pressed on and arranged a meeting 'for all those interested in Football (Rugby, British Association & Australian Rules) . . . for the purpose of making arrangements re: the forming of teams representing AIF Headquarters . . . and engaging matches etc'. Matches soon followed, but they were – perhaps not surprisingly – all games of rugby. Australian Rules was a game no other country played, and it demanded a large oval playing surface. Both considerations meant that whatever competition was hatched for Australian Rules in England had to take place between AIF teams at a venue that would not match the grounds in Australia.

But there was no shortage of interest in James's idea. It had to be sanctioned at the top before they even started to find a venue.

There was no doubt Monash would support it, given his determination to keep the troops occupied. He was quick to agree and helped get British authorities onside. Originally, the plan was to hold the match at Larkhill, but Monash wanted it in London. If the event was going to work, it needed to be something more than just a social occasion or an excuse for some football mates to get together and have a kick. It soon became clear that this match was going to become a showpiece of the Australian game.

Queen's Club in West Kensington, known more for its tennis but with a large stretch of ground, was chosen as the venue. Once Monash approved it, Beaurepaire, as the divisional sport secretary, was immediately given the organising task for the 3rd Division. The division's opponents would be the Australian training units, under the command of Sir Newton Moore. As a Western Australian, Moore was familiar with the Australian game. Organising the training units was delegated to the sports-mad Melbourne rower Lieutenant Harold Bartram. And, as Moore was the man in charge of the administration of the training facilities at Salisbury, it was entirely appropriate that the 3rd Division's opponents would be the training units of the 1st and 2nd Divisions that had been settled at Salisbury since June.

An office was established at the AIF Headquarters in London, and two senior officers, Colonel C.A.K. Johnson and Major C.W. St John Clarke, were put in charge to make sure there were no snags or red tape to prevent the game going ahead. The decision was also made to make the match a fundraiser for the British and French Red Cross Societies. In the same way Beaurepaire organised a sports day for the 3rd Division, Major Clarke and Bartram embarked on a similar program for the training units, which was held at Kimpton race track, near one of the camps, a month before the match.

Monash's aide Major George Wootten circulated a memo on 12 October confirming the game was going ahead in London on 28 October 1916, coincidentally the same day as the conscription referendum vote in Australia. Wootten's memo continued:

> All officers and men in this division desirous of playing in this match should be on the 10th Infantry brigade sports ground on Sunday afternoon, 15th instant, at 3 pm, and following afternoons at a time to be arranged, in order that they may train, and to enable the best possible team to be eventually selected . . . It is hoped to be able to raise a very strong team and League and Association players are asked to come forward for selection. Units possessing footballs should take them to the ground each afternoon.

Two selectors were appointed for the 3rd Division: Bruce Sloss and Jack Brake. Sloss knew there was a depth of talent in the division and forecast the final team would be made up of mostly VFL players. But as Beaurepaire demanded of the sports day, there had to be practice matches too, to help run the men in to some form. Units were pitted against each other. Sloss played for the 10th Machine Gun Company, which included the young Leslie Lee, former Richmond and Williamstown player. Some of the games turned into tight affairs. Sloss, forever concerned about his weight, grumbled about carrying too many pounds and his lack of fitness, but observers could still see the champion in him. 'He showed good form, and in the last quarter was the means of pulling his side out of the fire, securing victory by one point only,' Quartermaster Les Turner wrote to a South Melbourne friend.

Sloss was buoyed by the 10th Machine Gunners' undefeated run through the practice matches. His excitement for the Exhibition match was building. He and Brake settled on a list of 25 names. At least a dozen of them had played VFL and were known to both selectors from their playing days. Others had played senior football in Perth and Adelaide. It was a team ideally qualified to show off the skills required to play Australian football. They were all fit. None of them had been at the front line, so there were no wounds or injuries. The Training Units team was picked from the soldiers who were part of five training groups established at Salisbury. And that meant trainers such as Jimmy Foy, Jack Cooper and Stan Martin qualified for selection.

Enthusiasm was one thing but there were practicalities to be considered. What were the players to wear? Then there was the question of the football itself. There were some old balls that had been sent over with the YMCA but the teams needed something newer for the match. Making the football fell to one man, a talkative corporal who knew a fair bit about sport but even more about sewing. Claude McMullen was originally a tanner from Stawell, who moved to Melbourne and worked in Fordhams' sports goods store in Sydney Road, Brunswick, before enlisting. He started making balls when he was in Egypt, and footballers in the 5th Battalion with him swore by his handiwork. 'They were as good as any ball I have seen made and it was marvellous how they were made so true under the difficulties which Cpl McMullen faced . . .' one enthused.

The guernseys were a little more difficult. The issue was the design. Hewitt's runners at Epsom had worn a green singlet with red facings and 'Australia' in white letters on the chest when they had turned out for the cross-country meeting several weeks before. But both football teams were Australian – they couldn't both carry the name on their jumpers. In the end, the decision was made to use two symbols of the country: a map of Australia and a kangaroo. Sloss's team would have a navy-blue jumper with a map stitched on it, but – with what might have been a practical decision to avoid extra effort and material – no Tasmania. They would have navy socks and the era's favoured longer-style shorts. The Training Units team would sport a red jumper with a pale kangaroo down the left-hand side, red socks and dark shorts.

One of the other considerations was who was going to officiate at the match. Hewitt had never umpired in his life, but he saw running the boundary as an opportunity to build up his stamina for any future long-distance event. He made sure Beaurepaire put him down for the role of boundary umpire. It was perhaps a sensible choice – Hewitt was at least qualified to run, and follow the play, around the ground. And, of course, Hewitt instinctively recognised the match was going to be an 'occasion'. Just try to stop him taking part.

The other boundary umpire was Edward Watt, the central umpire who had reported two Victorian Junior Football Association players for striking him during a match in 1912.

The more important role was the main umpire. The decision was made to appoint two umpires, not to share the game at one time but to split the responsibilities between the first half and second half. The first selection was Corporal Edward Gray, a South Australian umpire. The other umpire was none other than the troubled and much-abused official George Barry.

Since Barry had left Australia, he had found a way to join the Royal Navy Air Service (RNAS) and, as he had promised his friends in Sydney, had started flying. The RNAS set up an aviation outpost in England's north-east after Germany bombed Hartlepool in December 1914. The region contained munitions factories among other key strategic targets, so defending England's coast was a priority. A site was chosen west of the Redcar racecourse in north Yorkshire, and the air base became a training ground and operational hub for sorties against German zeppelins and U-boats during the war. Between April 1915 and November 1917, there were 15 zeppelin attacks on the north-east. But the urgency of protecting the area meant the Royal Navy recruited a range of novice flyers, from England, Canada and Australia. George Barry was one of them. He joined the navy on 7 April 1916 and went straight to Redcar.

Barry schooled himself on the basics before he was accepted, which was just as well because training at Redcar often became real, when young pilots found themselves in the thick of the action. He was signed up for the duration of the hostilities and also spent time at the RNAS headquarters in Crystal Palace. The HQ was called the President, a 'stone frigate' that meant it was a 'ship' on land. It was there that Barry, somehow, was discharged from the RNAS. The reasons are unclear. The upshot was that his discharge papers were handed to him in London just five days before the Exhibition match. And Barry not only heard about the match but he also found a way to get picked as one of the two umpires.

The choice of the Queen's Club ground posed its own problems. Although it was regarded by some sections of the British press as 'the most vulnerable spot in the armour of the London pleasure-seeker', it wasn't the right size or shape for Australian Rules. It was about ten metres too short and also 25 metres too narrow for most Australian football grounds. Australian Rules, after all, demanded more open space than any other code of football. Trying to fit 36 players into that space would pose challenges for open play. The game could be compromised as a spectacle. But most of the Australians who played in any form of football since they left home were used to adapting to the various sizes and shapes of grounds. And the venue was central enough to encourage Diggers from all points around the city and surrounds to make the journey. The Queen's Club was actually keen to support Australian sport and volunteered the venue whenever the Diggers needed it.

Then there was the match as an event. There was an understanding from Monash down through the ranks that this game was an important exhibition of something that was unique to Australia and to the Diggers. There was pride in showing it off to those people who had never seen it. Here was an opportunity to reveal a new game, a truly indigenous sport that no one in the

Mother Country would find anywhere else in the world. The Exhibition match was a piece of proud nationalism, built on the Australians' growing confidence of their role in the Empire's war. But in a practical sense, it had the power to galvanise the football-following troops across London.

To ensure the flavour was entirely Australian, the organisers turned to a group of Australian artists to illustrate the match-day program. The notion of a program, containing the players' names, football gossip and news, was already part of football: *The Record* started in Victoria in 1912, and the *Budget* debuted in South Australia in 1914. Such publications were part of the match-day ritual for football supporters back home. This program would have something different about it, a souvenir of the cartoons of emerging Australian artists Cecil Hart, Laurie Taylor, Fred Lindsay, and husband and wife Ruby Lindsay (known as Ruby Lind) and Will Dyson.

This was a happy accident – especially securing Dyson, who had the greatest affinity with Australian soldiers of the artists of his generation. He drew them with empathy and wit, while never disguising his hatred of the whole sorry conflict. 'I never cease to marvel, admire, and love with an absolutely uncritical love our louse ridden diggers,' he wrote. Dyson and Lind, the sister of Norman Lindsay, left Melbourne, bound for London, in 1909. By the time war broke out, Dyson had established a reputation as a newspaper cartoonist in Fleet Street with an incisive wit that skewered German ambitions in new ways. Australian war correspondent C.E.W. Bean called Dyson the 'most intimate portrayer of the Australian soldier', and in his determination to do more of such work, Dyson was agitating to get to the Western Front.

He wrote to the Australian authorities to outline his desire to 'interpret in a series of drawing, for natural preservation, the sentiments and special characteristics of our army'. He even offered to do it for nothing and cede the Australian Government the right to own all his work. Australian High Commissioner Andrew Fisher approved the idea. Defence Minister George Foster Pearce agreed, with the caveat that the British War Office had to agree too. In the meantime, Dyson was allowed to go to Salisbury to begin 'pictorial records embodying the spirit and characteristics of the AIF training in England'. Inevitably, he found himself working on cartoons for the football program. Two months after the match, Dyson was granted a temporary and honorary rank of lieutenant (without pay or allowance) and became Australia's first official war artist. Then he was off to the Front.

The program also contained a one-page explanation of the rules for those who were curious onlookers and new to the game. The copies were free, but a group of 80 English girls volunteered to distribute them. The incentive was a prize for the girl who collected the most donations for the 'free' program on the day. The entrance fee was set at a shilling, 2/6 and 10 bob, depending on your rank. That took care of everything except the players. Sloss was made 3rd Division captain – another acknowledgement he was a leader in the making. Sloss's old club South Melbourne would have thought the captaincy entirely appropriate, and a precursor to the club conferring a similar honour on him. Sloss's opposite number for the Training Units was Red Wing Perry. Here were two God-fearing men in charge of teams who really had only two things in common: the AIF uniform and a love of football. And it was football that was the most powerful bond of all.

Two squads were named and printed in the program with the caveat 'to be selected from'. Perry's Training Units contained eight who had played or would play VFL football: Jack Cooper and Percy Trotter, at Fitzroy; Harry Kerley, a bulky forward at Collingwood; Stan Martin, the former Wesley captain who played for University despite his undistinguished academic record; Charlie Armstrong, who played 15 games with Geelong;

South Melbourne's George Bower; and Clyde Donaldson, a reliable defender for Essendon. James Maxfield, who debuted for Richmond after the War, was picked. Dan Scullin, the best player of the Western Australian Goldfields League and a 1914 carnival representative, was also selected.

Perry's team included a Norwood colleague, the power-fully built Ernest Beames, who had played at both ends of the field in Adelaide. There was also possibly the first footballer of Italian heritage to play Australian Rules at a senior level. Italo Cesari's football journey moved around the Geelong region, and he played in a Geelong reserves flag. But considering his back-ground, it was intriguing that he took up football at all. His father was a tailor and musician in Italy but he was enticed to Australia by the promise of a lucrative orchestra tour. Cesare Cesari was 31 when he signed a contract in Milan to go to Sydney and join a tour that would take him from Sydney to Melbourne, to Tasmania and New Zealand. Cesari would play the horn in Martin Simonsen's opera company, a massive group that numbered 85 – five prima donnas, four tenors, thee baritones, three bass, a 25-piece orchestra (including ten from Milan), a chorus of 35 and a ballet. The plan was to perform 18 operas, all under the baton of Italian conductor Signor Lombardi.

Cesari arrived at Williamstown in Melbourne on 13 October 1888. But the Melbourne season was a financial disaster and the tour was beset by angry exchanges between the conductor and the cast, including during one extraordinary performance of *Carmen* when the lead tenor stopped singing and walked off the stage. Cesari quickly signed on with Giovani Venturi of the Italian Society of Artists, which enabled him to stay on in Australia. He married Rosina Corra, who was also Italian, in Melbourne in 1892, and he became part of the orchestra at the Princess's Theatre. The couple had three children amid a stormy marriage. On 10 August 1893, Italo, the firstborn son, arrived.

The Game

This was to be, in many ways, the closest thing to an interstate carnival match. These were two strong teams, even though they were not selected on a state basis. And the competitive streak that ran through most of the 'name' players would be sure to come to the fore when they were pitted against similarly good opponents. There were no coaches: Sloss and Perry were de facto coaches in their role as captains. But it was also true the game had not changed since they left Australia, either in the rules or in the tactics. The VFL, in particular, was so denuded of talent there was no likelihood that the low-level competition would generate any significant alterations that could have been relayed to the troops. It meant the Exhibition match was going to be a contest about high marking, drop kicks, passing and even place kicks – a picture of the game as it was when the footballers left Australia. In that model, each footballer took responsibility for his role, and that role was heavily prescribed by the understanding of the accepted duties of the ruck, rovers, centremen and key position players.

While the match was, at one level, an exhibition for the Diggers and the curious onlookers, for the players it was something else – a chance to run around in the open air, to play the game they loved and test themselves in the way that they knew, body on body, running, jumping and kicking. It was a wonderful antidote to the dull routine of training and the anxiety of anticipation about what was ahead.

On the face of it, Sloss's team was the favourite. It had the bigger name players, including Minogue as vice captain. Seven of the team were in Sydney for the football carnival when war was declared: Sloss, Brake, Charles Lilley, Hughie James, Perth pair Jimmy Foy and Cyril Hoft, and James Pugh, from Tasmania. The view from home was that it was unlikely that a team either in Australia or overseas could be picked to beat it. But Perry's side had speed and dash. Percy Trotter might have been past his best, but a decade after he flashed across the muddied

161

Melbourne ovals, he still had the poise of a champion. Perry was a mobile big man, who could change a game with his peerless rebounding. And then there were the youthful speedsters Scullin and Martin. And Cooper, who had also been at the 1914 carnival, was a former Victorian captain. Wise judges thought it would be a closer match than it might have appeared on paper.

Sloss decided he would take Roy along for the game, as a trainer. On 25 October, Beaurepaire sent out a memo listing the men Monash approved to make the trip and, just as important, who was getting leave from match-day Friday until Sunday. Roy's name was included in the list of 29 soldiers who would leave Salisbury before midday on the Friday. The game was building into something remarkable. Minogue, whose name was on the list, thought the atmosphere was 'white hot'. Hughie James, who was at the school attached to the 3rd Pioneers, in Reading, was formally given leave to play and a railway warrant to get him to London and back. Carl Willis's, Bill Sewart's and Ned Alley's names were attached to the same memo, all of them at Reading with James and all selected in the 3rd Division squad.

Back home, the country was poised to vote in the conscription referendum. Billy Hughes relied on the troops to show the nation their support for conscription and organised for the vote to be held in France and at Salisbury 12 days earlier. Hughes used the October edition of the *Anzac Bulletin*, a troop newspaper, to spruik the need for conscription. But the threat of disbanding the 3rd Division to meet the requirements of the dwindling Australian frontline troops increasingly just looked like a deception to help Hughes's campaign for compulsory military service.

Pre-poll murmurings from the Front alerted Hughes that the support for conscription was not as universal as he expected, and the prime minister asked General Birdwood to send out a message to the troops advocating a 'yes' vote. Birdwood was reluctant to take a political stand but sent a telegram to the AIF command in France to delay the vote until they received his message. But Monash didn't receive the telegram until midday on polling day. By then, 80 per cent of the troops at Salisbury had voted, and Monash decided not to bother sending out Birdwood's message. The word from the troops, as it appeared in the papers at least, gave a strong pointer to the way they felt. 'It is pleasing for us to know that so many are enlisting in Australia,' the former South Melbourne footballer Wally Laidlaw wrote from his hospital bed in Malta. 'They need them all. If they at home only knew what the boys are going through they would not hesitate, but would come at once.'

By the time the two football teams walked out onto the ground just before 3 pm on 28 October 1916, Australians had already told Billy Hughes what they thought of compulsory military service. They didn't want it, although the margin of the victory was a narrow 72,456 votes and the states were split. Queensland, South Australia and New South Wales voted 'no'; Victoria, Western Australia and Tasmania supported it. It was a moment of compelling coincidence – here were 36 footballers who had been subjected to an oppressive and unrelenting pressure to enlist finding themselves less than 12 months later playing in an AIF-organised and sanctioned match on the same day Australians decided on conscription. It was a rich irony.

What helped to create a confused picture of the outcome was the way the soldiers voted – those who were in France or had seen action voted 'no' by as many as three to one, but those who had yet to see action, including those at Salisbury, voted 'yes'. The overall result was a narrow 'yes' vote among the AIF – hardly the resounding endorsement Hughes sought. He was as cranky as only Hughes could be at the soldiers' response. 'I can hardly forbear to rail at the Anzac vote, which could and it would, have pulled us through,' he steamed.

On the other side of the world, the Exhibition match struck a completely different mood. This was national service that had nothing to do with King and Country. This was an event about football and those who played it. For the afternoon, the men of the 3rd Division and the Training Units were players again, not soldiers. When the players turned up to Queen's Club, there was also a newsreel camera crew to record the occasion for British Pathé. The film would appear on Australian cinema screens eventually, but, for the moment, the camera caught the bustling, grinning, chiacking Diggers who found their way to Kensington for the match. There were buses, flags and bunting all around.

The film captures the players trotting out onto the ground in two distinct lines, Sloss leading one team and then Perry the other. Some are running; most of them are grinning. And in the time-honoured way, each team is photographed before the match. They line up haphazardly, not like soldiers at all, laughing with their teammates, looking up and around as if they are breathing in the fresh air of free men. Some of them, such as Carl Willis, look lean, almost without condition. But Brake and James are formidable: square-shouldered, impassive, immovable. Minogue's big head is turning this way and that. Here's a man who is built for competition. He's restless, ready to go, wanting to get out there and into the game. Sitting in the middle of the row is Frank Beaurepaire, cap set firmly, gaze fixed ahead and almost lost amid the larger bodies around him. He cuts a serious figure, like a school principal trying not to indulge his unruly boys. Sloss looks everywhere but at the camera, almost embarrassed that he finds himself in the centre of the picture. At one moment, he looks away, beyond his teammates and into the distance, lost in his thoughts. Sloss heard the King was coming to the match, but it is just a rumour. So too is the gossip that the Prince of Wales and the deposed King of Portugal are at the game. The Prince of Wales is in France. And as for the deposed Portuguese royal – in exile in England – no one can be sure of his whereabouts on the day.

When Perry's team takes its turn in front of the movie camera, there is less bonhomie, perhaps because these men do not know each other so well as Sloss's outfit. They have come from all over, different leagues and different divisions, so there are few soldiers who readily identify with them. Perry chews gum, a strangely modern moment, while his teammates stand quietly behind him. George Barry and Thomas Sinton Hewitt take their place in the front row of each team. Barry's hair is short, a cap perched on his head, but his clean-shaven face, although aged and lined, is still recognisable as the wild-eyed young man who was in the Claremont asylum. He holds McMullen's football, which designates he will start the game. Hewitt sits to his left, relaxed and clearly enjoying the moment, the performer awaiting his cue. And then Sloss and Perry go to the centre of the oval for the toss. The wind is blowing strongly down the ground to the northern end, and Perry opts to kick with it. And then, at 3 pm, the first overseas exhibition match of Australian Rules football is underway.

The crowd had been steadily growing throughout the afternoon. It reached 5000, many of them Australian soldiers but also a large troupe of English journalists who came along, intrigued by the Antipodean game. Minogue reckoned that plenty of the Diggers had managed to wrangle their leave to ensure they got to the game. 'Many and devious were the dodges worked by Diggers,' he explained. 'They had perfected to a fine art the very ticklish business of securing leave. On that illustrious occasion, they excelled themselves. They were there at the match, with bells on . . .'

The program was only of limited help to the crowd when it came to identifying the players – some of those named did not take the field, either through unavailability or injury, and were replaced by others. The replacements were no slouches. One of them, Billy Orchard, was Geelong's captain-coach in 1914, and slotted seamlessly in to the 3rd Division team.

The opening minutes were a blur of activity. Those spectators who had never seen Australian Rules football were struck by its speed and how the players hunted the ball, in congested packs, before a player burst clear with McMullen's ball or soared for a mark. There were moments when some players struggled to keep up. There were glimpses, to the trained eye, of handballs that never hit a target, or a pass that wobbled off the boot. Despite the conviviality of the football fraternity, some players struggled to know how their new teammates operated – which foot they kicked with, where the ruckman directed the ball, where the forwards liked to position themselves. It was understandable: most of them had never played together.

There was a chaotic undercurrent to those first few minutes, as the players searched for the pace of the game. Some, such as artful dodger Percy Trotter, slipped seamlessly into the groove of the match, able in a blink to sense the game's patterns. Others took longer, including Melbourne's Leo Little, who never quite managed to find his form. Behind this screen of febrile activity were, however, ribbons of connection, linking players from clubs and areas, junior teams and shared histories. Clyde Donaldson and Harry Kerley found themselves on the same team, at different ends of the ground, after starting their careers in a junior Victorian side before they went on to Essendon and Collingwood. Carl Willis debuted for South Melbourne against St Kilda, in what was also Harry Moyes's first match, for St Kilda; now they were teammates. Such coincidences only affirmed the resilience of the game's network of friendships and shared experiences.

The wind posed its challenges and tested the defences of both teams. Sloss's team kicked the first score, a point, but it was against the run of play. Perry's outfit responded with its own point and then quickly added another. For the next few minutes, Perry's team dominated the play. These were the sort of skills the Australians in the crowd wanted to see. There was clean possession, good marking and, best of all, some accurate foot passing.

The key was the stab kick, the short version of the drop kick, which had become popular in the VFL, particularly after Collingwood used it to great success earlier in the century. By 1910, the stab kick was an accepted part of football, providing a new way to keep possession with a series of short kicks and marks. The speed of the kick and its low trajectory made it hard for an opponent to intercept. It became part of the game's appeal. And Perry's men started to use it to great effect in the first quarter. The 3rd Division team struggled to win back possession, battling the wind and the assured foot skills of its opponents. Minogue couldn't help himself – he was struck, again and again, by the outbursts of applause from a crowd starved of football. He suspected the spectators were staggered by the spectacle and the fierce intensity of the opening quarter.

It was the first time Sloss and Willis played together. Although they were both nominally at South Melbourne in 1915, Sloss didn't play a game that season, which was Willis's first at the club. And Willis's opening moments of the Exhibition match were spent being dazzled by Percy Trotter. Willis was only a boy in short pants when he saw Trotter at Fitzroy. This time, he watched with admiration Trotter's display of skill. '[H]e showed us that he still retains his old dash; he was easily the best man on his side for that [first half],' Willis said. Trotter's VFL debut was in the far-off days of 1901, and he turned 33 a month before the Exhibition match, but age had not dulled his brilliance. He was still diving through gaps and skirting around packs, finding space that eluded everyone else. Trotter's roving in the first quarter was a reminder of how easy the game was to him. The infidelity of the bouncing football never troubled Beautiful Percy – the ball came to him with a faithful embrace that left his teammates and opponents wondering how he did it. Between Trotter and backman Clyde Donaldson, there were precious few moments for Sloss's men to cheer in the first quarter.

Donaldson was a lean man, with a face that always seemed on the verge of cracking into a lopsided grin. He had played with Essendon before the war and started to earn a reputation as a miserly defender, with a gift for anticipating his opponents' moves. But perhaps Donaldson's best asset was his deceptive speed, which propelled him through packs and enabled him to set up a chain of Essendon possessions from deep in defence. Forwards underestimated Donaldson at their peril – he could take on some of the taller ones or stick with the speedy goal-sneaks who wandered around the forward line, opportunists and pickpockets, willing the ball to spill from the pack at their feet so they could pinch a goal before anyone knew they were there. Donaldson treated both types of forwards with the same suffocating attention. While he applied his stranglehold to the 3rd Division's forward line, his team kicked two goals, to establish a 15-point lead at the end of the first quarter. The 3rd Division scored only two behinds.

No one doubted that Sloss's boys would come back hard with the wind, but, even so, there were precious opportunities. The first fell to Percy Jory, a bulky and strong ruckman at St Kilda, weighing in at 173 pounds and five feet 10 inches. Jory was fit, mobile and tough, as ruckmen needed to be to cop the punishment that came with the role. Towards the end of the 1915 season, Jory was reported for elbowing a Melbourne player and suspended for three matches. St Kilda had a bye and didn't play finals that season, so Jory would have missed the opening games of 1916 if St Kilda had been part of the VFL. Instead, he enlisted and found himself at Queen's Club with the ball in hand, kicking for the goal that would put the 3rd Division back in the game.

Jory could have opted to float a punt kick into the goal mouth, but the punt was an unpredictable tool for the job. He could have also chosen a place kick, an old-style approach that could give him distance. Jory's St Kilda teammate Dave McNamara was considered the best exponent of the place kick in the game, but Jory was not a regular forward like McNamara and didn't practise the place kick. Jory opted instead for the drop kick, to send the ball in a soaring, spinning arc towards the target.

The drop kick was a beautiful element of the game, either delivered at pace – such as Stan Martin's long kicks from the wing with University – or taken with several steps for a set shot. At its best, the drop kick went for yards and was the ideal kick for forwards wanting to mark close to goal. It rarely wavered from its path, and its end-on-end spin suited grasping hands in packs. But there was a problem: if it wasn't struck cleanly, the ball could veer yards from the target or just grub its way along the ground. Jory was not noted for his kicking, unlike his St Kilda teammate Harry Moyes, who was positioning himself in the goal square in case Jory didn't make the distance or duffed his kick.

Moyes was a successful goalsneak, who was suspected of not enlisting because he was too short at five feet 5.5 inches tall. (The speculation was wrong – in August 1914, the height restriction was five feet six inches, which was reduced to five feet two inches in June 1915. The reason for Moyes not enlisting earlier is not known.)

Jory went back to take his kick. He struck it sweetly. Moyes watched it go through for a goal. They were back in the contest.

The goal sparked a 3rd Division resurgence: Cyril Hoft, the Perth winger with his own dose of dash and speed, started to win more of the ball, while Brake managed to find some of the form that made him University's most decorated player. Before the half-time break, Sloss's boys had managed another goal and the 3rd Division led by three points. It had been a grim struggle; the 3rd Division had kicked two goals and eight behinds for the quarter, and Red Wing Perry's boys managed only several behinds. As the teams went off for the long break, Perry approached football-maker Corporal McMullen and asked if he could hang on to the football at the end of the match. McMullen agreed. He'd already given it a name – he called it 'the AIF Football'.

The crowd became more vocal. Barracking was loud enough for the players to hear individual barbs, almost always delivered with affection. Perry, the footballing padre, was given plenty of advice – 'cheery' too, according to one English observer – from Australian soldiers in the stands. The third quarter became an arm wrestle as both teams sought for an advantage. Once again, Perry's team surged with the wind and added another two goals to recapture the lead. They were classy contributions – Charlie Armstrong, the former Geelong and Melbourne player, was a solidly built, mature footballer. He debuted with Geelong in 1912, when he was a seasoned 29. He had the physical hardness required for the Exhibition match against the match-hardened bodies of the 3rd Division. Armstrong slotted a goal. Jim Maxfield, from Newbridge, near Bendigo, would play a few matches with Richmond after the war, and he added another goal to the Training Units to ensure they led, by 11 points, with only a quarter of football left to play.

The last quarter was a ferocious affair. Separate contests broke out across the ground. There was urgency to the match now. What might have felt like a social encounter earlier in the day had taken on the air of a grim and unrelenting contest. This was the fierce face of football, when footballers who became soldiers remembered their vocation and relished being back in a game. Everything except that moment when the ball bounced or flew through the air and into a pack receded from their minds. Getting the ball was the immediate priority. Winning the match was the end goal.

The 3rd Division's big men, including Sloss, Minogue, Hughie James and Jory, started to have an impact. Willis found some touch. Willis's great skill was to be where the ball was – an underappreciated but vital part of the game. But there were times when Willis's kicking let him down. When he was playing well, his disposal of the ball was clean and precise; on bad days, the ball simply refused to behave and passes kept missing their mark. The longer the match went, the better Willis became. He found teammates and won enough of the ball to kick two goals. Moyes was a proven goal-kicker with St Kilda, a clear and quick forward with a reputation for toughness. In his first game for St Kilda, he had landed heavily and needed several stitches in a torn lip. He had stayed on the ground and kicked four goals. This time, he added two goals to the 3rd Division's growing lead.

It became clear that fitness rather than just the wind was going to be a key factor in the final minutes. Trotter tired, and the spirit and verve he had given the Training Units around the ground in the early part of the game disappeared. The 3rd's big men – Minogue and James – were exerting an influence. Sloss roamed from deep in defence to the forward line, like a factory supervisor overseeing his employees' work. Yet the revelation was the young man from Richmond, Leslie Edward Lee. Lee did not give much away in height to Brake or James, but he was leaner and more agile. Minogue didn't know Lee at all and referred to him as 'an unknown follower', but Lee shattered that anonymity in the most eye-catching way. It was his turn to put on an exhibition.

Working up and down the ground, Lee was tireless. He grabbed contested marks, took on the bullocking work in packs, moved seamlessly between the rucking contests and kicked long, and usually to the 3rd's advantage. And he kicked a goal too. Wise fans who knew the game would have expected Hughie James and Minogue to dominate in the air. Instead, the boy they called Leggo did the job. Minogue reckoned Lee was the best on the ground that day, thrilling the crowd with some fingertip marking and drop-kicking.

Minogue could not disguise his desire to win. It was the thing that drove him, and so many of the footballers around him.

In those moments, when the game was in the balance, it was the will of the tough and seasoned competitors who determined the result. 'For my part, I know I never played harder,' Minogue said later. 'Hughie James and I toiled together in the ruck, playing as though for dear life.' This was football as it was meant to be played, with the intensity and desperation of a grand final. No wonder the crowd was thrilled. The 3rd Division added four precious goals in the final quarter to claw back the lead. Red Wing Perry was heroic, doing what he did with such success with Norwood, trying to engineer some opportunities coming out of half-back. But the ebb and flow eventually ceased. Perry's team could not bridge the gap. The final score was 3rd Division 6 16 (52) to the Training Units' 4 12 (36).

The English press marvelled at the athleticism on display but, not for the last time, struggled to follow the rules. The absence of an offside rule puzzled some onlookers. The *Sporting Life* identified the novelty of the exhibition itself. 'There have been fugitive matches in this country during the past two years between different units of the Australian military forces, but an attempt has not been made prior to Saturday to interest the public in them. It was encouraging to find a fair number of civilians in the stands at Queen's Club . . .' it said. The *Weekly Despatch* made the wise observation that, despite the quality of the footballers, their lack of experience playing together compromised a better display. And *The Times* was intrigued by a unique feature of the game – barracking – which it described as a 'cheerful running comment, absolutely without prejudice, on the players, spectators, the referee, the line umpire and lastly the game itself'. The war was just a source of more material for the barrackers. After one player dropped a mark, a voice from the crowd shouted, 'D'you think it's a bomb?' *The Times* was also struck by the 'classless' nature of the team selections. It betrayed the newspaper's mistaken assumption that because there appeared to be some similarities with the most establishment of

English games, rugby, the Australian 'version' was similar. They could not have been further from the truth.

In what would become a trend for decades to come, the Australian newspapers reported their English counterparts' verdicts, embracing some of the positive observations and being testy about some of the criticisms. But Jack Worrall, in *The Australasian*, revisited the old saw of a link between football and soldiering. 'There is no sport that I know of equal to our game of football for making the ideal soldier for pluck, self-control, resource, coolness, dash and initiative are its essential characteristics,' he wrote. It was an apt summation of the myth that had driven the public pressure on footballers to enlist. But even on that score, Worrall made his position clear. 'Footballers have answered the call well, and I trust there are many more to follow.'

The legitimacy of the shared qualities between Australian football and soldiering was an esoteric argument few of the soldier-footballers had any great inclination to discuss or even acknowledge. For them, the Exhibition match was like their football life on rewind, spooling back to the time when they could play the game without the fear of conflict and mayhem that beckoned them. Brake was so attached to the jumper he wore that he sent it home for safekeeping before he went to the Front. Stan Martin, elevated to sergeant after his training at Aldershot, wrote back to Wesley and referred to the match as a 'great game' between 'The New Division v The Old Heads'.

Sloss could not conceal his pride at being part of the game when he wrote to Tullie. 'We had a real match in London last Saturday,' he wrote. 'We had a great team, all League players, a team that would win any match at home.' In time, other players shared Sloss's view and reflected on the match as a highlight of their lives. Melbourne's Harold Moyes thought Sloss's team was the best side he ever played in. Hughie James called it 'a brilliant game of football'. Percy Trotter described it 'as one of the finest games it has been my good fortune to participate in'. Minogue simply said it was 'unforgettable'. Close to £1000 was raised for the British and French Red Cross, and the winning program seller collected £70 on her own, while overenthusiastically charging in to the 3rd Division dressing room in search of more sales. She retreated quickly, Dan Minogue recalled, a mixture of confusion and embarrassment at seeing 'big hulking soldiers' in varying states of undress.

The match became a model on how to organise such events. When HMAS *Australia*'s chaplain wrote to AIF Headquarters proposing a football match between the navy and the army, the response suggested Bartram could be one of the organisers after his efforts with the Queen's Club game. The plan was for Bartram to once again organise the training units into a team, but events conspired to prevent the match going ahead. But Sloss's team got another run, ten days after London, when it took on the division's second XVIII. There was talk of another divisional team to play an alternative training units outfit, this time in Salisbury on 18 November, with the gate fees going to the patriotic funds. But the same reason that prevented the army and navy match going ahead prevented the London rematch: the boys were moving. Monash had been given the signal to head to France.

Frustrated at the ongoing delays, Monash had complained to Birdwood in September about the lack of equipment for his troops. The message went up the chain of command to the British Expeditionary Force's commander-in-chief, Douglas Haig. He told the Australians that he wanted the 3rd Division on the ground as soon as possible, and the flow of equipment started immediately. Two weeks after the Exhibition match, Monash's troops were almost ready. The last route march was on 13 November, when the troops slogged it out for 15½ miles. Sloss was on a horse for most of it, and Roy didn't even take part, but it was gruelling for most of the division. 'This is the first long walk that our boys have done of late, so you can guess they were not too lively when it was all over,' Sloss wrote. 'It is pretty certain that we will be off this month to finish our training across the other side.'

Sloss wanted to let his family know how his life had changed since he left home. There were privileges to being an officer and he relished the luxuries that came his way. 'My batman is here building up a big fire for me . . . a nice little room, a nice fire and a man to look after me. Too easy.' The good news was the house Gladys's father had built for them was finished. 'What do you think of the house?' Sloss asked his mother. 'I have good reports about it, which is all they can be . . .' Now that the troops were about to move, Sloss was in such good spirits he had to share it. 'This is a wonderful life Mum.'

Part of the pleasure of the last few weeks in Salisbury came from Bruce and some of his unit spending time with a local family, the Hinxmans, who regularly invited them to supper. Bruce's brother Jock was firm friends with the family and introduced his brothers to their hospitality. On Sloss's final night before the troops moved out, he was with the Hinxmans, who asked him for a farewell song. Bruce picked a familiar hymn and sang it in his usual clear tenor voice. The men there never forgot it.

Slowly, the division began its move, heading for Southampton in 87 trains, over six days from 21 November. They would go to Le Havre on the French coast, and then to Rouen. The soldiers were delighted to be off, even if there was a growing awareness of the horrible conditions that were going to greet them. Birdwood had summoned the Australian Catholic Archbishop Clune to the Somme in November. The clergyman was appalled at the mud, dirt and general conditions he encountered. He found himself in a turnip field, addressing 1600 Catholic soldiers 'literally thigh-deep in mud'. 'I addressed the men for half an hour, the rain and snow pelting down on us piteously all the time,' he wrote. The Archbishop developed trench foot – a common occurrence among the troops at the Somme – and was treated in London. He got off lightly.

7

The Greater Game

Monash's division arrived in France in late November 1916 and set about getting ready for their turn at the Front. The troops were about to enter what became the worst winter in three decades. The vile weather coincided with the German aim to make 1917 the final year of the war, the year of victory. The new Diggers were taking up an important role at a critical time in the war. Their reputation in Europe still carried echoes of Gallipoli, and its emerging legend.

Monash was relying on his division's extensive training to help shape a different reputation and one removed from the growing legacy of the word 'Anzac', which Monash believed fostered an unrealistic view of his soldiers' achievements. Good training bred routine and reliability, not mercurial moments of heroism that grew wilder in the retelling. '[T]he Australians hate being called "Anzacs" as if they were some special breed. The name has acquired for us a nasty flavour, owing to too much boosting of the term in connection with exaggerated accounts of deeds of prowess.' Monash wrote. He was assiduous in keeping his men fresh for their turn at the Front, and implemented a system that meant each soldier would spend no more than 48 continuous hours in every 12 days on front trench duty. Monash estimated that, of a battalion of 1000, only 600 were actual fighting men at any one time. The rest were orderlies, stretcher bearers, drivers, grooms and messengers. His Pioneer battalion was scattered across the five miles of the Australian-controlled section of the 92-mile-long British line. There were brickies, such as Hughie James, blacksmiths, wheelwrights, carpenters, saddlers and plumbers, all carrying out their trade.

And in keeping with Monash's determination to ensure the troops were entertained and their morale was good, he established a troupe that would provide some Christmas comfort. It was Beaurepaire's work again – or, at least, he was able to take credit for it, after getting the support of the divisional brigadiers to revive a version of his Pierrots. Not surprisingly, given his predilection for performing and his experience with arts companies, Hewitt became the stage manager.

The Coo-ees, as they became known, lasted for almost three years, becoming a concert party that at its peak boasted 30 members and its own orchestra. There were songs, impersonations (even of Monash) and musical skits. But the troupe's first performance was far more modest. The six performers borrowed costumes from the local French villagers, and even the instruments were collected from a range of sources. '[T]hey made such a success of what was at first intended to be merely a brief raid in military histrionics, that they were ordered to dig in . . .' one of the AIF newspapers recorded. How much of the troupe's success is down to Hewitt is unknown, although it would be fair to speculate that he felt far more comfortable wrangling performers than Beaurepaire did. The swimmer was an organiser, interested in results, but Hewitt had the natural flair – and experience – to look after a group of performers. He would have loved the challenge of finding the equipment, costumes and instruments to ensure there was a first performance, let alone a string of them across the Front.

Many of the Australians were based in what they called 'the Nursery Sector', where recruits could do last-minute training in the comparatively quiet part of the front line around Armentières, near the French–Belgian border. In the first few weeks of his deployment, Sloss moved between the Nursery Sector and the Front. He was excited to find himself in action finally. On 11 December, he wrote home:

> I know you are going off at me for not dropping you a few pages of late. Well, you will be surprised to hear that we have been going all the time since leaving England . . . Don't think I'm complaining Mum, it's just the opposite. I have enjoyed nearly every minute of seven day's stay in the Front line.

Sloss admitted to enjoying commanding his unit, even though there were fatalities early on. 'I am sorry to say that I lost one of them the second day that I was in the trenches. Just a stray shot that got him. You know it would not be war unless that was repeated now and again,' he said.

Sloss's philosophical acceptance of the loss of life was common among the troops on the front line. They saw it all too frequently. He might have been in his first week in the trenches but he was quick to acknowledge the terrible cost and his inability to do anything about it. Once in France, he saw and felt the war up close. He was working on holding a line that had been the same impasse for almost two years, and there were regular strafing exchanges between the Germans and the Allies. Sloss saw how the Allies had managed to shape a bomb-struck neighbourhood from the horror. Much of Armentières and its hinterland had been bombed to pieces. Closer to the front line, streets and roads had been renamed by their new occupants – London Road, Australia Avenue, Spain Avenue and Panama Canal, which was actually a large drain. The damage was so extensive that, without names, soldiers would have been lost and disoriented. At a town not far from Armentières, the Allies set up military baths in an old brewery. Many of the Diggers made it a weekly appointment to have a bath and a complete change of clothes.

Sloss's respite came just before Christmas, when he went back to the billets well behind the line and was directed to some office work, where he stayed until 2 January 1917. He replaced William Algie, a 21-year-old from Neerim South, in Victoria, who was hospitalised with tonsillitis and was then sent to a machine-gun officer's training course. Algie had been a lieutenant, just like Sloss, but the Duntroon graduate and Wesley old boy had been promoted to captain in October, six months after he enlisted. Sloss found himself sitting in for the younger man. Roy was several miles further back, in a 'cosy' billet that was once a school.

Sloss found the adrenalin and danger a heady mix that made him feel engaged with life in ways he had never known. 'Have had more fun since I joined up than I had in all of my [life],' he wrote. Here was a mature man reflecting on his life, just days after his first encounter with the real dangers of warfare. It was exhilarating and harrowing at the same time. And he was well aware of the price of doing his duty. Sloss quoted his mother back to her, via his fiancée: 'Should have been married years ago, so Glad said you told her mum. Never mind. This has put easily 10 years on in only a few months time.' He wrote home again, on Christmas Day, marking down the time of 8.30 am. With the pang of knowing what he was missing, Sloss noted, 'You will be about having tea at home.' But his new role was so busy, Sloss had almost let the day slip past. 'Really did not know what the day was till one of the men helping the cook wanted to know what we were going to have for Christmas dinner. Had to drop everything and scoot off [to] . . . do a little bit of shopping.'

Another one of Bruce's machine gunners was killed in the previous fortnight, but Sloss admitted that the Front at Christmas was quiet. He was still in the office, and had been told to attend a machine-gun school that was on offer, but he found a way to get out of it. The decision was a fateful one. Sloss added a special Christmas card from the 10th Machine Guns to the Christmas parcel, stylishly printed, and sent that home too.

It was 4 January 1917 at the address the Diggers called London Road. Sloss was finally free of the office desk and was back at the Front. There were several men from the 10th Machine Gun with him, and 11 men from the 10th Field Engineers. The sappers were working above the ground, rebuilding defences under the blanket of a thick, cold night and relying on the machine gunners for cover. Percy Fairlam, a photographer from Cheltenham in Melbourne, was a sapper with the Engineers and learnt quickly what missiles to look out for, and which ones were less harmful. He wrote:

> It is rather a queer sensation in the trenches when Fritz sends over some of his shells. He has some they call 'minnies' they are terrors. They do not travel very fast but they make a hissing noise and come along in a wobbly course, generally three or four all sent one after the other. You can see them coming if you are quick, but it is hard to tell where they will land . . . [T]he only thing to do is to wait, then flop down flat and chance to luck. I tried it ten yards away from one and got covered in mud . . . They are not very dangerous but do a terrible lot of damage to trenches. Most of the chaps get shell shock from them . . .

Fairlam was more scared of the high explosives. He had seen the damage they could do. And on this night, the Germans were lobbing the dangerous missiles in Fairlam's direction. 'Fritz got busy and made it too hot to go on with the work,' he said.

Sloss, his team, and Fairlam's Engineers were ordered to get back to the safety of a rickety storeroom where the timber and iron for making trenches was kept. They started to move, ducking, to avoid the whistling shells.

Just as the men arrived at the storeroom, two shells exploded in front of them, quickly followed by a third. Fairlam had reached the safety of the storeroom doorway when a piece of shell struck him in the shoulder. 'I've got one,' he shouted at his mates. Bruce Sloss was heading for the gate beyond the storeroom, to a path that led back to the camp headquarters. He was called back for a moment and then turned again towards the gate when a shell landed at his feet. It killed him. He was 17 days short of his 28th birthday. Another half-dozen shells pounded the storeroom, shaking what was left of it, dislodging the plaster, but claiming no more lives. Fairlam was lucky. 'If there had been any more force behind [the shrapnel] . . . [I] would have been poking the daisies up by this time,' he said. Bruce Sloss had no such luck. Nor did three of Fairlam's Engineers and another officer.

It was the news Christina Sloss had dreaded. Bruce had taken on the responsibility of looking after his brother Roy. He had been the one to write home and keep up a steady stream of good news about the pair of them so Christina wouldn't worry. With James still a Turkish POW and information about his fate unreliable at best, Bruce had been the one connection between Christina and her boys overseas. And Bruce had discovered something liberating about military life: the sense of order, the joy of command, the adrenalin of danger. He had told them at home that he had never been happier. But he had a life planned for when the war was over: he and Glad would be married and then move in to the house at Nyora Street, Malvern. Glad was bereft at the loss of the man she loved. They had been together eight years. What would become of her now? What would become of the house her father had built? After all the hardship of the Slosses' family life, this was another hammer blow.

Tullie was in Trenton, New Jersey, looking after an American family when the telegram arrived on 17 January 1917. The cable simply read, 'Bruce killed in France.' 'I don't know what happened. I know I didn't faint but stood staring in to the looking glass when I heard and felt something snap in my head,' Tullie wrote. Her mind quickly turned to her brother James – known as Son within the family – who was still a Turkish POW. 'Presently, I could see Son in the mirror and my feeling came back to me. My thought was that we must not let Son know as I felt his biggest hold on life was to get back to Bruce.' In time, there was one consolation Tullie came to treasure about the circumstances of Bruce's death. 'His beautiful body was riddled with shell holes. So was his revolver and everything else which was in his pockets,' she confided to her diary. 'But his lovely face was left just as it had always been.'

The South Melbourne Football Club's grief was instant and heartfelt. Club secretary Herbert Howson sent a letter to Christina as soon as the news was known. 'The committee and players feel keenly for you and your family and hope that it will be of some consolation to know that your son fought as only brave men can and that he is numbered amongst those fallen Australian heroes whose great deeds will live for all time.' Yet there was something else the club lamented about Sloss's death – it was the character of the man, the rectitude, the commitment to the club, the desire for success.

The eulogies were sincere and extensive. The local paper called Sloss, '[A] fine stamp of a young man, good living, clever, and of a thoughtful, kindly disposition . . .' The obituary lapsed poignantly into the present tense as it concluded, 'He is as versatile as he is brilliant [as a footballer]. No matter where he is placed in the field, Sloss does credit to himself and the side. As with all champions, the ball is always his objective.'

Bruce's death galvanised Tullie into action. She decided she could not stay in New Jersey any longer. The USA was still not in the war and Tullie suddenly felt she needed to be doing something, anything, to help the war effort in England. She boarded the *Ryndam* on 28 January. The shipping routes were constantly under threat from German torpedoes, and the spectre of the *Lusitania*'s sinking exerted a powerful hold over shipping lines and passengers. The *Ryndam* was only 36 hours away from England when the ship was ordered to turn around and return to New York.

Tullie was back in New York on 14 February and tried desperately to find another ship to take her to England. She was offered a berth on the SS *Laconia* and she jumped at it, despite being told it was at 'her own risk'. 'Risk has never entered my mind if I wanted anything badly. So that night I was on the largest boat I had been on in my life,' she wrote. No one in the Sloss family would have been surprised at her decision. This was the woman who had business cards printed with 'Miss Sloss' and told her two sisters that she was the eldest and there would only be one 'Miss Sloss'. So they became Miss Mary and Miss Margaret.

The *Laconia*'s crew insisted on daily lifeboat drill and made sure passengers were either wearing their life jackets or at least had them nearby. At 9.30 pm on Sunday, 25 February 1917, the SS *Laconia* was struck by a German torpedo about 130 miles off the Irish coast. 'The ship toppled to one side and there she stayed with top side all broken ... The overladen lifeboats were let down. Some tipped whilst in mid air and went in to the water,' Tullie wrote. She found herself pinned to the bottom of her lifeboat by the weight of the rope that had held the boat to the ship, and then, in the dark, panicked passengers jumped into the boat, landing on her.

Struggling to her feet, she was given the job of keeping the flare going as a beacon for the other lifeboats. Another torpedo

The poster that set the tone for the bitter debate about sport and war
- the artwork shows an MCG full of football fans while a Digger stands
over a fallen mate. It was a powerful piece of propaganda.

From "THE WEEKLY TIMES," Melbourne.

W. SEWART

(1a) P. TROTTER.
FITZROY FOOTBALL CLUB.

G. Heinz, Geelong.

J. Cooper (Fitzroy).

WILLS'S CIGARETTES

CARL WILLIS
VICTORIA

BILLY ORCHARD

BRUCE SLOSS

HUGHIE JAMES

ST. KILDA FOOTBALL PERSONALITIES
(Series of Sixty-five)

No. 22   I. V. CESARE (Trainer)

COLLINGWOOD F.C.

D. MINOGUE

J. Cooper, Fitzroy.

P. JORY, St. Kilda.

A generation of sports fans came to know
their heroes from seeing their images on
cigarette cards. Although the men who
played in the Pioneer Exhibition Game
came from around the nation, the most
famous were those playing in the Victorian
Football League. Coloured portraits
like these created a vivid picture of
footballers as heroic figures, long before
colour photography was available. The
poses were always stiff and there were no
smiles: football was a serious business.

Top left: Handsome and inventive, with a wonderful tenor voice, Bruce Sloss was the youngest of eight and South Melbourne's best player when he joined the 10th Machine Gun Company in 1916.
Top right: Bruce's fiancée Gladys, who promised to wait for him.
Right: Bruce with sister Tullie, eldest of the Sloss clan and every bit as brave and brilliant as her brother. **Below:** The Sloss family and friends at Wonga Park, outside of Melbourne. Bruce holds the clock.

Left: Charged with doing Prime Minister Billy Hughes's bidding, Donald Mackinnon was a moderate voice in the feverish conscription debate. **Right:** Young fit sportsmen fitted the bill as AIF recruits. As casualty lists climbed, posters such as this one became a regular feature of the war at home. It was easy for the 'recreational' amateurs to give up their sport to enlist but the choice was harder for those who were paid to play.

Left: A young Dan Scullin, in a serious moment, away from the Boulder mine and the footy club he loved. **Right:** Leslie 'Leggo' Lee. Although he only played two games with Richmond, the yellow and black faithful embraced Lee as a favourite. According to Dan Minogue, he was best afield in the Exhibition match.

Left: Always ready for the stoush, Ralph Robertson was the NSW football captain when he became one of the first to enlist. He was in German New Guinea for Australia's first action of the War.
Middle left: Jimmy Pugh, athlete and footballer, born in Victoria but adopted by Tasmania. **Below left:** Richmond ruckman Hughie James, a born leader, and the most decorated VFL footballer of the War, winning the Military Cross and bar for bravery amid a 188-game career for Richmond.

LIEUTENANT HUGH JAMES

Above: Carl Willis, gifted cricketer and VFL star for University and South Melbourne, in France, 1917.

ADVANCE AUSTRALIA

Pioneer Exhibition Game

Australian

Football

In aid of

British and French Red Cross Societies.

3rd Australian Division

v.

Australian Training Units

At QUEEN'S CLUB,

West Kensington,

On SATURDAY,

OCTOBER 28th, 1916,

At 3 p.m.

YE HIGH MARK

LESSONS OF THE GREAT WAR.

Australian Rules Amended.

Football when the boys come home.

The souvenir program of the Exhibition match. It features cartoons
from some of Australia's finest artists, whose illustrations were a sly
insight into the Diggers' sense of humour in the face of grim conflict.

Ye Genial Goal-keeper

...Kick is an interesting

...the game.

...ng Home

WOOLOOMOOLOO KIWIS LOSE THE PREMIERSHIP.

"On the third day we exploded a mine under our opponents' goal."

9

SPORT AND WAR.

The advantage of the High Mark.

Pte. Ballup, of Wangaratta Dingbats F.C., collects a souvenir somewhere in France.

WIGHTMAN & CO., LTD., OLD WESTMINSTER PRESS, REGENCY ST. S.W.

Above: The soldiers in Red Wing Perry's Training Units team can't wait to end their military drilling and finally play some football.
Below: A relaxed and candid moment as Bruce Sloss's 3rd Division side gets ready for the team photograph before the match.

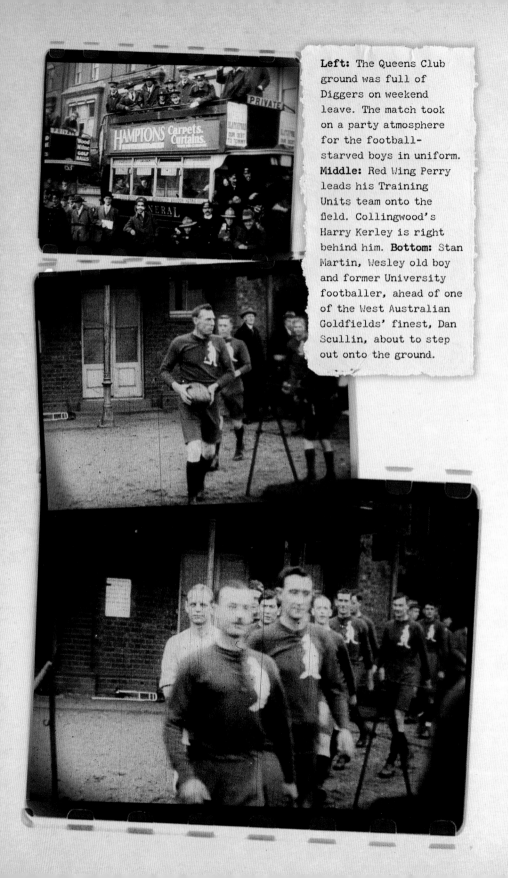

Left: The Queens Club ground was full of Diggers on weekend leave. The match took on a party atmosphere for the football-starved boys in uniform. **Middle:** Red Wing Perry leads his Training Units team onto the field. Collingwood's Harry Kerley is right behind him. **Bottom:** Stan Martin, Wesley old boy and former University footballer, ahead of one of the West Australian Goldfields' finest, Dan Scullin, about to step out onto the ground.

Left: Perry and Sloss reflect on the toss. Perry calls correctly and kicks with the wind.
Middle: Accomplished Essendon defender Clyde Donaldson kicks in for the Training Units.
Bottom: A goal-square scrimmage with the ball in dispute and the Training Units' defence under pressure.

Left: Dan Minogue's jumper from the Exhibition match. **Right:** Carl Willis, seemingly always relaxed, in a trench on the Western Front.

LEADER OF THE A.I.F.—THE LATE GENERAL
SIR JOHN MONASH.

Left: Tenacious Australian Prime Minister Billy Hughes insisted the nation's sportsmen do their national duty, whatever the cost.
Right: John Monash, iconic commander of the AIF's 3rd Division, saw sport as a vital part of keeping his soldiers fit and their morale high in the face of dreadful losses on the Western Front.

Above left: Frank Beaurepaire - Olympic swimmer, YMCA stalwart and John Monash's right-hand man in organising the Pioneer Exhibition Game. **Above right:** Billy Hughes's divisive conscription campaigns came at a price, not least to his own reputation. Here a Hughes dummy swings from a window behind the lines, for everyone to see. **Right:** Tullie Sloss, in her Women's Legion uniform, London, 1917.

Top left: Among the thousands of crosses and graves that fill France and Belgium stands one, suitably modest, as testament to the life of Bruce Sloss. **Top right:** Carl Willis, lean and grinning, in the jumper he wore for the inter-divisional football competition in Belgium, 1919. **Centre:** Dan Minogue had been Collingwood's favourite son ... until he joined Richmond and led the Tigers to back-to-back premierships. **Left:** After the War, Frank Beaurepaire turned his energies to business and politics, as Lord Mayor of Melbourne. He was knighted in 1942.

accounted for the listing *Laconia* and, soon after, the dark, shiny hull of the German U-boat surfaced near Tullie's lifeboat. The lifeboats drifted until they were sighted by three Allied warships at 3.30 am. It was another 90 minutes until one warship stopped to collect them. 'When all but three boatloads had been pulled on [board], the warship suddenly went off without any warning whatsoever leaving the other boats adrift. One boatload from the three left behind was picked up later but the others were never heard of again. The submarine was again after the warship . . .' Of the 75 passengers on board, six died, and six crew members also perished. Tullie made it safely to Ireland and finally arrived in London at 6 am on 1 March. It was a rare piece of good luck for the Sloss family.

Less than two months after Sloss's death, the South Melbourne Football Club held its annual general meeting. The previous year, 1000 people had turned up to hear South officials say that 12 current players, eight former players, 800 members, a trainer and a committeeman had all enlisted. This time, there were 40 stragglers and the meeting was over once the formalities were completed. The mood was sombre. The club asked the League to add any remaining dividends from premiership matches to the Patriotic Fund. 'Every effort has been made by your committee to encourage enlistment, and the heartiest support is being given to the present recruiting campaign,' the South Melbourne committee concluded. It acknowledged the death of three South Melbourne players at the Front, including Bruce.

One of Sloss's teammates from the Exhibition match, Carl Willis, had gone to the Military Cemetery at Armentières to visit Sloss's grave. He took a photograph of the headstone and sent it home to his father with the instruction to forward a print to Christina. Willis hoped South would plan a memorial for Sloss. 'If they are I think a suitable idea would be to hang an enlargement of [the] photo I took in France in the pavilion, say, besides a photo of Bruce,' Willis wrote to Brosnan. Willis was not a mate of Sloss's – they were, after all, radically different people – but football, and the club they played for, had nourished a common bond, for a game and a team. And Willis did share Sloss's sense of decency. But his idea for a Sloss memorial at South Melbourne failed to rouse the club into action.

January was a brutal month. Two weeks after Sloss was killed, the snow came. Temperatures fell, plummeting to 20 degrees Fahrenheit below freezing. The Australian sun was a dim memory. There was no way for the Diggers to get warm. Frostbite was insidious, physically crippling and corrosive to morale. The day's dawn cast only a shallow light on the night's carnage. In the midst of this bleak and frozen version of hell, James Pugh, the sprinter from Tasmania, found himself part of the 10th Brigade's nocturnal raid on German trenches. Pugh was a member of the 40th Battalion, the Tasmanian contingent, a proud group that had struggled to get established and then been slighted before it emerged in its own right.

Tasmania was expected to find enough men for a battalion, but, early in 1916, the numbers were so low that Defence Minister Pearce made it clear that it wasn't going to happen. 'The number of men enrolled in Tasmania was so small that it was found impossible to form a battalion,' he said. The barb drew blood. Within two weeks, there were more than enough Tasmanians to have their own battalion as well as reinforcements. Joined this time with a spread of soldiers from the 37th, 38th and 39th Battalions, Pugh and some of the Tasmanians were given the task of taking the Germans' first-, second- and third-line trenches. There were eight officers and 216 soldiers.

The operation was divided into three groups – one on the left, one in the centre and one on the right. Pugh was in the centre group, under the command of Lieutenant Stephen Suter, a clerk in the Launceston Magistrates Court, who had trained at Duntroon. Five minutes before the order to go was given, the Allies started an artillery barrage that was to be a diversion. The Germans responded, before the real Allied barrage started at 6 pm, when the Diggers started their raid in earnest. The right wing of the raiders worked through the wire protecting the German trenches and managed to gain vital yards before confronting a dual threat, from a German garrison and machine guns on their right. Only five of them were not killed or wounded. On the left, the Australians reached the wire, but it had not been cut. For 25 minutes, they grappled with finding a way through it. At 6.25 pm, they retreated with only one man wounded.

The wire was broken for Lieutenant Suter's group, and scouts discovered 20 Germans in the front line. The Germans turned and ran when they saw the raiders, but one German – a sniper or lookout – was shot as he tried to escape. The centre group split up – some went to the left in the trench network and destroyed four German concrete dugouts, and another group set off to the right and demolished another five dugouts. The telltale sound of steel doors being closed to the dugouts alerted the Diggers to the Germans' presence. These were sophisticated defences; one dugout was about 21 yards deep, with its own flight of steps.

The remainder of the group pushed on up a communications trench, blowing up one German dugout before reaching the disused second line of trenches. Moments later, they were at the third line of trenches. The light of the burning dugout revealed German reinforcements coming towards them. Suter and a fellow officer organised the Diggers to repel the counterattack and the Germans ran off.

After 40 minutes, AIF command let off a recall rocket, summoning the troops back to their own lines. Pugh helped marshal the troops back to safety, standing on top of a trench to lend a hand. An officer warned him about how exposed he was but Pugh just grinned and pointed to a nearby German, prone and done for. But the German was still alive. He found his weapon and shot Pugh in the back of the neck. Pugh died several hours later. Forty Germans were killed in the raid. Lieutenant Suter was awarded a Military Cross for his bravery. But one officer and another rank was missing, believed dead. There were 30 soldiers wounded, and Pugh was one of ten who died.

Captain J.W. Chisholm wrote to Pugh's parents in Trafalgar, about their eldest son:

> His personality, his soldierly qualities and unfailing good humour endeared him to all of us, and his platoon and the company as well, are much the poorer by his death. You have no doubt lost a splendid son, while we mourn the loss of one who proved himself a staunch comrade, a gallant soldier and a man.

These eulogies were the sad testimony many a commanding officer had to make to devastated parents, but with Pugh there was a sense that Chisholm's sentiment was heartfelt. Here indeed was the notion of 'a man's man'. What consolation that was to the Pughs is beyond knowing. They had two other sons at the Front: John, who enlisted in May 1916 when he was 27 and joined the 59th Battalion; and Victor, just 18 when he joined up four months after John and became part of the Tunnellers. Both survived the war. Pugh was 30, a man whose best sport might well have been behind him. But no one could be sure.

Jimmy Foy was so good at training soldiers how to use bayonets that his commanding officers wanted him to keep doing it behind the lines – even if bayonets were becoming less useful on the Western Front. It would have been safer for him, but Foy didn't want to be behind the lines; he wanted to be in the action. He told his mates that was why he had joined up. But every effort he made to get back to his unit was politely refused. Eventually, in early March, Foy's persistence was rewarded and he rejoined them. His 44th Battalion had impressed senior officers in Salisbury before it left, revelling in simulated trench warfare and trench-digging exercises. Now it was on the verge of a real fight. And when volunteers were called for a night-time raid, Foy put his hand up. He was that keen.

The 42nd and 44th Battalions were to be sent on a raid against the German trenches between the Armentières–Lille road and the railway line, in front of Grande Porte Egal Farm. The date was set for 13 March 1917, and there were 400 soldiers, including Foy, and six officers under the command of Captain C.H. Lamb. Although it was called a 'raid', it was a significant operation: dummy German trenches were built from air-reconnaissance photographs so the troops knew what they would encounter once they crossed no-man's-land. And the artillery barrage was to be the heaviest the 3rd Division had used up to that time.

The goal of the raid was to get through the first and second German lines, to capture prisoners and penetrate far enough into the enemy's territory to enable destruction of their defences. It was an ambitious plan, made even harder by the atrocious weather. It had been raining for days. The ground was sludge. In the forward trench, in front of the main German line, there was more than a metre of water, disguising barbed wire, and more deep, cloying mud. Captain Lamb wanted to postpone the raid because of the quagmire. But the schedule of what was known as the 'Travelling Circus' – the mobile heavy artillery group that was wheeled in to support each raiding party – wouldn't allow delays. The Circus would support the 44th, but only on the night of 13 March.

The operation was to start at 11.40 pm. Sustained trench mortar attack had cut through some of the heavy barbed wire in front of the German trenches, and regular machine-gun fire ensured the Germans could not leave their trenches to fix the breaches. In the days before the raid, the Australian howitzers had bombed the suspected enemy gun positions. It seemed all that needed to be done had been done. The men got ready by blacking their faces and hands with burnt cork. Their personal papers were handed in. Then they started, moving through the gaps made for them in the Australian line, to arrive at the assembly point in no-man's-land at 11.37 pm. But as Foy and the others lined up, a German searchlight picked them out and then remained on, about 110 yards north of where the Australians had gathered.

The barrage started two minutes later, when the howitzers started pounding the German lines. Then, on the stroke of 11.40, the rest of the artillery chorus joined in. Under the artillery cover, the troops moved about 55 yards forward, but the Germans were sending rockets and flares up to illuminate the pockmarked mud bath of no-man's-land, where the 44th were now pinpointed by the arc of the searchlight. The German artillery unleashed a fearsome barrage of shrapnel and high explosives that struck the front of the 44th, where Jimmy Foy stood. In the strange light cast by the flares, and the darkness punctured by the serial explosions, with the incessant boom of the guns, it was impossible to tell what happened next. But Foy was hit in the right thigh, a deep and fatal wound. 'Oh, I'm hit,' he told the men next to him. They tried to carry him back to the Australian lines but the pain was severe. He told them to leave him. Foy lasted only a few minutes more.

The order came to withdraw. Some were nevertheless determined to push on, but the turgid mud that surrounded the 44th was immobilising and made them easy targets for searchlights and shell fire. Even those who got through found the wire that cocooned the German trenches almost impossible to penetrate. One member of the 44th made it clear who the culprit was: '[T]he operation failure can . . . be attributed to one thing, and one only – not enemy shells or machine gun and rifle fire (heavy as they were) but mud, treacherous and slimy mud.' Lance Corporal Rowe agreed. 'The raid was not actually a success on account of the awful state of the ground, which was a mass of large shell holes filled with water, which caused us to retreat and I am almost certain that no one [entered] the enemy lines,' he wrote.

Forty-five men were wounded in the brief but horrible exchange, and 20 died. The confusion about Jimmy Foy's fate necessitated a Red Cross inquiry. An inquiry was always held to confirm the identity of a dead soldier, whether he was buried, his grave's location and whether it was registered. The Red Cross also asked soldiers who knew the dead man for a physical description to help prove his identity. Foy was one of many such inquiries. There had been some brave attempts to find his body during the raid but they failed during the sustained artillery barrage. It was several days later when his body was recovered and Foy was formally identified.

Second Lieutenant A.N. Birks told the Red Cross, 'I can hardly express the esteem in which Sgt Foy was held in his company, being recognised as a leader of merit by all ranks. He is sadly missed.' One of Foy's best mates, Sergeant J.E. Holmes, wrote to the Red Cross from his bed at Harefield Hospital in London, 'Sgt Foy was a personal friend of mine, one of the best friends I ever had. He was a particularly fine fellow with a wonderfully good personality and character. He was married about a month before we left Australia, his wife residing now I believe at Perth.'

It was an all too familiar tale of loss. Many of the stories were passed on to family without embellishment. Others were decorated with accounts of heroism and courage, perhaps to soften the blow at home. Foy's death became part of a tale spun later in the year when a returned man told how he saw Foy saving another soldier's life only moments before losing lost his own. It might have been true, but it was too hard to know. All anyone knew for certain was that Jimmy Foy wasn't coming home. He could have been an exceptional footballer, along with everything else that was denied him. It was less than five months after Foy had donned the jumper of the 3rd Division in London. He was laid to rest at the Bonjean Military Cemetery near Armentières, in plot 5, row A, grave 3.

The farcical 1916 VFL season was not going to be repeated in 1917. Geelong and South Melbourne waived their self-imposed exile and returned to the League, to boost it to a more interesting six-team competition. Geelong claimed its return was based on the premise that recruitment was more successful when the League had more teams playing, while South Melbourne's return was to help the financially stricken South Melbourne Cricket Club through ground-management fees. This was hardly a reason that would appease the recruiters but by this stage there was evidence of football's lack of commitment to the whole patriotic ideal. The four VFL clubs contributed only £282 to the patriotic funds in 1916 from more than £3000 in revenue. This was despite their supposed commitment to send all profits to the fund and not pay players.

Carlton was the worst example of the four clubs that played on in 1916, generating £884 of revenue but paying off debt instead of donating anything to the Patriotic Fund. The Blues put £99 towards recouping the losses players incurred for being absent from work, another £45 towards players' travelling costs and £57 to injured players. (Fitzroy paid £152 from £918 of revenue; Collingwood £40 from £664 and Richmond £90 from £614.) It sounded suspiciously like player payments under another name. The League did nothing to censure the clubs, triggering a wave of public cynicism at the VFL's position.

Billy Hughes went to the 1917 election with a stitched-up coalition of interests and prejudices after he had walked away from the Labor Party in the aftermath of his failed conscription referendum. The coalition was united by a single goal – to win the war – and Hughes played the card for all it was worth.

He was a mercurial politician, with an instinct for survival and a fierce capacity for hard work. He could change political direction with the assured footwork of a ballroom dancer but conjure division and opposition where there had been none. And then he would exploit the division to his advantage, while growing stronger on the pungent odour of discord.

Hughes knew in 1917 that one of his electoral assets was his resolute commitment to the Empire. Australians might not have voted for conscription but that didn't mean they had abandoned the Mother Country or the justness of the war itself. And as the Western Front became intractable and Australian losses grew, Hughes reasoned the country would finally have to embrace some form of compulsory military service, even if it was driven by the need to save the Empire. He went to the federal election on the shrewd promise that there would be no conscription without another referendum and only if it was an issue of national safety. Hughes might have been a Labor rat but he read the mood of his countrymen – the Hughes Coalition won 53 seats in the 5 May election and Labor only 22.

Recruitment plummeted to 2617 men in December 1916. Desperate to boost numbers, the government took responsibility for national recruiting away from the Defence department and gave it to Donald Mackinnon. It might have looked like a vote of confidence in the job Mackinnon did in Victoria, but the truth was that he was in no way a vocal advocate for conscription. Why Hughes and Pearce put someone who didn't really believe in conscription in charge of recruitment remains a mystery. Mackinnon's public views were no secret, although he was prepared to concede that a protracted conflict made conscription more likely. He also believed the threat of conscription was an intimidating incentive to recruiting. 'It has come under my notice that demands for conscription are stimulating the enlistment of many who are apprehensive that conscription will become law,' he said.

One of Mackinnon's first acts was to write to sporting associations to ask for their help: 'Through you, if your executive will apply its influential weight, very many sportsmen and supporters of sport will be moved to take an active part in the campaign . . . it is confidently expected that the call to sportsmen has only to be sounded to bring forth a hearty and unanimous response.' Mackinnon believed sportsmen already at the front would act as a suitable inspiration for those who were still at home, playing a different game. But he could not have anticipated the extent of bitterness that was at the heart of the issue and how hard his job would become.

May 1917 was the month when football reached a new level of notoriety. On 19 May, recruiting officers were sent to Melbourne football grounds to address the crowds at half-time. According to the recruiting officers, it was a shameful disaster. '[R]acecourse crowds are better than football crowds – one lot are gentlemen compared to the others. Gentlemen because they will at any rate listen to recruiting officers. Football crowds will not only not listen, but they would get you down if they could and put the boots in,' one said. Another complained that the Fitzroy committee gave him no help, other than access to the grandstand. All the officers – whether they were at Collingwood, South Melbourne or Fitzroy – complained about the crowd's hostility and jeering. One at South Melbourne claimed, 'They said I had no right to go there and spoil their sport. I had to leave the ground, as they threatened to deal with me.' The Melbourne *Age* was appalled. 'These are narratives in plain language of heartless, vicious and detestable actions on the parts of individuals who class themselves as sports people . . . It is another big blot on football.'

The situation was certainly dire, if that was what actually happened. But the reality was somewhat different. It appeared the recruiting officers' high dudgeon was just cheap rhetoric and another shot in the conscription conflict. And the two

Melbourne morning papers, *The Age* and *The Argus*, were in lock-step with the government on the issue, quick to back the recruiting officers and run extreme, probably erroneous, tales of the football crowds' behaviour.

Gerald Brosnan, the former Fitzroy premiership player, University coach and football correspondent for *The Winner*, was at South Melbourne and witnessed the recruiting officers' address:

> I . . . listened, with others, for a time, to the speakers, and barring a few interjections (and these by returned soldiers) I can honestly say nothing in the nature even of an interruption took place. I have also the word of gentlemen, on whose honor I can implicitly rely, that neither at Fitzroy nor Collingwood were the speakers harassed in any way whatever. Far from being so, they were given an attentive hearing in both places.

Brosnan could barely contain his outrage. He was affronted at the allegations about the game he had given his life to, and the players – many of them already at the Front – whom he had coached and counselled:

> Football, as a sport, comes in for a lot of undeserved criticism but rarely has such a glaring case of pure mendacity come under notice as that regarding the experiences of the recruiting officers. It has not even the merit of highly-colored exaggeration because it is wholly without foundation in any instance. It is purely and simply a fabrication, and a deliberate one at that, one calculated to do an irreparable injury to the game by reason of the vital interests at stake.

There was no hiding what Brosnan thought about it, but for many readers of the two morning newspapers, it confirmed what they already thought about football supporters. The recruiting officers' so-called testimony was a brutal escalation in the public battle over sport's role in the war. 'The harm has been done but it is a thousand pities that the great national sport of the people should have meted out to it such unfair treatment,' Brosnan added two weeks later.

The club officials, under increasing scrutiny from the State War Council, were courageous enough to doubt the recruiting officers' recollections. The Fitzroy delegate to the VFL thought the recruiting officers were given a good reception. At South Melbourne, the lieutenant was 'cheered'. Geelong delegate Charles Brownlow said he received a letter from the recruiting officer 'telling me how pleased he was at the way our committee had received him'. Collingwood's Ernie Copeland made the salient observation about the absence of reports in the papers about such an alleged fracas. 'The reporters do not miss anything like that,' he said. But, he could have added, the leader writers certainly took it upon themselves to pass judgement. Nonetheless, the League's president and former University delegate Mr Owen Williams resigned, largely to placate the growing anger at the League's issues around the patriotic funds, rather than over the treatment of recruiting officers.

The State War Council wrote to the League pointing out that if it was going to honour its commitment to donate all its profits to the patriotic funds, it was necessary for the League to apply to the War Council for permission to play games. Failure to get permission would be an offence under the *War Precautions Act*. The League was neatly skewered now; it needed the State War Council onside to play, and it needed to hold games to generate money for the Patriotic Fund. Brownlow, who stood in as chairman after Williams's resignation, said there was 'nothing very dreadful in that' but the League still decided to have a meeting with the War Council, ostensibly to put its position but in truth to come to an agreement on how to navigate the new landscape they now confronted. The meeting went ahead on Wednesday, 6 June, but there was no public comment from either group until the War Council released its motion almost two weeks later that clubs could not raise money for the Patriotic Fund without submitting their estimated expenses to the Council.

The Council would also approve a scale of 'reasonable expenditure' for holding matches, as submitted to them by the clubs. In the next ten days, the League responded. The Council appeared to be taking a tough line, but, somewhere between the Council's first statement and the League's response, a resolution emerged that did nothing to dispel the public cynicism surrounding the League. The VFL explained to the Council that it was only an 'honorable understanding' that the clubs would pay money to the funds. 'How well that misunderstanding was not honored is now a matter of history,' *The Age* sniffed.

The League also pointed out that it had raised £4600 since the war started, which might have impressed some but paled against the effort of the state's schoolchildren, who raised £100,000 for the war relief fund by the end of 1916. But Brownlow did note that club memberships fell from 28,365 in 1914 to just 3469 in 1916. It was not surprising with only four teams playing that revenue had also plummeted from £17,423 to £2785 pounds in the same period. The War Council decided to take no further action against the VFL. Indeed, the League was given the right to decide its allocation to patriotic funds later in the season. The War Council's motion that it had circulated with such certainty days earlier was now left to drop quietly by the wayside. It was a stunning victory for the League.

There were still some concessions to be made. The scheduled round 13 in the 1917 season was delayed a week so that recruiting officers could go to grounds on 4 August. But the steady increase in spectators with two teams back in the competition helped give the League some much-needed leverage. The League might have retained control of its financial destiny, but there were larger forces at work that it couldn't stop. Two months after the recruiting officers' visits, Prime Minister Hughes made a formal announcement on recruitment. 'The Government is of the opinion that in the best interests of the nation, measures for the restriction of sport must be introduced. The heavy financial burdens caused by the war must make it necessary that the resources of the Commonwealth should be most carefully husbanded for national purposes,' Hughes explained. '[S]o much time is given to sport in Australia where many look on and few participate, that the safety of the nation is in danger. Many are indeed so obsessed by sport as to ignore altogether the grave danger in which this country stands.'

So Hughes wanted Australia to believe that being a sporting spectator was actually imperilling the nation. This was Hughes's wild rhetoric at its best. It was as plain as day that he was going to deride, cajole, misrepresent, blacken and wheedle any impediment to recruitment. He directed his Defence minister, Senator George Foster Pearce, to convene a conference in each state with sports organisers to 'submit suggestions to give effect to the Government's proposals'. The politics were crude and underscored by an unmistakeable desire to intimidate sport into surrendering its players and its fans to the recruiting office.

Hughes was also, more profoundly, setting up the circumstances to revisit the conscription issue. While he maintained that he honoured the previous year's result, he left open the possibility of a second referendum if national safety became an issue. The average number of new recruits for the first six months of 1917 was 4750 a month. Hughes wanted to bump that up to 7000 a month. Mackinnon didn't like the idea at all and felt that Hughes was risking too much for the sake of the difference between 5000 and 7000 recruits. 'It is a question whether Australia should be again plunged in to a bitter political combat, the issue of which is uncertain and the consequences of which are so grave, for the sake of 2000 men?' Mackinnon asked. It was an entirely fair question posed by a man who understood that the forces Hughes unleashed in the first referendum would only become more seismic, more profound at a second attempt. But Mackinnon's common sense was lost in the fury of the debate.

Sportsmen and sports fans had to make their mark, according to the Hughes doctrine. All those sportsmen – the footballers – who were already in uniform were not enough. There had to be more, Hughes insisted. The cracks that had appeared in football just 12 months before seemed mild in comparison with the splintering Hughes and his supporters were now intent on driving through the nation's recreations, including Australia's own game.

Yet on the Western Front, games of football went ahead, free from politics but not from danger. 'The playing field was within shell range. Every inch of it had been won from the enemy by the hardest fighting, of which evidence lay all around,' *Argus* journalist Lieutenant L.G. Short wrote from the Front about one match. He went on:

> The centre was marked by enormous shell holes, with two 5.9 shells (unexploded) lying beside a sand bomb at the bottom of one . . . But the saddest and most realistic touch of all lay behind the goal post on the southern end. It was a small heap of earth – the grave of dead soldiers – with the simple but sublime superscription 'To Unknown British Heroes'.

This time, there were no jumpers with Australian symbols – the officers wore sheepskin jerkins, with socks where their puttees used to be. The non-commissioned officers wore their standard-issued cardigans. Short did not see much to inspire him about the football. How could it be otherwise, with the snow melting and the ground becoming slippery and treacherous, and the men out of condition and out of practice? But Short knew the game's value. 'It is impossible to chronicle all the wonderful events of that most stupendous game,' he wrote. 'That night saw officers and sergeants again to the front line on a tour of inspection previous to another term of duty in the trenches. But it is certain that the game gave them fresh heart. It had carried their thoughts vividly back to those happy days when football was played in certain Melbourne suburbs they called "home".'

There was an implied equation at work: the worse things became at the Front, the more important, the deeper the connection, the greater the need to find ways to do the things that reminded the men of home. Football was a cornerstone of it. 'And it is in such happy thoughts and memories that we soldiers live,' Short concluded.

8

Those Who Are Left

The rumours of Hughie James being missing wouldn't go away. The big Richmond ruckman had been in a big stunt in France and no one could find him. And none of the family knew anything – missing, killed or alive. It was a constant problem for families on the home front. Often, their anxious waiting was a prelude to the worst possible news. A few were lucky and the 'missing' turned up 'found'. The rest of the families just kept waiting for months until there was no other conclusion to be reached, that their son, or husband, father or brother, was dead.

James's father and cousin got wind of the rumour and, rather than wait for any formal notification, decided to take it on themselves to find out just what Hughie was up to. They went to the Base Records Office in Melbourne and asked whether there had been any word about Hughie. A cable was dispatched to London in January 1917. The reply came back: 'James well at latest.'

James was not only alive, he was thriving. He had been promoted to lieutenant, in the Pioneers, after excelling in a series of examinations in Salisbury. He had impressed many fans at Richmond with his understated but impressive capacity for leadership. Now, he was demonstrating it again, in the most difficult of circumstances. Here was a man who felt at ease with himself, someone who was able to work with soldiers and the ranks. It was a valuable skill. And those around him wanted Hughie to do well. 'All Richmondites, I know, are aware that Hughie James is now wearing a star on his shoulder,' a young Richmond soldier, Tom Lacey, wrote from the Western Front about James's promotion. 'He is just as popular here as he was in Richmond. All the lads here wished him luck when they heard of his promotion. Wouldn't it be appropriate if he went back home a captain?'

In the build-up to seeing their first action, Willis and Minogue found themselves back playing football, this time against each other. The match took place only 1000 yards from the trenches and was played on a 'small rectangular patch' in the heart of a town where the Australians were billeted. It was a world away from the ceremony of the Exhibition match. 'The goal posts were those used for the British Association football,' Willis wrote. 'The behind posts were empty army biscuit tins ... The "pavilion" was in one corner of the ground and had most evidently been a stable until the concussion of shell had settled the tiles on the roof.' One team wore shirts and the other 'cardigan' jackets. There were no studs on the boots, so players slipped in the mud and some crawled around the ground in pursuit of the football. 'Later in the afternoon three of our planes made their way over the enemy lines and came under the fire of his anti-aircraft guns. This effectually [sic] put a finishing touch to the unrealness of the whole thing,' Willis explained. The result and how Willis and Minogue performed was not recorded but Willis, not for the last time, would lament how stiff and sore he was after the encounter.

Stan Martin, the would-be doctor turned dentist, who couldn't quite find a way to turn up to university, had an appointment he wouldn't miss. It was with the Germans at Bullecourt, one of the most savage and debilitating encounters the Australians faced during their time at the Western Front.

Martin had grown a moustache and looked too young to have it, let alone go to war. But he was 25, and part of the seasoned 22nd Battalion that saw action initially at Gallipoli and arrived in France in March 1916. It endured Pozières, Ypres, and then returned to the Somme for the onset of the winter.

Martin was spared most of it because he was seconded to the 6th Australian Training Battalion, working as an instructor in physical training and bayonet fighting in England. He had done his own training at the Imperial School at Aldershot before returning to Salisbury. From there, he was selected for the Exhibition match. But when the time came for the 22nd Battalion to take its place at the Front, Stan Martin was there.

The Allied grand plan was built around the French and the British attacking Champagne and Arras in a coordinated push. The British at Arras would seize the high ground and force the German reserves away from the French at Champagne, leaving the Germans vulnerable and fighting on two fronts. The Australians had no main role in the bigger picture but it was thought they could make a difference if they could attack the German flank.

In February and March 1917, the Germans made a strategic withdrawal for ten to 30 miles to the Siegfried Line (or, as the Allies called it, the Hindenburg Line). As planned, the British launched its offensive at Arras on 9 April, and the Canadians fought a bloody and successful battle to secure the high ground at Vimy Ridge. The Diggers, part of the British command under General Sir Hubert Gough, were given the task of attacking the Hindenburg Line around the heavily fortified town of Bullecourt, ten miles south-east of Arras.

Gough planned his first attack for 10 April. But the early artillery attacks did little to break through the German wire where the Australians were going to launch their attack. Rather than wait for more artillery support, Gough decided to use a dozen tanks to bludgeon their way through the German barbed wire – which was 33 yards thick in places – with the infantry coming up behind. It was a flawed plan, not only because the tanks were slow and unreliable but also because they were positioned some distance away from the front line. When they didn't arrive in time, Gough postponed the attack until the next day.

It just delayed the carnage by 24 hours. The Germans, well aware of the aborted plans from the day before, raked the uncovered Australians with ceaseless machine-gun and artillery fire, while the tanks – black, lumbering silhouettes against the snow – were blown up and burning all around them. The Diggers were pushed back to their own lines, with massive casualties. Losses included 1170 Aussie prisoners, the largest number of Australians taken in a single battle to that time. Charles Bean lamented that the Australian 4th Brigade, part of the 4th Division at Bullecourt, was 'a magnificent instrument recklessly shattered in the performance of an impracticable task'.

Gough tried again on 3 May. This time, he was better prepared. It was a major British assault with 14 divisions on a 15-mile front, accompanied by heavy artillery bombardment. The Diggers wanted to have nothing to do with tanks after they proved useless in April. This time, the 2nd Division of the AIF was used alongside the British troops, rather than the 4th, which had suffered such losses. And that meant Lance Corporal Stan Martin was about to see action.

Martin's 22nd Battalion was on the left of the Australian push, and was the most exposed to the German defences in Bullecourt. One of Stan Martin's colleagues in the 22nd, Eugene Gorman, explained the build-up to the attack:

> For no other struggle had the preparations been so complete, the rehearsals so thorough, or the general organisation so apparently perfect. Yet, within a few minutes of its commencement, the combat developed in to a pell-mell of violent hand-to-hand struggles, where the 6th Australian

Infantry Brigade met the flower of the German Army, and beat it in to quiescence.

Gorman, a 25-year-old Catholic barrister from Melbourne with a gift for the criminal law, won a Military Cross for his bravery on the day. It was that kind of attack – only the foolhardy and the lucky would survive.

There were 21 officers and 615 other ranks, including Stan Martin, who all moved into position at 3.25 am on 3 May, 20 minutes before the attack was to start. It is hard to imagine the nerves and anxiety that gripped them. A bright moon hung around in the early hours, making it easy to see shapes in the dark. But it disappeared in the final ten minutes, blanketing the troops in deep darkness. Finally, when 'zero hour' came at 3.45 am, the Allies launched their attack with the cover of heavy artillery.

Only four minutes had passed when the Germans responded with a targeted barrage of shells and heavy machine-gun fire across the 22nd Battalion line. These were crack German troops behind the guns, the Kaiser's favourite 'Cockchafers', whom he had personally picked to hold the Bullecourt Garrison. The waves of Australian battalions, which included the 21st, 23rd and the 24th as well as the 22nd, merged in the chaos of the opening moments. The noise was brutal. Gorman believed the battalion was exposed to the most intense machine-gun fire it ever confronted. 'The noise of the bullets and the rattle of the machine guns that strewed them were distinct sounds, that rose above the din of the barrage,' he wrote. The 22nd was leading the advance on the left flank of the assault. Martin was in the thick of the pounding artillery and the endless white-hot chatter of the machine guns. The German shrapnel barrage started to cleave the battalion's advance.

Captain Joe Slater had played football for Geelong and was a cherished son of Corio, a gifted athlete of genial nature.

He played all sports well – cricket and athletics in particular – but it was football where he was most effective, thanks to his dash off the half-back line. Slater was mentioned in dispatches for his courage at Pozières and was leading his men again at Bullecourt. Slater and Martin had been opponents several times when Stan was with University. Now they were on the same side, trying to find a way through the piercing din and deadly fusillade that surrounded them in the dead of night, miles from home.

Slater was hit by shrapnel, and then machine-gunned, while stuck in the horrible embrace of a trench's barbed wire. Martin, the impish winger with a trademark running drop kick, was caught in the machine-gun fire and fell. He was one of 56 men of the 22nd Battalion who died in the awful moments before the dawn. Many who were wounded could not be rescued because of the intensity of the German machine-gun fire. Some took shelter in the massive shell holes that offered some safety. One Digger waited 16 hours in a hole before he finally made his way back to the Australian lines. The casualties were so severe that, at about 4.30 am, those who were still able were 'compelled to retire'. The 22nd was all but wiped out – 16 officers and 422 soldiers perished, the most of the four Australian battalions in the first 24 hours of the attack. Yet despite the carnage, some Diggers got through to the Hindenburg Line and established a precarious hold. The Germans mounted 13 counterattacks throughout the day, ensuring the ground gained was constantly under fire, but the Australians held on.

At the end of the first day, however, the only objectives reached and held were those of the Canadians in the extreme north and the 6th Australian Brigade in the extreme south. The pressure to consolidate the gains was becoming more intense, with mutinies breaking out in the French Army and the lack of Allied success. On 4 May, the Australian 1st Division replaced the exhausted 6th Brigade while British troops attempted to take Bullecourt. Three days later, the British captured some of what remained of the crumbling, bombed Bullecourt.

The battle wasn't over, though, and it continued for another 13 days, with seven German counterattacks. On 10 May, the Australian 5th Division was brought into the fighting, and ten days later the Germans withdrew. The two Bullecourt battles cost 10,000 Australian casualties in another cruel example of military folly. Back home, Hughes and Pearce, who had agitated for a sixth Australian division three months earlier, came to realise that the extensive losses and the continuing recruitment shortages meant a new division was not possible.

Something snapped within Irvin Martin when he was told the news of his son Stan's death. It was the final indecency of a war that had torn the Martins apart. Three months after war was declared in 1914, Arthur Martin became the first man in the family to enlist. He was sent overseas and attached to 1st Australian General Hospital in Heliopolis. But in November 1915, when Arthur was working as an orderly at the hospital, he had what doctors described as an epileptic fit. Arthur had no history of epilepsy but he was invalided home and sent to the Royal Park psychiatric hospital in Melbourne in March 1916. While he was there, he contracted broncho-pneumonia and died. He was 31.

Stan had already enlisted and was overseas when his brother died. So too was another brother, Hector, aged 39, an accountant, who was taken into the 45th Battalion and was badly wounded at Pozières. Irvin described Hector's predicament in graphic detail:

He was shot through the chest, the piece of shell coming out the back of his shoulder, a piece as big as a billiard chalk passed through his steel helmet; he was 'splathered' with bits of shell over his face, arms and legs, was buried (explosion of shell) from 10pm 'til 5.30am next day when he was dug out. His comrades on each side of him were killed.

Metal splinters were removed from Hector's face and head some time after he was wounded. He was invalided back to England and applied his accounting background to work in a military pay office. But Irvin was worried that his eldest son was going back to the trenches. Not only that but the family's only daughter, Mabel, was nursing in France. There were no children left at home. Stan's death convinced Irvin that Hector had to come home. He wrote to Senator Pearce and the army, pleading for their understanding. 'My wife is in a deplorable state – nearly blind and in a serious state of nervous breakdown,' he said. '[Hector] has fairly done his bit and we as a family have done ours . . . and if anything happens to [Hector] it will be the death of his mother.'

Everything the Martins had left as a family was invested in getting Hector home. Hector was 'no shirker' and his father, desperate to overcome any obstacle the government might put in the way of his return, volunteered to pay whatever it cost to get his son back to Australia.

The Defence department went through its practice of verifying Irvin Martin's claims about his family. Local police initially made inquiries and then passed on the result to the relevant military district authority. Another son, Leslie, was married and living in New South Wales, but it was concluded that the Martins were in 'good financial circumstances', were living alone and were aged. The recommendation to Defence Secretary Tom Trumble was to bring Hector home. On 5 July 1917, two months after Stan died, Trumble sent Irvin a letter confirming Hector's return. 'The Minister desires me to convey his appreciation of the splendid patriotism displayed by your family in the present national emergency.'

Hector came home on 27 July 1917. At least Irvin and Mary Martin had one son back, amid the constant reminder of the two they had lost. Stan had appointed Irvin and fiancée Olive Weaver as the executors of his will. But there were precious little belongings to send home – it was only razor blades, some training manuals, three collars and a tie.

It was a sad fact of the Western Front that a soldier's life existed on a short line of extremes that ran from dread to boredom. The weather was another kind of enemy. One soldier wrote about the horrible winter: 17 degrees Fahrenheit below freezing at night. 'To go for water means to take a pick and a bag, break up the ice, carry the lumps back in the bag and stack them outside the door of the hut ready for use. In the morning the bread is frozen as hard as a board.'

But when the thaw came, there were other things to do behind the lines, and it was often football. Wally Laidlaw, a driver attached to the 24th Battalion, had played a couple of matches with South Melbourne. He captained his unit's football team that played seven games in the space of several weeks and won five of them. They even played against a Western Australian team that included Percy Trotter. 'Beautiful Percy' was still turning it on. 'They beat us by seven points. Percy has accumulated some weight but played well getting three goals,' Laidlaw wrote. Then there was the usual reflection on how many footballers he saw at the Front. Even with the war so ever-present, there was still time for the game and to celebrate the fraternal football bonds that had been established back home.

Frank Beaurepaire was still doing his best to entertain Monash's 3rd Division. In an engineering lecture theatre of a technical school, the École Provisionelle at Armentières, Beaurepaire ran a 500-seat cinema. The entrance fee was half a franc. The YMCA paid £170 for the projectors, chairs and lighting, but the three months' revenue of £630 went straight into the corps fund for the benefit of every soldier. 'You might stroll one evening at 6 down towards the cinema hall – quite a pretentious building, with posters on the walls – to find a long queue waiting to again admission,' one correspondent wrote. 'Many have to be turned away before a "full house". It is a good hall and up to date, if it was a bit "shell-holey" before the Australians took it. It is well tucked away, moreover, from the shells that now come floating around. You can see a change of pictures three times a week and Pierrot items once a week.'

Hewitt was inevitably part of the entertainment that led Monash to describe the Pierrots as 'real artists'. It was Hewitt who insisted on exotic scenery, lighting – electricity was sourced from the tramways in the vicinity – and plenty of theatrical pomp. The troupe was made up of working soldiers; one, dressed as a lady, appeared on stage with shrapnel still in his neck. Many of the jokes were at Monash's expense but it didn't matter to the general, as long as they were in good taste and made the troops laugh. In the first three months of 1917, the attendance for the show was 40,000 soldiers. On the most basic of calculations, that meant each 3rd Division soldier had seen the show twice. These entertainments were not just confined to Monash's division. The Anzac Coves, a musical troupe similar to Hewitt's boys, developed a higher profile and performed for the Prince of Wales, General Birdwood, General Gough and the Australian High Commissioner Andrew Fisher. One correspondent estimated 150,000 Diggers had seen the Coves, and they even performed in pouring rain with 15-inch shells landing within 100 yards of the show.

Beaurepaire's health, however, was failing. He went on ten days' leave to England, returned to the front and was then declared sick with trench fever. Back he went to England to recover. 'It appears I had been sickening for weeks, and I know my ten days' leave was nearly all "non bon" for me as I was too seedy most of the time,' Beaurepaire wrote home, with forced levity. Trench fever was a curse on the Western Front. Although nowhere near as debilitating as trench foot, the fever's symptoms resembled typhoid or influenza and caused skin rashes, head-aches and leg pains. The ever-present lice were the culprits, and the impact could, in some instances, incapacitate a soldier for up to three months.

One of the consolations for Beaurepaire was a letter he received during his recovery from Monash:

> I need not say how very sorry I am not only that the state of your health necessitates this, but that the division will be, for a period, deprived of your very able services . . . As organiser of social work within the division, of comforts for the troops in the trenches and of sports and amusements, your work has been on a uniform plane of excellence. I trust that the gratitude felt towards you by all ranks will constitute some measure of reward for your labours.

Beaurepaire saw the letter as an endorsement of how indispensable he had become. He was desperate to return but, once again, his body let him down. He found himself back in Australia, undergoing an operation for damage caused by gas.

Beaurepaire was lucky it wasn't worse. Hundreds of gassed Australians suffered for years, but Beaurepaire was only exposed to a draught of gas that went through a nostril to the back of his left cheek, which had turned septic. Surgery was done to remove some of the affected small bones. Beaurepaire insisted he was not badly off. 'Had I been severely gassed I am afraid I would have suffered considerably more than I did. I am thankful to be able to say, however, that two doctors have given me "all clear" so far as chest and heart is concerned. The gas had evidently not got any further than my nose and face,' he said.

He went into the private hospital Somerset House in East Melbourne just before Christmas 1917 and was well enough to take part in a 100-metre exhibition swim at St Kilda baths on Boxing Day morning. His rivals on the day were equally indisposed – Frank Fitts, a former 100-yard Victorian champion, was recovering from being gassed in France, and Melbourne Swimming Club champion T.W. Mason was recovering in hospital from wounds he had received on the Western Front. Mason was so incapacitated that he started in the water while Beaurepaire and Fitts were on the starting board. Mason won the race by half a body length. The swim was enough of an indication to Beaurepaire that he was sufficiently fit to do at least something for the war effort. Early in the New Year, he embarked on an interstate tour to spruik the YMCA's role at the Front.

Monash's support for Beaurepaire's entertainments made it easy for the YMCA representative to institute new recreations and maintain some of the old ones. It gave the YMCA a privileged place in the Australian 3rd Division. And Monash's confidence was contagious. The results, after all, were plain to see. Phillip Schuler, who covered the Gallipoli landings for *The Age* and then enlisted to see action on the Western Front, found himself charmed by the impact Beaurepaire had on the men around him. '[D]isregarding for the moment the military side of the question, the cheery optimism of the officers, the interest in the very weapons of war, its arrows, bombs, shells and explosives, there has been one man the general [Monash] has turned to and in whom he has placed a well-merited confidence – Frank Beaurepaire,' Schuler observed. 'Frank Beaurepaire was well known over Australia as the champion swimmer. Illness compelled him to "go slow" for a while, but his spirit took him amongst the troops, and now when "go slow" has changed to "hustle" each day . . . he could ill be spared from work he so enthusiastically carries out.' Schuler's story appeared in the paper his father, Frederick, edited, just a week before Schuler died of wounds on the Western Front.

Leslie Edward Lee, the baby-faced boy from Richmond who had played so well in the Exhibition match, was sent to hospital in May 1917 with pediculosis. It was an ailment that thousands of soldiers dealt with – lice infestation. It was often treated by a bath in the converted old brewery vats Monash had set up behind the line, along with issuing fresh uniforms or at least ironing the old clothes to kill the parasites. But sometimes the infestation was too severe for such remedies. Lee's was a bad case. The trenches were a petrie dish for any kind of bug and bacteria. Men had to sleep under groundsheets or tents in the bottom of trenches and latrines were often in the front line trench, creating an odour as well as a cesspit. In winter, the trenches were full of snow or ice and the men huddled together for warmth. The lice jumped between the shivering bodies. Lee was in hospital for several weeks but was deemed well enough to return to the 10th Machine Gun unit towards the end of May, as preparations were being finalised for the 3rd Division's first major role.

One of Lee's best friends was Private Francis Ignatius Joseph Coffey, from Albert Park in Melbourne, who described himself as a 'gentleman'. It was a grand label for a 23-year-old Catholic with a penchant for trouble. The two cast an uneven shadow – Lee, at six feet, with his strong physique, clear skin and rich, curly auburn hair, and Coffey, six inches shorter, nimble grey eyes, brown hair and the air of the feckless teenager. Although Coffey and Lee had left Australia together on the troopship *Ascanius* on 27 May 1916, their military careers took radically divergent paths. Lee was a quiet character, considered and private, but Coffey felt an instinctive need to test where the boundaries were. He soon found out. In Salisbury, he was fined for impersonating a sergeant. He broke out of hospital, used obscene language, was drunk, and went absent without leave. None of these were great transgressions but they reinforced the image of Coffey as a serial offender, a wild, restless and often reckless young man. Lee was serene in comparison. And each time Coffey crossed the boundary, the penalties increased, from fines to days locked up. The Army Provost Corps, which kept an ever-alert eye on Coffey, approached Lee to see if he would swap his soldiering for a safer time working for them and policing the Diggers in England. But Lee declined the offer and opted to stay with the Gunners. And when the time came, Coffey would provide an eloquent testimony to his friend's character.

The grand offensive that the Allies had planned had ultimately failed. The British plan became focused on Flanders, with a two-pronged attack to liberate Belgium and to push through the German line to free key ports, such as Ostend. Monash and his 3rd Division had been at Armentières, in France, just before the Belgian border. The new priority meant they moved over the border, near Ploegsteert Wood, and a manoeuvre was devised to capture the Messines–Wytschaete Ridge, where the Germans held an elevated view of their enemy.

The ridge had been a sore point for the Allies during the previous two years. Its elevation gave the Germans clear views of what was going on, and it had become a key defensive position. A frontal attack would be madness, so the Allies had decided on using tunnellers and mines. The plans were detailed and extensive. The topography, the trenches, the ditches, the fortified positions were all mapped. Large models were constructed so troops could familiarise themselves with what lay ahead. Canadian and British tunnellers had started laying mines deep under the German lines two years earlier. Their payday was coming. The next part of the plan was a week-long artillery barrage that was to keep the Germans occupied and perhaps dispirited before the real show started. Twenty-one mines were set to go off for the attack on 6 June.

This was to be Monash's 3rd Division's first battle. All those who represented the division at Queen's Club – with the exception of Bruce Sloss – were scheduled to be part of what would become known as the Battle of Messines. The Germans got in first and shelled the wood where the Australians had gathered with gas, creating mayhem and causing at least 500 Australian casualties.

214

War correspondent Charles Bean wrote in his notebook, 'As we went up thro [sic] wood . . . gas shells began to fall fast – pot, pot, pot all around. We stopped and put on [gas] helmets . . . trenches were pretty well steeped in gas.'

Carl Willis found himself in the midst of it. Gas was his worst fear – more alarming to see its effect on other soldiers, more confronting the thought of it infiltrating his nose, mouth and lungs than being struck by gunshot and shells. 'There is no chance of mistaking the gas shell when you have once seen or heard one,' he said. 'The first time one lands you will probably think it is a "dead" shell [one which has not exploded] owing to there being no report; but soon you can distinguish them easily as they have quite a different sound in the air to the ordinary shell. Instead of a scream or whirr, the gas shell seems to make a buzzing sound, and when it hits the ground there is simply a dull pop . . . The gas is fairly heavy and easily visible in small white clouds hanging to the ground like an early morning mist, which is being gradually dispersed by the sun.' Although the soldiers were given gas helmets – and trained in how to use them – marching or running with a full kit made breathing difficult. Even the AIF artillery brigades had to wear masks as they pounded the German lines, just in case the gas cloud came their way. This time, the gas attack struck the Australians as they moved through the wood.

Despite his mask, Willis somehow breathed it in. 'I can honestly say that I got the one thing I was really frightened of . . . I was not bad from it when one considers what some of the other fellows got but quite bad enough for my liking. I would sooner see men blown to pieces than see them die from gas. It is a most ghastly death,' he said. Willis believed gas was 'just about the most awful invention of a diabolical brain'. But both sides used it and Willis made no judgement about that, other than to invoke the horror of its effect. 'Somehow in war you expect to see terrifying sights such as men with extensive wounds and men cut into pieces by shellfire but to see them gassed is unnatural. A man comes toward you rolling and staggering about for all the world like a drunken man.'

Willis finished up in hospital for several weeks, under the care of the former South Australian footballer Fred Le Messurier. From there, he was redeployed back to Salisbury, to the dental unit. It had been two years since Willis had practised dentistry. He was not going back to the Front. The gas was Willis's vile souvenir of the Western Front, one that he carried for years.

The tunnellers did their job expertly at Messines. The horrible impact of the 450,000 kilograms of explosive tore the German line apart. 'Nothing could have withstood such an onslaught, and nothing did,' a soldier said. Even Londoners miles away heard the roar. The carnage was instant, killing several thousand Germans. It was still before dawn, and the dust and smoke from the explosions infiltrated the darkness, making it even harder to see the extent of the damage or the openings in the German line. Some officers used compasses to find their way. There was little German resistance and the Messines Ridge was a stunning success for the Allies. But the hard work for Hughie James and his bridge-building mates in the 3rd Pioneer Battalion had barely started.

The Pioneers had a vital role. The Douve River, a slender strategic waterway, flowed around the front of the Messines hill, to the southern end and back towards the German position. The river, perhaps more of a stream in high summer, marked the boundary of two German armies. And some Australian troops had to cross the Douve to join up with New Zealand and other Australian troops north of it. Bridges were built and carried to the river. 'It was a complicated task,' Bean said, 'and almost sure to be heavily opposed sooner or later by the army whose territory they invaded.'

Lieutenant James had two key tasks – not just to help get the bridge in place but also to repair the shell-riddled Messines Road to ensure the Allied troops could get through. The work had to be precise and rapid but the pressure from intense German shelling posed a continual threat. Somehow, James kept his crew assembling the bridge and repairing the road. The 3rd Pioneers' chaplain Cuttriss could not hide his pride in the men: 'A pioneer battalion is a unit of specialists – mechanics, engineers, drafts-men, carpenters, ironworkers, electricians, analysts and so on. Their work at times is very hazardous and frequently exposes them to a merciless rifle or shell fire. Their disregard for danger, capacity for work, patience in pain, spirit of comradeship and sense of humour afford material for volumes.' That was Hughie.

On 17 July 1917, Lieutenant James was recommended for the Military Cross. The recommendation read, 'On the 7th and 8th June, 1917 at Messines Road he reconnoitred and repaired this road, and constructed a bridge over the river Douve under heavy shell fire. His devotion to duty under the most trying circumstances was a fine example and inspired his men with confidence.' Lieutenant James's Military Cross for 'conspicuous gallantry and devotion to duty' at Messines was gazetted on 24 August 1917.

No victory on the Western Front was without consequence, no matter how good the plan. Monash's 3rd Division recorded 4100 casualties at Messines, and, as the battle ebbed during the next day, there was another soldier who could not be found among the living or the dead: Leslie 'Leggo' Lee. The mystery became more compelling with each day. No one at the Front was sure of his fate, although a few of Lee's colleagues had a good idea that it hadn't ended well.

The Lee family in Richmond had been told Les was missing, but there was no official information, simply because the military authorities didn't know what had happened. In desperation, Lee's aunt put an advertisement in *The Graphic* on 30 November 1917 asking for anyone who knew anything to get in touch with her. The Red Cross undertook its usual inquiries but found verifiable details hard to come by. Francis Ignatius Joseph Coffey imposed himself on the inquiry, with a predictable flourish. 'He was an intimate friend of mine and his disappearance for a long time mystified me,' Coffey told the Red Cross. 'I was continually making inquiries but received no tidings whatever until recently when we received some information, which while not quite convincing, must, I think, be accepted as final and conclusive proof of his decease.'

Coffey's reasoning was sound, if his testimony to the events lacked the ring of authority. Coffey recalled being at Messines and hearing that there were only two survivors of the 10th Machine Gun Company. He believed Lee was wounded and set out to find him 'at the first opportunity'. Coffey found Lee badly wounded but there were no stretcher bearers who could bring the young man back to the 3rd Division line. Eventually, Lee was lifted by another soldier out of the trench where he was found and put on a parapet awaiting a stretcher bearer. That was when Coffey left him: 'Our numbers had been sadly depleted and not a man could be spared from that position. I had been convinced that, since he was carried out, we would eventually hear of him from some dressing station.' What Coffey found out later was that Lee's solid physique had been too much for the stretcher bearers and they had carried him only a small distance before dropping him. Engineers found Lee the next day, moments before he died.

Coffey's description of events is sadly plausible. Lee was indeed a big man – five feet eleven and a quarter inches and twelve stone three – who would have tested stretcher bearers, especially if they were under fire. But the flaw in Coffey's testimony is that he was probably nowhere near the battle. Several days earlier, he was charged with drunkenness, being absent from his billeted area and not being in possession of a gas mask. Coffey was put in confinement for three days, awaiting trial. His saving grace, however, was his unfailing regard for his friend, whom he described as 'brave, affectionate and lovable a comrade as was ever numbered in the ranks of the AIF'. There was something appropriate that Lee's chief witness on his death presented such a complicated testimony. It was an echo of the tangled family that Lee had left behind, an echo that became louder in the weeks that followed the definitive announcement of his passing in February 1918.

It started with the formal death notices that were inserted by George Lee and the woman who was actually Les's mother, Isabella Barnes. After returning to Richmond, she had married Arthur Roberts in 1910, and gone to live in South Yarra. Les's half-sister Laurel Isabel was born the following year. George, whom Les had nominated as his father on his attestation papers, placed a death notice in the local paper, the *Richmond Guardian*. Les was George and Eliza's foster son, the notice read. In another newspaper, Isabella Barnes claimed Les as her own. That was true. And she set out making sure the Defence authorities knew it.

When Isabella wrote to the Military Records Office in search of the Memorial Scroll and acknowledgement from King George of her son's sacrifice, she was told that several months earlier Eliza Lee had come into the office to notify them that she was Les's mother and she had changed her address in Richmond. Isabella was having none of it and fired off a letter, high in indignation:

> My son made Mr George Lee . . . his next of kin, being his father [but he] was not his father. He was his uncle by marriage, being the husband of my sister, Mrs Eliza Lee. She had <u>no right to tell you</u> she was the mother of the late soldier Leslie E. Lee . . . he was boarded out to my sister for 4 [*sic*] years when a little child, then went to live with my sister Mrs A Simcock . . . Some of the time he lived with me but as he had a step father he preferred to go back to my sister Mrs A. Simcock from whose house he left to go into

camp . . . as for making Mr George Lee his next of kin, I can quite see he was influenced in to it. I have made myself quite clear in claiming the right of being the mother of the late Private Leslie E. Lee.

Isabella said she had supported her son until he was able to look after himself. And she allowed him to take the name 'Lee' because of the time he spent with the family. Isabella was told she had to sign a statutory declaration to ensure military records were corrected. On 8 July 1918, she obliged. To commemorate the second anniversary of her son's death, Isabella Roberts placed a notice in *The Argus* and *The Age* under the name of 'Lee':

In loving remembrance of my dear Leslie, Killed at Messines, 8 June, 1917; also his dear comrades of the 10th Machine-gun Company, who fell in action.

Thus why should our tears run down
And our hearts be sorely riven
For another gem in the Saviour's crown
And another soul in heaven.

Inserted by his loving mother. B. [*sic*] Roberts.

It was perhaps testament to Lee's positive impact at the Richmond Football Club that it lent its support to the increasingly fractured family. The Simcocks placed a bereavement notice in the local paper that thanked 'the Richmond Football Club, the committee and members of the Richmond Central Junior Football Club . . . for the consideration and kindness they extended in our time of sorrow, which helps to lessen the great burden we have been [put] upon to bear in the loss of one who was dear to us'. The club made its own sense of loss plain in its 1917 annual report:

> We regret to announce the death at the front of L. Lee, one of our former players, 'Leggo' Lee, as he generally was known, respected and esteemed by all . . . [H]e was a whole-hearted supporter of our club and looked eagerly to the time he would once more don the uniform and do battle for his district, but it was not to be and poor 'Leggo' is now 'sleeping the sleep of all time somewhere in France'.
>
> One of the many who have made the great sacrifice in the supreme cause of the Empire, we will treasure his memory as one of the boys of the Richmond Football Club who did his duty nobly and fearlessly, and we tend [*sic*] our sincere sympathy to his family in its sad bereavement.

The club had seen something of quality in Lee, and as a local it was entirely appropriate that he would contribute to the local team. Even though he left the club to play for Williamstown, Richmond still claimed him. But perhaps the saddest part of Leslie Edward Lee's short life was that his end was so uncertain. One witness to the Red Cross inquiry explained there were only two men missing from 10th Machine Gun unit on 7 June 1917; one was a Private Revel and the other was Leggo Lee. Revel was later tracked to a hospital in France, where he was recovering from wounds. But about two months after Messines, the unit was told on the parade ground that one of the missing machine gunners had been found, carrying the unit's colours. The Pioneers buried him but the body was too decomposed to be recognised, and there was no other identification. It was concluded that it could only have been one person – Leggo Lee.

Messines was the first stage of what would become the gruesome road to Passchendaele, a campaign that would occupy the Allies for months. The only good news was that the United

States of America had finally committed to the war on 6 April 1917, and the boost in manpower, albeit untrained, was a vital part of regenerating the Allied efforts.

After helping the British with a smaller strategic operation on 31 July, Monash's 3rd Division retired from the front line, to join the other Australian divisions resting and regrouping. It was late summer, and by mid–August all the Australians, bar the overworked artillery, were recovering. The next stage of the Allied plan was to resume in September.

9

The Great Brotherhood
of Sport

Harefield Hospital in London was a common enough destination for wounded Australians. Some never made it home but others convalesced before returning to the Front. One of them, though, undertook an unusual activity to help his rehabilitation. Claude McMullen, the man who made the footballs for the Exhibition match, was recovering at Harefield and found time dragged. What did someone so able with a needle and thread do? They learnt needlework. McMullen became so good at his new craft that he issued a challenge to any man in Britain that he would out-stitch him in plain or fancy needlework. It was a brave challenge, but no one took him up on it. McMullen, who was secretary of the 5th Battalion's sport and amusement club, knew a fair bit about competition. He probably also knew that if he was in a needlework contest, it was never going to be a fair fight.

In early 1917, Gerald Brosnan was one of the few voices to publicly defend the interests of footballers and the broader role of the game. Most of the mainstream press routinely mined the war and sport debate for evidence of shirking and happily fell in line behind the government's recruitment push. Brosnan's feelings might have been well known to both sides of the debate, but he was never opposed to the war and defending Australian interests. What he objected to was the constant suggestions that footballers had not done the right thing. Footballers – at home or on active duty – were his people, and he wouldn't abandon them. But his claim that three-quarters of the AIF was made up of sportsmen was impossible to verify.

Brosnan's column in February 1917 was a measured, logical but passionate explanation of the fact that many of the young men he had coached – and some of the older ones he played with – had made their commitment. Brosnan didn't criticise the 'average man' outright. Instead, he blamed their mistaken impressions about footballers on 'certain writers for the Press'. Brosnan was talking about writers such as Reginald Wilmot – 'Old Boy' in *The Argus* – who fulminated against professionalism and, from there, alleged that the money was a reason not to enlist. Brosnan was having none of it, estimating that before the war there would have been tens of thousands of footballers across every level and region of Victorian football clubs. 'And now look at the present position of affairs. Not one country or provincial club able to muster a team, and in the whole of Melbourne not more than 300 players – and the large majority of these married men or ineligibles.' Brosnan continued in the same vein, but he acknowledged that professionalism had 'been the cause of all the trouble'. For all of that reasonableness, Brosnan was still susceptible to the hardy myth that footballers were ideal recruits.

No matter how indiscriminate the carnage and regardless of the vast numbers of talented soldiers from a range of backgrounds, the fiction about footballers' physical prowess as the ideal qualification for soldiering endured. 'Owing to the training necessary to become an expert (and everyone aspires to be an expert) and the physical fitness and endurance required to take part in a game of football, our players should, and from the letters received, do, make the best soldiers,' Brosnan wrote.

'From all sides one hears glowing accounts of their discipline, ability to do long marches and quickness and resources in dangers and difficulties. This is exactly what one would expect but unfortunately these very qualities place them in positions of the greatest danger, and day by day the footballers' death toll grows until by now it assumes alarming proportions.' Perhaps it was the only way football people could explain the enormous pressure the players were put under to enlist. Footballers had to be worth that effort, didn't they? But for all of that, they were as vulnerable as any other soldier. The war was indiscriminate; football talent didn't offer any protection from a bullet or a shell.

Brosnan's lament was shared by Percy Trotter, the man regarded by some shrewd judges as being the finest footballer of his era. Trotter wrote to Brosnan from Perham Downs, one of the camps in Salisbury, awaiting his return to France. 'It was with great regret I heard of Bruce Sloss . . . being knocked out. This grim war is taking very deadly toll among our best athletes.' Trotter saw Sloss up close in the Exhibition match, and, like all good sportsmen, Trotter knew a champion when he saw one. Sloss was a footballer on the cusp of a great career. His death had prompted Trotter's reflection, a wistful sadness about the loss of talent.

Trotter, though, was finding comfort in football and was playing as often as he could. He played several matches in France, on rough, shell-struck ground, but was pleased the game still prompted enthusiasm among the troops. On the second anniversary of the Gallipoli landings – an event Trotter called 'Our Day' – there was a football match at the camp. 'I hope you will not think I am boasting when I say that we showed them a little bit of decent football,' Trotter wrote.

Reunited with some former Fitzroy teammates, including Herb 'Boxer' Milne, Trotter couldn't disguise his pleasure in rediscovering that the cogs of cooperation that oiled the best teams had started to turn and whirr again when the boys were reunited. 'I am going back to France with a good heart, and I will do my best to hold my end up.' Brake too felt the absence of the game, telling Brosnan, 'I could do with a good game of football now Gerald.'

Dan Minogue felt similarly about the loss among the football fraternity. When he sat down to write a letter home in early 1917, it was not far from where 'poor old Bruce Sloss was killed'. Collingwood kept in touch with their former player, sending Minogue a parcel wrapped in one of his own old guernseys, a joke that worked a treat among Minogue's football-loving mates at the Front. Many of the footballers kept up to date with the sport news from home through copies of newspapers. Mail deliveries might have been infrequent but match results, in particular, prompted letters back to the papers, creating a long-distance conversation about players, teams, ladders and premierships. One correspondent was bemused to find a copy of *The Winner* in a German trench. What the Germans made of the 1917 football season or the last race at Flemington was anyone's guess.

The escalation in Brosnan's rhetoric reflected the widespread anxiety that something finally had to be done to spirit sportsmen away from their games and into uniform. Brosnan claimed there were 'roughly 10,000 playing the game every week prior to the war. Now there are scarcely 350. Surely containment could go no further,' he wrote in 1917. But such arguments failed to convince the government, or the game's resolute critics. In reality, there was still no way to get footballers to enlist other than by cajoling, shaming and persuading them. Demand for recruits had never been higher, driven by the appalling losses the Allies incurred throughout the year. This time, though, there was an edge of desperation to the debate, especially after the failure of the conscription referendum the previous October and the divisions it revealed within the community.

A day was set aside to induce sportsmen into uniform: Sportsmen's Recruiting Day, which was held on 27 July 1917.

Prime Minister Hughes had lost patience with sport and the men who played it. He appealed to sportsmen's sense of duty and the conventions of sport itself. 'Sportsmen of Australia, to you is given a great opportunity, upon you rests a heavy responsibility. As you have played the game in the past so we ask you to play the greater game now,' Hughes said. 'This is your day. Its success or failure rests with you. You are wanted today in the trenches far more than you were ever needed in the football or cricket oval . . . I ask you to be true to yourselves, and to prove yourselves worthy members of the great brotherhood of sport.' Hughes was hoping a combination of shame, duty and the fraternal bonds of sport would work. Enlistment posters featuring the former boxer and Victoria Cross recipient Albert Jacka were printed to spruik the Sportsmen's Thousand, with the kicker, 'Show the enemy what Australian sporting men can do.' But that wasn't the only strategy.

The time Carl Willis spent recuperating from being gassed gave him the opportunity to think about what he'd seen at Messines. He pondered the role of luck, the place of the soldier in a war's grand scheme and the conversations he'd had with veterans of the Western Front. He joked that the 'big stunt' was really a matter of 'Fritz knew that it was coming off. We knew that he knew, and we knew that he knew that we knew.' It wasn't original but it summed up Willis's feelings. The people who didn't seem to know what was going on were the soldiers themselves. 'I have not the least idea how many of our senior officers knew the exact day [of the operation] but I can say for certain that none of us in the ranks did . . .' he wrote. The ignorance was compounded by the nature of battle itself:

> I noticed again and again, throughout the day . . . how little the men actually fighting knew of what was happening. All kinds of rumours kept coming through from what was our new line, and thereabouts, and you had to try and

piece things together from several entirely different yarns. Anyway, they only knew what was doing on their one tiny sector.

Willis had identified an issue that even cartoonists found to be a source of grim humour. And he appreciated the joke: 'One drawing I would like to have . . . would be a couple of men in a shell hole, with shells falling like rain around them, and one reading out of a paper the heading: "Germans short of ammunition".'

But surrounded by a constant sense of mortality, the agnostic Willis raised the issue with one of the padres. The padre replied, 'You know my boy, we men of religion are placed in a rather difficult position over here. It isn't much good talking Christianity to men when 6 and 9 inch shells have been falling around thick for an hour or two.' No wonder Willis admitted that the more he saw of war, the more fatalistic he became.

Donald Mackinnon's role as head of recruiting required exploring different ways to bring pressure to bear on men to enlist. The question was just how far would he and the government go? The mood, even among sporting organisations, was hostile towards men who refused to sign up. At a meeting of Victorian sports associations in January 1917, there was a motion put 'that all governing bodies or committees of clubs be required to debar all eligible men from taking part in any matches or competitions'. The proposal was extreme and cared little for spectators who were prepared to pay to see the best players in their chosen sport as a simple afternoon's entertainment. But the overwhelming majority of the sporting associations were amateur bodies that had no interest in generating revenue for the sake of paying players. Mackinnon's representative at the meeting, G.W.S. Dean, promptly told the members that compulsion was not an option, and if Mackinnon considered the idea coercive he wouldn't support it. Mackinnon was entirely consistent in his view, but there was a sense he was swimming against the tide.

It soon emerged that Mackinnon's plan was to return to the idea of two years earlier, to establish a sportsmen's unit (or units). This time, though, Mackinnon decided that he might get better results by co-opting someone else to put pressure on the sportsmen. His strategy was the 'arousing of interest among the womenfolk associated whether directly or indirectly with sport'. He went on, 'Clubs, and especially football clubs, have a great many lady friends and supporters. I am convinced that the women element is going to save the situation in this recruiting campaign.'

Mackinnon understood, perhaps better than others, that football in particular had a strong female following. It always had, dating back to its early days. Female fans became notorious for a time, occasionally spitting or deploying long hat pins against umpires, but, in the main, they were loyal and committed fans. South Melbourne members, for example, numbered 3838 full members on the eve of war, but there were also 623 women and boy members, and that was down 285 on the previous year. But their interest went beyond supporting teams, and there was a small but dedicated group of women who also played football during the war. Some of them played with teams attached to the larger retail outlets. Games were played, admission was charged and all the money went to patriotic funds. As a variation on what was going on with men's football, it was distinguished by an employer using the matches to show they were committed to the war. That, and what spectators saw as the novelty of the contest.

The notion of getting women involved to pressure their husbands, sons and brothers away from sport and into uniform was also being tested in Sydney. In preparation for the national Win the War day on 24 February 1917, representatives of 'Lady Women Swimmers, Ladies Amateur Swimming

Association', golf, rowing, and croquet, among others, were to be given a stand to enable them to spruik for recruiting. In Melbourne, the Sportsmen's Recruiting Committee sent a circular to several women's sporting organisations outlining its intention to draw on 'devotees of sport – both men and women' to help enlistment. In the letter to women's tennis players, it said, 'Taking in to consideration the number of lady tennis players in the State, it is felt that their efforts, if properly organised, would effect [*sic*] very materially the progress of the recruiting campaign.' Rather than be so bold as to pressure the players into asking sportsmen to enlist, the circular advocated calling an urgent club meeting to discuss being part of a local recruitment committee and doing 'all that you can' to make a recruiting meeting held in the local area a success. It seemed a fairly innocuous circular, but Mrs Helen McBride, a seasoned charity worker from Brighton, leapt onto the cause with the passion of a true believer. She circulated a letter among Melbourne's women tennis players that spelt out the problem, as well as the 'solution':

> The sporting community, and, in particular, the tennis community, has not been behindhand in responding to our country's need, but it is felt that more might yet be done. It is generally acknowledged that it is with the women of Australia to send, or to hold back, the men. It is realised too, that the sacrifice of the women who send their men is in many cases greater even than the sacrifice of the men who go. And yet in spite of that we appeal to you to do all in your power to send men. Whether we wish it or not, we share in Australia's glory; we must be ready to share in Australia's sacrifice.

Mrs McBride was just clearing her throat at this stage. Then came the nub of it:

The call for help comes from many quarters, but there is one call which comes with compelling force – the call from the trenches; the call from the men who, through long weary months have borne the burden of the conflict – men who need a spell and can only get that spell if others come to take their places . . . And that call must not go unheeded. Will you therefore use your influence, not only with the men belonging to your club who might enlist, but with all whom you know, that our debt of honour to the men who have gone may be paid, and the end of this terrible war brought nearer.

McBride was Mackinnon's experiment to see whether sporting women were able to push their men into uniform. Without the aid of any other compulsion, it was a clever ploy that was partly based on women's generous – and often spontaneous – work for the Red Cross and the Australian Comforts Fund in supplying provisions for Australian soldiers. So there was no doubt that women would help Mackinnon's plan if they could.

The other powerful clarion call contained in the appeal was to the wives and mothers who were dealing with the anxiety of their husbands and sons being still at the Front, or the grief of them never coming home. They too could be transformed into powerful advocates for recruiting. Mrs McBride's problem was, however, that she was hardly a working-class figure – she lived in a well-to-do part of the city and played a game that was hardly a sport for the masses, unlike football or cricket. It was highly unlikely that a long-winded plea for help from the ladies' tennis fraternity would trigger a rush to enlist among the footballers in Richmond, Carlton, Collingwood or Fitzroy. Nonetheless, Mrs McBride's vigour and pragmatism enabled her to say what few men would dare to. The hastily erected image of the epitome of manhood cast in the shape of the Anzac soldier suddenly looked a little rickety.

The female push arrived with more vigour north of the Murray. At a special meeting of the New South Wales branch of the Sportsmen's Recruiting Committee, 113 largely middle-class women from amateur sports committed their services to effectively 'enlist one man by appealing through my Woman-hood to his Manhood'. Women were given a badge to pass on to a man who was willing to accept it and enlist. Once he had enlisted, the woman received another badge. None of this was supposed to get in the way of any other work a woman needed to do. 'This duty will not interfere with the ordinary daily duties of any lady, nor will it cost anything,' one newspaper reassured its readers. 'A handsome diploma is also issued to each lady and this can be hung in the homes as an indication of their interest in reinforcing their brothers over the other side.' What the newspaper neglected to mention was that the badge contained a message, written in French, that translated as 'He who excuses himself, accuses himself'. And in a more extreme move, the National Council of Women resolved that all women and girls should refuse to play tennis, golf or any kind of sport with eligible men. One women's magazine put the position clearly: 'It seems incongruous and callous to see virile athletic men who would seem to be dissipating so much energy in games where [there] is so much work calling them.'

The plan in Victoria was a little less strident. The president of the Victorian Croquet Association, Mr N.B. Were, wrote to the Sportsmen's Recruiting Committee that his membership was predominantly female. Mackinnon jumped on the opportunity, telling his colleagues:

Taking in to account the great influence that could be wielded by an association of a thousand sportswomen, ... [I] invited their co-operation in the Sportsmen's Recruiting Campaign. I am pleased to state that although the majority of the ladies have been already engaged in patriotic work they are taking effective steps to organise the association for most efficient recruiting services.

But attempts to follow through on it failed. There was also talk of establishing a women's sub-committee of the Sporting Recruitment Committee, but that too never got off the ground. It was becoming increasingly clear that meetings and recruitment drives were not working on sportsmen. A recruiting rally held in West Melbourne in March, featuring boxing and vaudeville, drew more than 3000 people but only 20 new recruits. After three meetings at Melbourne Town Hall in October 1917, there were only five new recruits. St Kilda Town Hall fared a little better, managing 26 enlistments in a fortnight across the same month. It was hard work. Sportsmen at home thought they had done enough. Not even plans for a Sportsmen's 1000 football club were enough to generate sufficient numbers. Every scheme that was tried had little effect. Many were discouraged from enlisting by the news from the Front, while others remained exempt.

As a former Fitzroy captain and premiership player, Jack Cooper took particular delight in sharing the news of the club's 1916 premiership. The fact that the club cabled the result of the grand final to the Front only made it more special. Cooper played for his state at the 1914 carnival, captained Victoria and played all his 135 senior games with his local team, Fitzroy. He was 26, a storeman, when he enlisted and still capable of another couple of seasons in his chosen role in defence. Cooper had a reputation for being tough – he played on during one game in 1914 with a broken rib after a heavy collision and seemed to show no ill-effects. In his younger days, he had been suspended for 12 weeks for charging and striking. But as he matured, he revealed a capacity to thrive in important games. A grand final was Cooper's stage. He was also deeply committed to the club. He helped organise social events and weekends away for the players. At the unfurling of the 1913 premiership flag, Cooper's infant daughter presented the president's wife with a bunch of flowers. Like Sloss, Cooper found that army life suited him, and he was soon identified for higher duties and sent to the Officer's School at Aldershot in England.

He was at the Front twice and sent back to England to recover each time. The first time, Cooper was gassed after only a brief spell in the trenches. He was well enough to join the guard of honour at the royal presentation of a silk flag and silver shield to the Australian command at Wellington Barracks in London in July 1916. Cooper thought it was a grand spectacle and happily went off to Salisbury, from where he was selected in the Exhibition match in London after being attached to the 2nd Training Battalion. 'I am in the best of health and spirits, and that the change of life and the work agrees with me is borne out by the increase in my weight from 11st, to 13st. 2lb. – fairly substantial,' he wrote home. He was put in charge of German POWs near Salisbury. 'I have to watch and control 26 German prisoners, and from the appearance of several of them the job is not going to be any sinecure. However, I intend to take no chances.' Cooper anticipated that the rising list of casualties meant he would be soon rejoining his unit at the Front. Cooper was right. He was indeed recalled, but his throat had been so affected by the gas that he was sent back to England a second time, in autumn, to recover his lost voice. He left England in June and rejoined the 8th Battalion in Belgium. In August, he was made lance corporal, just in time for the Battle of Menin Road.

The official title for what occurred in the autumn of 1917 was the Third Battle of Ypres, but thousands knew it by the name 'Passchendaele'. Ypres was a medieval town, in the middle of a bowl, although after continuous shelling that almost levelled the place it was hard to believe it was ever that shape. The Allied plan had grand goals that would break the Hindenburg Line, capture Passchendaele Ridge, and ultimately give it access to the Belgian ports where the Germans had stationed their U-boats.

The British troops embarked on the first phase on 31 July, on a 2.5-mile front between Ypres and the Passchendaele Ridge. But stout German resistance made progress slow. Three years of constant shelling had destroyed the field drainage and, combined with heavy rain, turned the lowlands into a bog. Heavy artillery took an age to manoeuvre in the mud. Shells fell harmlessly, neutralised by the swamp. Progress was slowed by the constant delays in trying to move the bulky artillery from one muddied spot to the next.

After several fruitless weeks, Allied command under General Haig decided to recast the offensive. The new plan involved a total commitment of 11 British, New Zealand and Australian divisions (all Australian divisions were to take part) to attack the Germans across an eight-mile front. An unprecedented artillery attack would start almost three weeks before the main attack, to disable and destroy the German strong points: pillboxes, concrete machine-gun nests and fortified farmhouses. This was a massive strategic challenge. As Willis so correctly identified, the infantry soldiers, such as Jack Cooper, knew little of the bigger picture. What they came to know was that 'Passchendaele' translated into Valley of the Passion. There was indeed something Biblical about what happened there.

Cooper's 8th Battalion was part of the two Australian divisions enjoying some rest and recreation near Amiens. There was sport, of course, and plenty of time to recuperate. They left there for Passchendaele in what became the first time two Australian divisions fought side by side. Although the British artillery outnumbered their German counterparts by a ratio of four to one, the pre-battle barrage failed to eliminate the German artillery threat. Low cloud hampered accurate aerial sighting of the German artillery positions, and some incompetent gun placements among some of the Allied artillery meant that intended German targets were not located until two days before the infantry attack. Rain started to fall when the soldiers began to move into line for the 20 September offensive, filling the shell holes and adding yet another layer of sludge to the shifting mud under their feet. But this time, their goal was to gain the ground that the artillery could safely cover – not 4375 yards but the more manageable 1640 yards. The infantry was the second wave at Menin Road.

Cooper's 8th Battalion moved off at 7 pm on the evening of 19 September and reached its assembly point 90 minutes later without incident. Then the rain came and slowed progress. Cooper found himself stuck behind the 7th Battalion for two hours. They were now hopelessly behind schedule. But there was no panic, even after the German artillery pounded the soldiers from the 7th Battalion. The objective of securing the lines of German trenches remained in place. The battalions kept moving, meeting little resistance and instead finding Germans surrendering. The Diggers secured the position and awaited the inevitable German counterattack.

German aircraft tried to bomb them but failed to make an impression. There was shelling at 2 pm that claimed the regimental sergeant major, but there was no concerted German response to impede the battalion's progress. For some, such as Private George Radnell, it was a bit of a lark. 'Hop out and lads done well,' he wrote in his diary. 'Collected some fine souvenirs there . . . gas in one pillbox. Two wounded Fritzs in one and helped them to the dressing station.'

But Jack Cooper didn't make it. When it happened is not clear, but, some time after the dawn, Cooper became one of 40 8th Battalion fatalities at Menin Road. It was not in a sense-less charge or a folly tucked away in the corner of some general's grand plan; it was a death, like so many others in the war, recorded as a cost to be paid for the greater goal. Or so the great theory of sacrifice went. *The Football Record*, in its 1917 grand final edition previewing the game between Fitzroy and Collingwood, couldn't help but make the connection between the war, football and its own distinctive blue printed product: 'It is gratifying to the proprietor to know that there are club members who, unable to get away to the war, are keeping the gallant boys in the trenches supplied with copies of *The Record* . . . Jack Cooper, the former captain of Fitzroy, has written out expressing the pleasure he feels when the Little Blue Book comes along. "It makes us feel that we are back home again," he wrote the other day. "May they all be back before next season opens fit and ready to take up the game, and play it as nobly as they have played the game against the common enemy of the world on the bloodstained battlefields of France."' Unbeknown to all those who bought *The Record*, Cooper had already perished. Fitzroy lost the grand final and, soon after, had to mourn its former captain.

'Mr Cooper was a native of Fitzroy – a resident of this city all his life – and for eleven years a prominent player of your club, in 1912 holding the position of captain,' the club said in its 1917 annual report. 'His fame as a footballer was known, throughout Australia, he having represented Victoria both in interstate and carnival matches. On two occasions, he was captain and vice-captain of Victorian teams. Jack Cooper was a most ardent worker in your interests, both as a player and committeeman, and by his genial manner endeared himself to all with whom he came in contact. Not only has your club sustained a loss, but our winter pastime also has lost one of its most able exponents.'

The Allies had to follow up the success of Menin Road. Nine days after the initial assault, in the stunted, shell-sheared forest known as Polygon Wood, the Diggers regrouped for another brutal instalment. The two Scullin boys from the Western Australian goldfields – Dan and Patrick – were there. Daniel was the stand-out footballer of the family, the young man who had played for Western Australia in the 1914 carnival in Sydney.

Goldfields football had been struck hard by the war. Mines Rovers, one of the strongest teams in the competition and Scullin's team, gave up 15 players to the war after the 1915 season, and Railways had lost 22, plus its club secretary. Boulder had only five men left who were able and fit enough to play. By the time the 1916 season rolled around, the League administrators were wondering what to do. 'Personally, I think it would be a very great pity if the league were allowed to lapse,' the president said at a League meeting. 'We could do a considerable amount of good by playing and devoting the proceeds to the war Fund, patriotic Fund, and any other funds we might decide on. We have it on the very highest authority that it's not desirable to go in to sackcloth and ashes over the war.'

What the 'highest authority' might have been was never disclosed, but the president's words were a vibrant echo of the VFL's determination to continue. Discussions reached the ludicrous position of the Goldfields League deciding on a starting date for the 1916 season without agreeing on how many teams would be playing – four, as in previous seasons, or three, allowing for two war-affected teams to amalgamate. The season finally got under way with three clubs but the organisation of the games was so haphazard that the ball was forgotten for the first match. It was no wonder that the competition ceased by June and was not revived in any form until 1918, when it stuttered into life to host fundraising games for the war effort. The League's decision to end the competition underlined how much of an impact recruitment had on regions that were dependent on young, fit men to drive the main industries.

From the turn of the century to the outbreak of war, Kalgoorlie was one of Australia's most prosperous towns. Gold drove it all, from the migrants who travelled from southern Europe to the prostitutes who set up shop in the main street. In 1907, five mining companies in the Kalgoorlie goldfields paid out more than £200,000 in dividends, a result that outstripped the nation's banks. Sport was important, especially if it involved a wager. Kalgoorlie and Boulder each had its own racecourse, with grandstands, lawns and a society of racegoers. Kalgoorlie even had its own Cup. Professional foot-running and billiards – often featuring Fred Lindrum Jnr, older brother of Walter (Walter Lindrum was born in Kalgoorlie) – were regular pastimes too. The area was a huge, noisy, churning, apparently endless source of money and precious minerals. But some companies had started to look elsewhere, such as South America, to diversify their interests and to protect themselves from doubts about the quality of the ore in Kalgoorlie and Boulder.

The war's arrival peeled away what remained of the gloss, and then much of the profits. Many of the European mine workers were moved on after war broke out, and hostilities arose against German speakers and their allies. The absence of 600 mainly skilled workers caused a 10 per cent decline in mine output by 1916. However, the larger, global problem was the price of gold, which had been fixed. By the time the Scullin boys left Boulder, it was not the place it had been in its heyday.

The parlous state of football in the Goldfields was worthy of comment in the local paper in April 1917. 'The truth is, with the number of its old devotees now away taking their part in the sterner game in France, there is no chance of reviving the sport till they come back,' *The Kalgoorlie Miner* said. 'Football, at the present time, with the approach of the third season since the war commenced, has been for the time being relegated to the hands of the younger generation.' The paper went on to name the League footballers who had gone to the Front. Several were already dead, a few were still missing. From Scullin's team, there was only one fatality and one missing Digger, but such outcomes were about luck, pure and simple.

Football united the Scullin family. Patrick was handy but didn't have his older brother Dan's class. The boys' other brother,

John – who was known as Jack – had also played. The boys didn't look similar. Jack had fair hair and dark-blue eyes, and a solid physique. Patrick was about the same size but had dark hair and brown eyes. Dan was the biggest of the three boys, over five feet 11 inches and a shade above 11 stone. All three of them were born in Balmain in Sydney, but the family moved to Boulder for the work. The Scullin parents, Daniel Snr and Kate, hated the idea of the boys going. The family had come so far, had settled so well and carved out a life in the goldfields. It was an immigrant dream made real. One day, Daniel and Kate caught one of the boys by surprise on the train platform. He was in uniform and ready to go. Both parents pleaded with their boy to stay but when the train came, he got on board.

The first batch of bad news came about Jack. He was initially described as 'missing' in the murderous action that was Pozières, but was later found dead. The date of his death was given as 29 July 1916. Dan had played the Exhibition match in London with that grief a fresh burden on his spindle shoulders. Patrick was recovering from a wound sustained in April – a gunshot to his back and shoulder. He left England for France on 22 October 1916, just six days before the game. The two remaining Scullin boys were reunited in France and found themselves close to each other as the Diggers marched on to Polygon Wood.

The 4th and 5th Australian Divisions replaced the 1st and 2nd divisions at Polygon Wood for what was over a 1600-yard advance. The Australians were well versed by now in pacing themselves behind the wall of artillery fire, to ensure they were protected by it, even if there was a constant cloud of shell bursts. Once again, the artillery barrage that preceded the attack was formidable. And once again, it paved the way for the greater military success.

The Scullin boys' 51st Battalion was a latecomer to a battle that had been going for almost two months. Despite Messines, the larger goals were still to be met. The Hindenburg Line held.

The preparations were thorough. Dan and Patrick Scullin were each given 220 rounds of ammunition, two sandbags, two bombs, two full water bottles, two days' rations and one emergency ration. There was a choice between a pick or a shovel and every man was given a waterproof sheet. At 3 pm on 25 September 1917, the battalion made its final preparations. A meal was served at 4.30 pm. Then they were off, across roads lined with broken artillery, dead horses and abandoned wagons.

By the time the evening drew in, the 51st found its cover, in a range of shell holes that were a sanctuary for only a few hours, before the final whistle. Ahead of them, in the front line of trenches, the other Western Australian division, the 52nd, covered their advance. At 1.30 am, the 51st started towards Polygon Wood, crossing over the Diggers in the trenches by a plank bridge. Pockets of light erupted in the night with each German shell. Then came the whizz-bangs, the smaller explosive bombs, which cut through the men as they assembled in anticipation of the sign to go. It was a long and bloody wait. Few of them had the comfort of sleep. All of them were stung with anxiety. At 5.50 am, the Australian gunners let loose a brutal cacophony and then, at the command 'Fix bayonets', the Diggers leapt forward into the smoke. Out of the haze emerged startled Germans, their arms thrust up, surrendering to their fate of prisoners of war. The Diggers reached the German front line without meeting any great resistance. And then they kept going.

By 8 am, the 51st had taken 12 prisoners and a machine gun. Support lines were set up, barbed wire rolled out and trenches connected. It was the Diggers' turn to install their own Lewis guns. The Germans mounted counterattacks but were repulsed. On the night of 30 September 1917, the 51st Battalion was relieved and moved back behind the lines, but Dan and Patrick Scullin were not with them.

It's unclear exactly when the cruel moment of fate for the Scullin boys arrived. Patrick had been shelled and Dan raced to help, crossing the pitted ground that was racked by machine guns and more shells. Dan reached his brother but, at that awful moment, Dan too was struck, dying instantly. Both boys had perished in the same place, perhaps only moments apart. The situation suddenly became complicated – Patrick was identifiable but no one was sure about Dan.

The parish priest, Father Donagher, made his way to the Scullin family home in Pirie Street, Boulder, to pass on the news about Patrick. That was bad enough but perhaps there was hope that Dan had made it, by some grand piece of fortune. Dan had written home earlier in the year, exulting in his luck when his helmet saved him. He still had a head wound, but it could have been a lot worse, he reassured his parents. This time, the Red Cross made its inquiries. It seemed to take forever. The Scullins waited and prayed. The report was brief by the Red Cross's exhaustive standards. Daniel Scullin had died trying to look out for his brother. There was no doubt. Back went Father Donagher to the Scullins, eight months after Dan had died, to extinguish all hope. The boys' sister, Meg, recalled years later the moment when she saw the priest walking down the path to their front door. It was something she could never forget. What can be said to the parents of three fallen sons? Nothing, nothing at all.

Two officers and 28 other men of the 51st Battalion died at Polygon Wood. In the overall scheme of losses on the Western Front, it was a small number. But such statistics are meaningless to those who are left to mourn. The Scullins went on remembering their boys; on the anniversary of Patrick and Dan's death, a notice from the family was placed in the local paper. 'In sad and loving memory of our dear sons Private Dan and Patrick Scullin, who were killed in action 26th September, 1917, somewhere in France. So sadly missed.' They had died together, and they would be remembered together.

10

'The Boys Are Dead Against It'

September was football finals month – a frivolous notion when men were dying half a world away. But there was still a keen interest among the Diggers in what was happening to the home teams. One of Collingwood's stalwarts from the 1915 losing grand final, Malcolm 'Doc' Seddon, sent a souvenir back to the club from France, to help inspire them. It was a horseshoe made from part of a German shell. Seddon had inscribed it with 'Good luck' and 'to CFC. From Doc. France 1917'. He also sent a letter: 'I hope this shoe will bring the boys to the top of the tree this year.'

Seddon's gesture turned out to be a more potent omen than Minogue's keepsake that he had sent to Victoria Park the previous year. Minogue had found a metal piece from a German zeppelin shot down over London and sent it to Collingwood. But Seddon's horseshoe was perhaps just the inspiration Collingwood needed against Fitzroy in the final. It was a hard and physical contest, but the Magpies won by 35 points, to record their fourth flag.

In Australia, the Hughes government's determination to restrict sport did not come into full effect until after the September finals series, ensuring that there was still sufficient patronage to drive revenue to patriotic funds. In its way, it

243

was also an acknowledgement that recruiting footballers and their supporters was a job for the off-season. It seemed too big a challenge when the competition was on. Implicit in the timing was the government's understanding of how important football was, especially in 1917. The huge loss of Diggers in France and Belgium, the influx of returned soldiers with chronic ailments, injuries and mental scars, plus the sense that the war was no closer to an end combined to create a prevailing sense of gloom across the nation. Football was a more powerful diversion than ever.

Nonetheless, when George Foster Pearce announced the sporting restrictions on 12 September 1917, he made it clear that there were only three sports under consideration: football, horseracing and boxing. Of those, horseracing was restricted in each state, although the number of New South Wales metropolitan meetings was only scaled back from 134 to 97, and from 80 to 78 in Victoria. The number stayed the same in South Australia and was actually increased by two meetings in Western Australia. (Queensland was the worst affected, going from 136 metropolitan meetings to 64.) Pearce's dubious explanation was that 'in the interests of horse breeding' it was advisable to keep the industry going.

There was far less compunction about boxing, which was restricted to one 20-round contest in each state every fortnight. Amateur bouts would not be restricted. And those promoters who tried to get around the restrictions by mixing vaudeville with fisticuffs were warned that any mixed bill had to have at least half the program taken up by vaudeville or pictures. Any bout was to be no more than ten rounds of two minutes, and admission prices were capped.

And football? 'It was not considered necessary to take any action at present regarding football,' the report stated.

It was, by any measure, a half-hearted attempt to convey an idea that sport was still a nefarious influence on recruiting.

Instead, it looked like it was aiming for just two sports that had other social issues, such as gambling and drinking, associated with them. There was some evidence for the suspicion. In 1915 and 1916, all states, except Western Australia and Queensland, had introduced early closing for hotels. Sobriety was somehow one of the pillars of national rectitude, alongside morality, patriotism and doing one's duty for one's country. Not for the first time did some of the working class think that the government was actually trying to restrict all kinds of entertainment, not just sport.

The overall impact, on a nation trying to cope with the divisions of the first conscription referendum, was toxic. It was left to a few senior statesmen, such as the former New South Wales premier Sir Joseph Carruthers, to point out the dangers of restricting sport to his political colleagues in Melbourne: '[W]e have the liquor trade against us; we have also the Irish Catholics with few exceptions; we have the trade unions, very largely; and we are making bitter enemies of the Sporting Fraternity except for a favoured few. This latter class is more numerous than you imagine. Moreover it includes tens of thousands who are just as loyal as you or I.'

Carruthers believed that the resentment these actions caused actually slowed recruiting, rather than boosted it. And recruiting was, again, the dilemma Hughes was facing. The time had come to revisit his election statement – that he would only raise conscription again if the nation's safety was at risk. Hughes believed that time had arrived.

Monash's 3rd Division's next appointment with the Germans was Broodseinde, in October 1917, in what turned out to be the third instalment of the Passchendaele saga. It began again with an Allied artillery barrage, although the Germans gained an early ascendancy when they anticipated the Australian attack. The Diggers were stuck in the rain and exposed to a sustained trench mortar attack. There were 6500 Australian casualties but, despite the losses, the Germans fared worse, referring to it as a 'Black Day'.

The follow-up attack eight days later, designed by Allied command to take advantage of the successes, proved more problematic. The rain had once again turned the ground to sludge, which anchored the Australians and New Zealanders as they tried to capture the Passchendaele village. The stasis was symbolic of the state of the war. No one was moving. Each grim day seemed anchored in mud and mire. It was the final evidence to compel the Allied generals to delay further action until the weather improved. The Australians were slowly withdrawn and the Canadians stepped into the breach. On 15 November, all the Australians were back in the relative calm of the Messines front for the winter. For Monash, the respite was the ideal time to get the troops thinking of other things.

He decided to implement 'a comprehensive football Tournament throughout the Division'. The idea was a big one – to play Australian Rules and rugby matches with soldiers representing state-based teams. Each state had to field a team in both football codes. Once again, the YMCA would be integral to the competition; it would present two cups, one for each tournament. A meeting was held to refine the idea and devise a selection plan. This was a highly bureaucratic exercise built on the success of the Exhibition match. A series of three-man sub-committees was set up across the division to investigate potential players for football and rugby. The sub-committee would provide a player's name, his home state and his previous football performance. Not surprisingly, Hughie James was appointed to the Australian Rules sub-committee.

But the tournament didn't take place. There is no evidence as to why it didn't go ahead, but perhaps the most compelling reason was the cost 1917 had on Australian troops. There were 55,000 casualties that year, including 38,000 at Passchendaele. Put another way, 35 Australians died for every metre of ground gained. It wasn't just the physical cost but the dreadful impact on morale. Six of those men who just a year earlier had played in the Exhibition match in London were gone: Sloss, Pugh, Foy, Martin, Cooper and Scullin. The men who were left hoped for peace but prepared for the worst.

Christina Sloss made one rule after Bruce died: the family had to talk about him. No one was going to ignore who Bruce was and what he had done just because he had not come home. There might have been an enormous gap in the family but silence would not honour Bruce's memory. Christina had been comforted by the condolence letters and messages. Several weeks after Bruce was killed, a black-framed envelope arrived at the Sloss family home in Armadale. It was the formal letter from Governor-General Munro Ferguson on behalf of the King, expressing his sympathy and regret at Bruce's passing, 'a gallant officer, who fell fighting for his Country and Empire'.

More personal letters arrived too, from Bruce's next-in-command Captain Harold Ordish, who was able to tell Christina that Bruce was buried in the Military Cemetery the day after he was killed. Roy and four officers not on duty were there for the burial. Jock was still in England but took two weeks' leave immediately after he heard the news. 'We would none of us wish for a better death, if it has to be, than "Killed in Action" when it comes as sudden as your dear boy's loss,' Ordish wrote. He reminded Christina of the conversation they had at Port Melbourne when she farewelled Bruce and how pleased Ordish had been to have Bruce alongside him. Since then, Bruce's reputation had spread throughout the army: 'He was known more widely through the AIForces [sic] than any other officer or man, and to know him at all was to respect and admire him as a man and a soldier, and to love him as a comrade.' It was vivid testament to Bruce's decency and a personality that triumphed over circumstance. No mother could have asked for more from a son.

Bruce was sending money back to Christina, but after he died it only lasted a further two months. She applied for a war widow's pension and eventually managed to scrape enough money together to buy the house Bruce and Glad were planning to call their own. In time, Christina and the rest of the family moved in.

Gladys, however, struggled with the grief. Her fiancé's absence was a powerful force in her life that worked away at her. On 15 January 1917, a notice appeared in *The Argus*. It read:

> In loving memory of my dear friend, Lieut. Bruce M.F. Sloss, who was killed in action somewhere in France on 4th January, 1917.
>
> Sweet is the memory left behind
> Of one most noble, true, and kind.
> His fight is fought, he stood the test,
> All his life he was one of the best.
>
> Inserted by his loving friend, Gladys R. Hamilton.

'A loving friend', after eight years together and engagement? Perhaps Gladys was trying to distance herself from the memory of the man she had promised to marry.

In the midst of her grief, she was swept up in Tullie's restless energy and determination to never let sadness settle like a shroud. Tullie enlisted Gladys as a travelling companion, but Gladys was never quite the resolute traveller. On a shipboard cruise that went from Melbourne to Fiji and then to Hawaii, Gladys struggled with seasickness, while Tullie, seasoned and without any time for such inconveniences, remained intent on experiencing everything on offer.

There were several such trips before Gladys married Alfred Lester, a widower from Malvern. Lester's first wife – also called Gladys – died in 1912, leaving him with a son and daughter. Gladys married Alfred in 1928 in a ceremony conducted by the Slosses' long-time Presbyterian minister, Reverend Donald Macrae Stewart. Eleven years had passed since Bruce died. Gladys was 37; a family of her own was possible but unlikely, and, in the end, it didn't happen. But Bruce's memory was never extinguished. Gladys kept their engagement ring and, years later, when her stepson became engaged, she had the ring cut in half. She gave one half to her daughter-in-law; the other half was a keepsake that Gladys never surrendered.

But Christina's worry was not over. Australians were still fighting against the Ottoman Army in the Middle East, and trapped somewhere in the heat of the desert was James McKenzie Sloss. It was September 1916 before the family knew that James was a Turkish POW, 18 months after he'd left Australia. But no one doubted that it was remarkable James was still alive. After the Siege of Kut, the 11,900 prisoners from Britain, Australia and India were subjected to a 1200-mile trek through Mesopotamia and the Syrian Desert, back to Turkey. Many were already sick before they began the march. Others soon joined them. Death was commonplace. James Sloss recounted losing 18 men in just one's day march. Dysentery and diarrhoea claimed many. Some fell and were whipped by their captors following behind on camel trains to get them back to their feet. Others never got up. Food was rudimentary and water elusive. But James kept marching.

'Hours before we stopped, I thought I could go no farther but I tied my wrist to a cart and was pulled for about thirty yards,' James wrote later. 'No longer did any sense of feeling exist; my entire energies were concentrated on keeping my feet moving. I got through the remaining five stages by donkey and horse riding . . .'

They stopped at a village in what is now Syria, and Sloss was given supervised work in an engineering business. But after hearing Australian warships were active nearby, he hatched a plan with several prisoners to head for the coast to try to make contact with them. Sloss and some other prisoners went on the run and managed to make it to the coast nine days later, only to find the Australian ships were some kind of cruel mirage. Exhausted and dispirited, Sloss surrendered and was promptly imprisoned in a Turkish military jail. In January 1917, when Bruce was on the Western Front, James was perilously ill with typhus in a Turkish hospital.

Tullie was doing munitions work in England, and experiencing the war up close, with its food shortages and frequent air raids. Her extraordinary luck held. One raid blew off part of the roof above her bedroom and deposited a huge piece of shell on her pillow. She saw Roy and Jock, who came to visit her in London. Roy adapted so well to the constant danger and incessant bombing at the Front that when he was told to take shelter during a London air raid, he sat on his kit on a train station platform and went to sleep. While Tullie was bemused by her brother's antics, she couldn't escape the random moments of grief that brought her undone. 'Roy and Jock go back to France: I, to London, feeling more dead than alive. In . . . tea room today the little waitress who waited on me was so like Gladys that it upset me for days afterwards.'

In September 1917, Hughes's director-general of recruiting, Donald Mackinnon, publicly 'prohibited' his state-based counterparts urging the introduction of conscription. He had been vocal about conscription for some time, telling his local paper that he wished talk about conscription would stop because it was childish and inimical to recruiting. But Mackinnon's statement so angered some state recruiting committees that they resigned in protest.

The Charters Towers committee in Queensland was forthright and 'emphatically declined to allow themselves to be gagged, and the onus of adopting the necessary means of procuring reinforcements to save the slaughter of our men at the Front must be borne by the Prime Minister and Mr. Mackinnon'. Mackinnon was in an awkward position, caught between a personal reluctance towards conscription and a prime minister who saw no other way.

Hughes had his own dilemma, which was more political. It was becoming clear that the rickety coalition of interests he assembled in the name of winning the war was only good enough to win him an election. There were sizeable rents in the thin fabric that bound his Cabinet together. In August, New South Wales was riven with a massive general strike that started with railway workers and soon spread across the state. It was the nation's worst strike. Strike-breakers and police pushed through picket lines, while food riots erupted. The movement spread to other states. Businesses that took a tough line on rehiring strikers in Melbourne had their office and shopfront windows broken. The bitterness and discord was palpable. Hughes was isolated, suspicious of his colleagues, and increasingly anxious about losing power.

And the man who helped coalesce the Irish-Catholic, largely working-class opposition in Australia to conscription, Archbishop Daniel Mannix, was becoming more vocal, revealing a sharp political tongue and a shrewd sense of timing in deploying it. Hughes admitted after the first referendum, 'I am now worn with the storm and stress of a conflict – the most severe the most bitter Australia has ever known.' In the face of all of that, Hughes decided once again to hold a referendum. And once again, the role of sportsmen would be central to the debate.

Sectarianism became a festering point of division during the second referendum, and, once it was called for what it was, it wouldn't go away. In the aftermath of the vote, a Protestant and a Catholic in Armidale, northern New South Wales, came to blows after the Protestant blamed the outcome on 'the three Cs; cowards, the c[—] and the Catholics'.

Mannix was not archbishop during the first conscription campaign, but there was no doubting his abhorrence at the violent response of the British to quell the Easter Uprising in his Irish homeland. When the second referendum campaign was in full swing, Mannix had the platform of his office to campaign against conscription. The 'yes' voters demonised Mannix and dropped the conscription outcome at his feet. It was easy to sketch a cartoon contrast between Mannix, tall and lean in clerical garb, with a studied air and enigmatic smile, and Hughes, the small, tight coil of a man with manic energy. Hughes threw barbs and Mannix deflected with a passive but penetrating logic. Hughes called Mannix 'a man to whom every German in the country looks'. Mannix responded, 'If you surrender your freedom by accepting conscription, what assurance have you that the rights you give away will be used to the best advantage of Australia?' The overall effect of these tempestuous exchanges was to increase Hughes's anxiety. He wrote to his confidant in England, journalist Keith Murdoch, that he was 'like a swimmer in a vast ocean without the friendly shelter of even a dilapidated hen coop'.

The referendum date was set for 20 December 1917. The question, slyly worded, was, 'Are you in favour of the proposal of the Commonwealth Government for reinforcing the Australian Imperial Force overseas?' The word 'conscription' was noticeably absent. But the intent was plain, even if the proposed scheme, on the face of it, was full of exemptions and qualifications. Conscription would only be activated when there was a shortfall of the monthly target of 7000 volunteers. The men conscripted would be single, without dependants, and aged between 20 and 44. And they would be selected by a ballot. But the foundations of the argument – and the visceral hostilities that went with it – had taken on a more public form since the 1916 referendum. Most Australians knew where they stood on the issue. Another 12 months of war, and all the grief that accompanied it, had only made the feelings rawer, even deeper. The 1917 campaign ushered in a lacerating national debate that entrenched many of the political and sectarian divisions for years to come.

Herbert 'Boxer' Milne, a Fitzroy and South Melbourne footballer who was in France with an ambulance brigade, had the same position on both referenda. In early 1917, he wrote home, 'Was very pleased to see that conscription was knocked out. There are enough over here now.' A day after the 1917 vote, he was equally direct: 'The boys are dead against it. If they left it to the men who are doing their bit, there would be no talk of conscription.' Boxer was known to have a touch of the satirist about him. The letter didn't disappoint. 'Of the 27 men in the hut where I am, only one voted "yes". We know the reason. He had been knocked on the head by a piece of a shell and is therefore not responsible for his actions.'

Milne's sentiments were probably in line with most of those on the front, just as in 1916. Wally Laidlaw, who urged men to sign up from his Malta hospital bed in 1915, had changed his mind after 18 months on the Western Front. No one should have to do what he had done, he said. But AIF support staff and troops in the English training camps again swung the vote narrowly in favour – the soldiers voted 'yes' by 91,642 to 89,859.

But the referendum vote was lost, worse than the 1916 result, because in 1917 Victoria changed its mind and voted 'no', along with New South Wales, Queensland and South Australia. Hughes had promised that he could not govern without conscription, so, after the vote, he tendered his resignation to Governor-General Munro Ferguson. The governor-general looked at the composition of parliament for a replacement. Neither Labor's anti-conscriptionist Frank Tudor, the Richmond Football Club's former president, nor Sir John Forrest could command sufficient votes to present themselves as alternatives. So Munro Ferguson rehired Hughes for the top job.

The governor-general had come some distance since he raced from Sydney to Melbourne for the declaration of war in 1914. He had worked with previous prime ministers Joseph Cook and Andrew Fisher but found in Hughes some traits that resonated with his own world view. Hughes was 'always dauntless, cheery and patriotic to the core, while his dash and genius lend charm to a wild career'. Munro Ferguson's main problem was Hughes's capacity to occasionally not tell him anything. 'He has all the arts of a crab. When he does not wish to be drawn, he withdraws within the impenetrable shell of his designs, or literally disappears in to space . . .' But on the issue of conscription, the Scot and the Welshman were in fierce agreement, and they were in no doubt about what each other thought on the matter.

The limitless energy that distinguished Frank Beaurepaire on the Western Front was now obvious in Australia as he embarked on a series of lectures around the country, spruiking the value of the YMCA to the war effort. In April, it was announced there would be a fundraising drive to collect £22,500 to ensure the YMCA could continue its work at the Front, and Beaurepaire became one of the ambassadors for the June fundraising event. He also made a tentative return to the pool, after almost four years without dedicated training. Beaurepaire entered the 440 yards handicap at the Abbotsford Baths in a competition organised by the Victorian Amateur Swimming Association but finished about 43 yards behind the winner.

But the truth was that Beaurepaire was desperate to return to the war. The disappointment of missing out the first time because of appendicitis had been too challenging; Beaurepaire had a thirst for action, not for organising sports meetings and theatre troupes. He had already approached Monash the previous year, but the general told Beaurepaire that his work with the YMCA was too valuable to be spared. So he tried to enlist again.

This time, Beaurepaire's enlistment application included a letter from a doctor who had treated him for rheumatic fever when he was a boy. The doctor identified some potential heart issues, particularly a condition known as 'cardiac hypertrophy', where the actual heart muscle thickened. Beaurepaire was only 26 and working his way back to some level of fitness. But the doctor's recommendation was clear – Beaurepaire was not suitable to enlist. Rejected twice, Beaurepaire went back to the water, but his war was over.

On the other side of the world, and far closer to the front, Hewitt and his Coo-ees, without Beaurepaire's guidance, were basking in the patronage of the recently knighted 3rd Division general, Sir John Monash. Monash could barely contain his pride in how the troupe had grown from one to four – one for the division and one each for each of the infantry brigades. An officer was given overall control of the troupes. He had nothing else to do but organise them. There was a full 24-piece string orchestra, under the command of a lance corporal. 'My troupes are real artists, and their performances are a high-class musical treat, staging operatic scenes and putting on their numbers with full orchestral accompaniment and all the adjuncts of good scenery, lighting and appropriate costumes,' Monash wrote, adding that the 'entertainments' were 'of incalculable value to the troops'.

Monash also had two soldiers who dressed up as women, and he even sent them to London to get new wigs, gloves, shoes, hosiery, frocks and jewellery. 'Both have beautiful clear soprano voices, and in the concerted numbers the combined effect of voice, bearing and gesture is all that could be desired,' he wrote, with satisfaction. One of the female impersonators, Lance Corporal Fred Watsford, had been in the 10th Machine Gun Company with Bruce and Roy Sloss.

Hewitt was still organising running competitions but finding some of the talented runners he knew were gone. He turned up to a 10th Infantry Brigade event behind the lines for a mile race that was to include former East Malvern Harrier, Aaron Goldstone. 'I did not know of [Aaron's] death until last Tuesday when I went to the 10th Brigade sports, expecting to compete with him in the mile championship,' Hewitt explained.

His surprise at the loss of fellow sportsmen receded with every brutal day at the Front. Three months later, Hewitt wrote home about the death of another runner, Jack Lynch, shot by a German sniper. '[P]oor old Jack. He was a good sport. We came from Victoria together in the same platoon. In fact he took my place as sergeant when I was put on duty with the concert party. He is the third member of our English cross-country team to make the great sacrifice.' The longer the war went, the more sportsmen succumbed. It was a simple proposition – no one was immune.

By June 1917, recruiters in Sydney had embarked on trying to find another sportsmen's unit. There was such confidence about finding another 160 men that recruiters even speci-fied how many men each sport should contribute – including 15 boxers, 15 general athletes, 15 cricketers, 40 footballers (ten each from rugby union, rugby league, soccer and Australian Rules), 15 golfers, and 15 surfers and swimmers. There were even plans to establish a 'barometer' at the George Street recruiting offices showing the number of new recruits and the number needed. The recruiters didn't manage to get the numbers, and neither did their counterparts in Melbourne. Eventually, a thousand men were recruited under the auspices of the Sportsmen's Recruiting Committee, but it never reached the kind of numbers it sought. Part of the reason was a lingering tension between the Sportsmen's Committee and the general recruitment committee, fighting as they were over the same dwindling number of resources. The Victorian sportsmen's committee certainly tried. Given the state's avowed passion for sport, it would have been a dereliction of the committee's purpose not to. A prominent member of the Victorian Parliament, Mr Agar Wynne, notified the Sportsmen's Recruiting Committee that he would offer £500 to the first member of the Sportsmen's Battalion to win a Victoria Cross. Agar was a former federal minister who had been elected to the Victorian Parliament in 1917. He had been president of St Kilda Football Club and relied on his extensive business and grazing interests to fund his generous offer. But it made no difference: if you didn't have a Sportsmen's Battalion, there could be no incentive. And perhaps the simplest explanation of why none of this worked was that, by 1917, all the Victorian sportsmen who were going had gone. The rest were staying at home.

The long European winter of 1917–18 gave way to a mild spring, and, for many of the Australians who were resting behind the lines, it was another opportunity to compete in a sporting competition. Boxing and football came to the fore. The view that the teamwork required for football in particular helped to develop a similar mutual reliance at the Front was growing in acceptance. The reason was partly to do with the alacrity with which the troops played football – and their determination to find any pockmarked, shell-struck, pitted, open ground to do it – combined with the AIF's growing reputation within the Allied armies and among the Germans for producing formidable fighters. Although the premise that linked football teamwork with soldierly reliance might have been stretched, there was no doubt that the way Australians went about their sport was an obvious contrast to the British in particular. The classless nature of the Australian approach to sport meant the officers had little impact once they were selected in a team. '[I]t is indisputable that the levelling influence of all branches of sport had much to do with that spirit of comradeship between officers and men which was so marked a feature of the AIF,' Newton Wanliss, whose son Harold was killed at Polygon Wood, wrote.

Carl Willis found the tedium of the Dental Corps hard to bear. He might have been safe from the dangers of the front line, but he struggled to deal with the sense that he was doing nothing of real value for the war effort while he was in an English camp. After just three months with the Dentists, he wrote home about how much he missed the company of the men with whom he had forged a particular bond in the most trying of circumstances. '[A]m deadly sick of it already, it is so monotonous, especially after the other side of the Channel, but that is the trouble about this game. It is either terribly dull or too damned variegated,' Willis wrote. 'I thought when I got a "movement order" to proceed to England that I would never in my most instane [*sic*] moments wish to be back again, but somehow in spite of yourself, you get thinking sometimes, and wish you were back with the boys, even if there was trouble about.'

What compounded Willis's feelings was that most of his work was treating mouth disease. Australia, New Zealand and Canada led the Allies in instituting a dental corps because they realised the growing problem among the troops of trench mouth, in particular. The ailment started with a lack of hygiene, and the resulting bacteria could, if untreated, spread beyond ulcerated and bleeding gums to lips, cheeks and jaws. It became a significant problem in 1917, and there were more than 500 cases hospitalised at any one time. There were no antibiotics, so rudimentary treatment with hydrogen peroxide or salted water was a common way to cleanse the infection. It was unpleasant, routine work and a fair distance from the dentistry Willis had learnt at the University of Melbourne. He allowed himself to dream of a better place to be, and France became that destination. 'I think when this war is over they should call France "The Land Of Good Fellowship" for it undoubtedly is. There you get away, to a great extent, from the average pettiness and jealousy of military life,' Willis said.

But there was no escaping the military life for those still caught up in the conflict. Red Wing Perry was attached to Jack Brake's 8th Field Artillery Brigade and found the work of ministering to the men difficult with the continual movement of troops. Rather than try to offer regular services, the padre opted to work with individual soldiers and offer them counsel. It was a smart move but it also struck Perry how interested some soldiers had become in spiritual matters. He put it down to the constant danger they had been exposed to during the previous year. They were confronted every day by life and death. Mates, acquaintances, strangers, all of them lumped together in mortal danger. Not all of them could survive. Perry understood it and tried to help.

Brake's 8th Field Artillery Brigade was positioned near Corbie, near the Somme River in France, in April 1918. The Germans were hanging on, showing no signs of giving in, despite the arrival of American troops and the Allied gains. Brake was in a dugout when he heard aircraft overhead. He looked up in time to see a distinctive Fokker red tri-plane that belonged to Manfred von Richthofen, otherwise known as the Red Baron, the leader of the team of lethal German air aces called the Flying Circus.

The Red Baron was the pre-eminent air ace of the war. In the grim shorthand used to describe his achievements, he had 80 'victories'. He was just 25, an aristocrat of the air, and a man who seemed to defy gravity and mortality. Around 11 am on that day, 21 April, the Baron was caught between two Canadians, chasing one and being chased by another. There could only be one outcome.

But what Brake saw was a fatal change in the Baron's luck. Years later, there would be debate about who finally ended the ace's life – whether it was Canadian airman Roy Brown, nagging at the Red Baron's tail, or an Australian gunner, who fired from the ground and got lucky. Either way, it was a testament to

Richthofen's life that there were plenty who wanted to lay claim to ending it. Fatally wounded by a solitary shot to the chest, the Baron struggled to land in a field near the village of Vaux-sur-Somme. His famous plane banked, started to quiver and shake, and then limped to the ground in a clumsy landing.

Brake looked out from the dugout and saw something of the red plane, but a fuller view was obscured by nearby trees. 'We saw R[ichthofen] overhead and turning northwards . . . R then circled round and crashed out of our views . . . I am certain there was not any plane behind R as we emerged from the dug-out,' he recalled. Brake and his men raced out to have a look. But the German artillery nearby understood what had happened to their air ace and kept firing at the spot where the plane had gone down. The barrage was an act of optimism in case a wounded Richthofen needed some cover to escape the Australians. It also gave the rest of Richthofen's Circus time to circle their fallen leader's wreckage, just in case. They flew over the downed plane four or five times before flying off in one final sombre salute.

Once Gunner Hugh Hawes and three of his mates arrived at the plane, they found another soldier and a medical orderly, Queenslander Ted Smout, checking the body in the wreckage for signs of life. 'The orderly declared the pilot dead,' Hawes explained. 'He also produced a gold watch with the Baron's name inscribed on the back. So we were the first to know who the pilot was.'

Hawes and his mates started to help themselves to some of the wreckage, but they were soon joined by other Diggers who had run from dugouts across the area, suspecting that the red plane was indeed the Baron's. Hawes grabbed a lump of laminated mahogany propeller before too many of his mates turned up. Men came from all across the 8th Field Artillery position in search of souvenirs. But just before the looting got out of hand, a tall and dignified man with an Australian accent strode into the scene. It was Red Wing Perry, who moved among the men, calming some of them, joking with others and lecturing the remaining Diggers that it was entirely inappropriate to be souveniring a dead's man property. While looting of the dead was not uncommon, Perry made it clear that there needed to be some dignity attached to the Baron's demise. Perry took it upon himself to collect all the souvenirs to ensure none were lost or sold.

Despite Perry's intervention, very little of the Red Baron's wreckage survived. Lieutenant John Warneford, of the 3rd Squadron Australian Flying Corps, managed to keep the Baron's left overboot, a knee-high, tailored leg covering, made from animal skins and featuring red wool trim sewn around the toes. The boots were mandatory for warmth when flying. And Monash souvenired some of the Fokker's fabric and some of the propeller. On 22 April 1918, the Baron was buried with full military honours in the Bertangles cemetery.

The 1918 football season started with the readmission of Essendon and St Kilda in the VFL. That left only Melbourne of the prewar clubs not back in the competition. Six of the 12 Association clubs resumed competition after the War Council agreed that the Association could start on the same conditions as the League. The six largely working-class clubs – Brunswick, Footscray, North Melbourne, Northcote, Port Melbourne and Prahran – had spent two years in cobwebs. Now they would resume, with all profits going to the patriotic funds. Association clubs had an ulterior motive – their five-year agreement with the VFL to limit player clearances was about to expire, and if the Association was to have any future, it needed to be able to find a way to retain its talent.

The old divisions, though, remained. Brunswick, one of the less well-off clubs, pushed for a resumption at its 1918 annual general meeting, with the all players in the VFA appearing as amateurs. All surplus money would then go to the patriotic funds. One man at the meeting even suggested that football should not have been stopped, and if the Association didn't resume in 1918, then other clubs should form a breakaway competition. The Association's vice president, Alf Woodham, was keen for the competition to resume, he told the meeting, but it was up to the War Council to decide whether playing football impeded recruiting.

The War Council did not mind and allowed the competition to go ahead. It felt the same way about the VFL. Richmond secretary Bill Maybury claimed the Council was always of the view that playing football would not affect recruiting and that it would also provide much-needed patriotic funds, plus much-needed entertainment. If that was the case, the Council had failed to make its case in the face of the alternative point of view.

On the eve of the 1918 season, details were released on just how many footballers had enlisted the previous year: Fitzroy 32, Richmond 31, Carlton 22, South Melbourne 18, Collingwood 16 and Geelong 14, or 133 VFL players. The numbers were impressive. An analysis of the total number of players who turned out for the six clubs in 1917 reveals there were still 178 footballers left playing. Just how much the war had affected football was captured by the massive decline in club membership figures, down from 28,365 across the League in 1914 to 3469 in 1917. Even allowing for teams coming and going during the previous three years, it was a significant decline. The number of matches, inevitably, was slashed, from 90 in 1914 to 45 three years later. In the four-team competition of 1916, the clubs had generated only £2785 in revenue. At Richmond, players' expenses amounted to two shillings and sixpence to cover transport fares. Everything else went to the patriotic funds. It was no wonder the clubs thought they had done it hard for long enough.

Yet the message was slow to permeate. *The Argus*, that paragon of patriotism and amateurism, marked the start of the season only with a simple listing of the games in the first round but no other details. Halfway through the season, *The Winner* was silenced by war-driven paper shortages. It was initially explained as 'suspended' publication but the newspaper never returned after its final edition on 12 June 1918. For many weeks during the war, it carried at least a half-page broadsheet report on sportsmen at the front. It was a compelling reminder of the fate of the sportsmen who had enlisted. Even in the final edition, there was an ad at the bottom of the page urging sportsmen to 'Enlist and Play The Game'.

Resurgent football crowd numbers could not save *The Winner*. The attendance figures from the 1917 finals series were good enough to fill the VFL with optimism for the following year. Finals attendances in what was the worst year of the war were well up on the four-team competition of the previous season. *The Football Record*, a more aggressive supporter of the game than Brosnan's measured defence, was clear about the reasons:

> The military authorities have decided not to restrict football for the present. This, presumably, is the result of what football and footballers have done in war matters. It has had the effect of enabling people to feel that they are doing nothing improper in patronising and supporting the game, and so they attend and enjoy themselves, as they are entitled to do.

And it added:

> By the way, there is a big number of members of the M.C.C. who are rather inclined to regret that they had decided to give up football, seeing that other clubs who continued playing in the face of the attempts of the newspapers to squelch the game have not suffered in the public or official estimation.

Donald Mackinnon's war soon became touched by the same awful tragedy that gripped thousands of Australian families.

His son, Brice, had been at Melbourne and Geelong Grammar, and a member of the school's first cricket and football teams. He had been a prefect, a debater and then an MCC member, destined for a storied career to rival his father's. Brice Mackinnon enlisted in the famous 42nd Highlanders in England, the Black Watch, and won a Military Cross for leading a raid in Salonika. The good news was communicated to his family on 1 July 1918. But it was soon followed by bad: Brice became ill with dysentery and died in a French hospital on 5 August. Lieutenant Brice Bunny Mackinnon was 20.

His father rarely spoke of the pain of his loss. His public face never cracked and his resolve never wavered. Donald Mackinnon had a job to do, and he would do it to the best of his ability and to the end of the war. But from 5 August 1918, it was a loaded argument – Mackinnon had a stake in the greater game, and a sad stake at that.

Hughie James had a charmed life. How else would you explain being wounded twice in a week and still being around to tell the tale? He was lucky; no other word for it. James was initially wounded in action in October 1917. But throughout the following April, he was in the front line with the Pioneers, wounded on 23 April, and then suffering a gunshot wound to his arm and back a week later. These were the dangers associated with trying to recapture ground taken around the old Somme.

The war's strategic situation changed after the Russian Revolution in 1917. The Germans brought back soldiers from the Russian front to bolster their plans for the rest of the European war. English forces were exhausted and suffering from extensive losses. The Australians, comparatively fresh from a winter behind the line, and united for the first time into an Australian Corps, were given the job of trying to support the British and save their positions in what was the old Somme battlefield.

At a village east of Amiens – Villers-Bretonneux – a decisive battle took place that incurred a gruesome loss of men on both sides. The action was launched at night on 24 April 1918, the day after Hughie James was wounded. Perhaps his greatest fortune was not being there for the 'stunt' that cost thousands of lives, but the battle in the end ensured the Allies held the village and the valuable Amiens rail junction. The signs were becoming clearer of Germany's falling morale. Their troops were spent, struggling to deal with the fresh men and energy the Americans brought to the Allies, and the growing sophistication of the artillery and tanks.

With increasing speed, the Allies consolidated their progress, at Hamel and Amiens in August. But there was a host of smaller, intense battles breaking out across the Western Front, as German resistance was redoubled for what seemed to be the build-up to the final denouement. Between 7 and 14 August, there were 6100 Australian casualties across four separate conflicts. But these engagements were a different kind of war – liberated from the brutal, sapping, intense stalemate of trench warfare, the Australians found themselves fighting on open ground. It at least felt more familiar than the mud, frost, grime and glue of the previous years.

Willis grumbled again about missing the action:

It gets very monotonous being in the same spot so long, and never getting away from here for more than a couple of days at a time. I am satisfied that a man is missing the best part of the war by being on this side at present. All the lads coming through here as convalescents say they have enjoyed the recent fighting immensely, compared with the old days, when they were stuck in the trenches and never saw Fritz for a week.

He was maudlin. Too much time on his hands made him ponder what the future held. Willis was gloomy about returning to football, fearing that he – and the other footballers at the Front – would struggle with the game when peace came. 'I am afraid that I would not last long in the team now: in fact, none of us, in my opinion, will ever be much good again. We will all be pavilion players, talking about what we would have done with the ball under the same circumstances.' It might have been Willis's disillusionment and boredom speaking, but he was sincere enough in what he saw of the physical and mental impact the war had on the soldiers around him. His mood was not even leavened by the continued good news from France.

This time, it was the Allies who redoubled their efforts and devised a strategy that would, ultimately, break the 6,500-plus-yard-long Hindenburg Line. On 22 August, the Australians were part of the push to drive the Germans further back to the Somme. Lieutenant Hughie James was in an attack west of the village of Bray. Nine artillery brigades began the barrage just before dawn on 22 August, and then the infantry began to move with the support of 24 tanks. James's platoon came under heavy German machine-gun fire from an entrenched position. James saw many of his men shot but he pushed on, defying the guns, to reach the German line with the rest of his men. Thirty Germans surrendered. James was given a bar to his Military Cross. '[I]t was only by his courage, cheerful disposition and total disregard of danger that the consolidation was completed successfully,' the citation read. 'His fine example, great gallantry and devotion to duty was an inspiration to all ranks and contributed largely to the success of the operation.' The honour made Lieutenant John Hugh James, of Ascot Vale, the most decorated VFL footballer of the First World War. 'I knew he'd do it,' one proud old Richmond fan stood up to tell the club's annual meeting.

The Australians continued to make significant strategic victories, especially in the Battle of Mont St Quentin and the Battle of Montbrehain, the last Australian infantry action of the war, on 5 October 1918. Then they were all withdrawn to rest, leaving the British, French and Americans to land the final blows that brought an end to it all. The Australian Corps was exhausted and threadbare. It might not have been able to make it back to the front if the war had continued.

The Armistice came on 11 November 1918. Finally, after four long years, 62,000 Australian deaths and 156,000 wounded, imprisoned or gassed Diggers, the war was over. Just in excess of 416,000 Australians had enlisted. Many of them were sportsmen and some of them were footballers. The silence gave everyone time to grieve.

11

The Final Siren

There was lingering tension over recruitment when the 1918 VFL season opened, but by finals time the issue had eased, with the growing expectation that an Allied victory was imminent. A month before the last Australian action of the war, South Melbourne defeated Collingwood by five points to win the flag, with 39,000 fans watching. Pundits, led by the former Carlton and Essendon coach Jack Worrall, saw promising signs in the renewed spectator interest. 'While it is freely admitted on all sides that the great playing standard that existed in prewar times has not been maintained during the war's currency, the season just concluded has been better sustained than any of its immediate predecessors,' Worrall wrote.

The return of clubs that had not been part of the previous two years' competition helped boost patronage. However, if there was one element that liberated fans, it was the perception that finally there was no shame attached to playing or watching the game while the war was headed towards its conclusion. Of course, the state of the war failed to extinguish the resilient faith of the torchbearers for amateurism, but their power was receding.

Instead, there were separate discussions about trying to enshrine a distinction between those footballers who 'played

269

the greater game' and those who didn't serve. *The Football Record* was lobbied to place a star in its team lists against the name of footballers who were returned men. An alternative notion was to encourage footballers who saw action to wear a special badge on their guernsey. Neither idea was taken up. Fans and footballers just wanted their sport to return to what it was before August 1914. But everything had changed. There was no going back.

On 22 May 1918, Tullie Sloss left Liverpool in England to return to the USA. Just before she departed, she received a letter from Gladys. The pair had been in regular contact, and inevitably the letters focused on Bruce. 'I'm feeling terribly sad today,' Gladys wrote. 'Lieut. Fraser, as you know returned today, and, as he passed, I thought if it were only Bruce – if I could only see him – but still I must not worry you . . .' Gladys had met a gunner from Bruce's 10th Machine Gun Company 'and like all the others, [he] loved Bruce'.

But there was bitterness and anger at the base of Gladys's mourning for her fiancé. Bruce had made the ultimate sacrifice but there were still men eligible to serve. Gladys had no tolerance for those who didn't sign up or those who agitated against conscription. She had joined the Women's Auxiliary Army Corps in the hope of getting to France but lamented the government would only allow women to be part of the home service. 'Of course, I suppose it's impossible to let the women go from here yet as there are so many eligible's [men] left but once we get rid of these degenerate males, I'm sure the WAAC will be recognised,' she told Tullie.

But she saved her strongest vitriol for Archbishop Mannix, who she said had refused to remove his hat on St Patrick's Day when 'God Save the King' was played. 'I wish I had been near him. I would have helped remove his head I think,' she wrote. 'I hope he will be deported soon. I'd like to put snakes all over him.'

Gladys's view of Mannix was not uncommon. The conscription debate had few bystanders. Tullie, for her part, remained resolutely proud of being Australian. She was given dispensation to wear the Australian rising sun button on her Women's Legion uniform and she told her mother how proud she was to have it. 'It is about the only thing I have ever swanked over in my life,' she said.

Tullie became ill while she was nursing in England, and New York seemed the best place to recover. Her illness had stripped the weight off her. She was only 78 pounds in her heavy nurse's uniform when she left England. The privations in England were strict. Simple foods were rare and luxuries unheard of. When Tullie saw a plate of white bread and butter being circulated among diners on her first night at sea, she became desperate. 'How my eyes followed that bread platter. I was so afraid it would be all gone before it came around to me again. The officer at the head of the table told me afterwards that he knew I had been without B[read] & B[utter] by the greedy way I followed the plate.'

Back in New York after having to deal once again with the threat of mines on the journey, Tullie censured the carefree mood in America, where food was bountiful and the war seemed a long way away: 'How I prayed that the Germans might drop a bomb on New York to waken its people up. I hated leaving the others behind in England, and . . . I felt miserable and restless and wanted to be right back [in England] again.' She resumed her life as a governess. When 11 November arrived, it took Tullie by surprise.

'WAR IS OVER! . . . For the last four years everything we did or wanted to was when the WAR IS OVER and here it is over now,' she wrote, 'and all I can do is go to my room at the sound of the first bell, grasp Bruce's picture and call to him WAR IS OVER!' The war's end prodded Tullie to reflect on its impact on her family. 'SON: [James] On the way from Turkey

271

to Egypt reported . . . as dying; ROY: in hospital in France. JOCK: still over there; BRUCE: In heaven (the best off of all of us); HECTOR: home ill. MA, BIDDY AND COOKIE: Worn out and tired from the weary endless watching and waiting and MYSELF: Not fit to be on duty not to mention the suffering of those near to us.' Even before the war, the Slosses suffered, but they found a way to endure. The war, though, almost broke them.

Tullie's understanding of James's predicament was off the mark. He recovered from his bout of typhus and was moved from one village and town to the next, spending three months in one, a few weeks in another, working under supervision on occasions, being confined to hospital with diarrhoea or recurring fevers. It wasn't until 3 May 1917 that James received his first letter from the family, a note from Tullie. 'The life of a prisoner-of-war seemed to dull one's sense to most of the things one used to enjoy,' James explained. 'No wonder we became tired of it all, body and soul.' He predicted the Americans would bring an end to the war but not until 1919. James prepared himself for more time in captivity. But in September 1918, rumours of peace started. Turkey and Bulgaria were out of the war, and on 22 October James found himself in a place called Paradise. It was a British settlement, near Smyrna. James McKenzie Sloss was free to go home.

The silence that burst across Europe after 11 November 1918 was a novel experience for the war-weary Diggers still stuck in France. They had no one to fight and nowhere to be. Another winter beckoned. The past four years had imposed a discipline and routine on them that couldn't just be turned off once the guns stopped smoking. What to do with the men, so many of them burdened by the grief of their experiences and either damaged or injured by battle? Or, as one of their number noted, 'What greater problem can there be than that of keeping a couple of hundred thousand home-hungry men content?'

Even if the men (and their families) had been able to be moved, there were massive problems with congested French and Belgian train lines, while troopships were in constant demand. By the end of the year, 15 troopships were on their way to Australia with 13,000 men. But the rest had to take their turn and wait.

What to do with them? The answer, not surprisingly, was sport. '[W]hile the [Australian] Corps was on its way back to the line [in late 1918], the order to ceasefire came along. Everybody said a fervent "Thank God" and thoughts turned again towards – well, first of all, towards HOME and then towards SPORT'. It might seem hard to comprehend that sport would have been such a prominent concern, but, for many soldiers, the physical release of sport – free of mortal threat – was a powerful antidote to all they had seen and done. And training for sport was the ideal transition from the military training that occupied the time of many soldiers between their stints at the Front.

The plan to stage competition across a range of sports went beyond the AIF. In the absence of the 1916 Olympics, the program of sports took on an international flavour that involved soldiers from England, France, Canada, Australia and New Zealand. There was boxing, athletics, rowing, rugby union, shooting, cricket and soccer. The locations were France, Belgium, England, Palestine, Mesopotamia and Egypt. The AIF established a Sports Control Board to coordinate fixtures, organise funds and resources, and manage the massive task of moving teams around a still-heaving Europe. The competition devolved from the international to the inter-battalion, inter-brigade and inter-division. This became the best way of running a competition of Australian Rules, simply because no one outside the AIF could play it.

As the competition in other sports became more intense – and international – football became less prominent. The Sports Control Board didn't even put football on its agenda of planned competitions, choosing, pragmatically, the international sports of rowing, rugby union, golf and tennis. But there was still an organised roster of matches, for the Australian divisions. None of the competitions could happen without support from home. So Australian sports fans were asked one more time to make a wartime donation. The Victorian Racing Club gave £100, John Wren the same, and Collingwood Football Club £50, in what was the first gesture of a VFL club to the cause. The VFL sent footballs and the Australian YMCA donated a cup for division and corps troops competing in football, rugby, boxing and cross-country running. The winner of the cup would be decided by a point system, with points accrued on the basis of performances across each sport.

The AIF Headquarters in London's Horseferry Road was the clearing house for sporting inquiries. Every soldier who wanted to play sport had to report to the Sports Section at Horseferry Road, and they were then passed on to the relevant sporting section for a trial. If the soldier was not deemed suitable to play, he went to a repatriation camp.

There was no shortage of men wanting to be part of the competition. One of the reasons for their keenness was the AIF generals' continued support for sport behind the lines in France. It ensured their troops were never completely cut off from activity or interest, regardless of the equipment, grounds or conditions. It was this encouragement that meant the sport program could spring to life with such vigour despite the exhaustion of war. The other reason was the soldiers' recognition that they needed something to do while they were waiting to get home.

While most of the press attention was on rugby, boxing, athletics and rowing, the AIF footballers found themselves playing inter-divisional matches at Charleroi, in Belgium. Despite the war's devastation, the town was in good order. Its trams were running, so soldiers could get around easily. But prices were high for those who were billeted nearby, including

Carl Willis. The dull time in England was over for Willis. He was delighted to be on the continent and happily engaged with the football. 'I have had a great time, really, since I've been in this area,' Willis wrote home. He had leave in Paris when his brother Jack married his Italian fiancée. It was the first time the brothers had been together since Jack left Sydney with the navy, four years earlier. Willis loved Paris and was dazzled by its spirit, colour and flair, but was horrified at how much it cost. '[N]othing but lack of funds got me back as soon as I did come,' he wrote. 'It stands alone in every way from all the other cities I have seen . . .'

Hughie James and Dan Minogue didn't start the war as mates. They played for different football clubs, with the rivalry that went with that. They weren't even like-minded souls who suddenly found they had something in common. Minogue was a rough-hewn, instinctive man, with a healthy larrikin streak. James was shrewd and strategic, given to thinking, then acting. Both played tough football – physical but within the rules. They were big men, solid and imposing. They played together in London at the Exhibition match and they were back in harness for the 3rd Division in the inter-division postwar games at Charleroi.

Although Sloss, Lee, Pugh and Foy were gone, there was still plenty of talent for the 3rd Division to pick from. But this time, the competition was across the five Australian divisions. Each divisional team played at least four games before, depending on results, progressing to the finals. Before the 3rd played the 5th Division, James teamed up with Minogue and between them worked on converting young soldier Len Gale from rugby to Australian Rules. Gale was a pugnacious character, a potter from Melbourne, who after the war joined Fitzroy as a rover. James, Minogue and Gale formed a formidably bruising ruck combination for the 3rd Division.

When the time came for the game against the 5th Division, there were few backward steps. Lieutenant James observed that he put some of his opponents off when he turned up to the game in his officer's uniform. 'I noticed one or two of the Fifth Divvy fellows nudging each other. It was not hard to imagine what they were saying: "A blinking officer! A la-de-da!"', James recalled. Perhaps it was enough to put James in a 'mood'. Soon after the game began, he 'stopped' an opponent:

> That was only the start. Dan Minogue stood four square and Len Gale went a bit further. We fought our way through two quarters when without warning the fight began in earnest. That finished the football. We were hard at it, hitting where a head bobbed up, when who should walk out on to the ground but His Nibs – brass hat and all.

James didn't identify the general who turned up to sort out the fight. 'Now cut this out,' he said, 'this is a game instituted for the good relationship of the corps. Fighting is strictly prohibited. If it does not stop, I'll cancel the whole affair.' The general turned on his heel and walked off.

'We lost the football and the fight was a draw,' James concluded. The truth was, of course, no one was sure what the sanctions were in these matches. The men were still in the army so the usual discipline could have applied, but, then again, it was peacetime. Who would know how the brass would react to an outbreak of fighting in a sanctioned sporting contest? These men had been fighting for months – their aggression couldn't be turned off, like a tap.

For all Charleroi's charms, it was difficult to find a sufficient clear patch of ground to hold a football match. Australian Rules demands open spaces. And the winter, once again, was harsh enough to make for challenging conditions. Willis sent a photograph home, taken before one of the matches. 'I can't understand what has happened to my legs, unless they were entirely shrivelled up by the cold. The ground we played on was half-frozen, and after the game was over you could have scraped some square yards of skin off it,' he wrote. Willis lamented his poor form, which explained why he didn't play in every match. But he wasn't alone. Many of the soldiers were in poor physical condition after months at the Front, short of decent nutrition and regular exercise. Willis might have been in the comparative safety of the Dental Corps but it was no preparation for football, in freezing conditions.

The round-robin football competition began on 2 March and finished on 18 March. The games were low-scoring, although the 1st Division team kicked 11 goals and 12 goals in two of its games, and no other team cracked ten goals or more. That explains in part why the 1st Division won the competition, from the 2nd and 4th Division teams. The 3rd Division – the men who had played with such flair in London – was equal third. It is worth remembering that the 3rd Division in October 1916 had not seen action. Arguably, the losses the 3rd incurred after that match meant it was unable to reach those heights again. The YMCA Australian Corps Sports Cup went to the 1st Division by half a point from the 5th Division.

The lure of an international athletics program was too hard for Hewitt to resist. He had a wife and baby boy he hadn't seen in Melbourne, but he put that aside to train for what was billed as the Inter-Allied Games in Paris over June and July 1919. The Games were the Americans' idea of demonstrating their friendship with France. The US came up with the concept and then built the stadium for 25,000 spectators at Joinville-le-Pont on the outskirts of Paris. The one thing the Americans couldn't control was the French themselves, and labour issues conspired to threaten the stadium being ready.

The program featured a mini-Olympics of nations: the US, Australia, Belgium, Canada, Czechoslovakia, France, Guatemala, Hedjaz (in the west of present-day Saudi Arabia), Italy, New Zealand, Portugal, Romania, Greece and Serbia. England could not find sufficient athletes to make up a team – an understandable outcome in the circumstances. Hewitt had been in England and ran a full marathon from Windsor to Stamford Bridge athletic ground. He was, all things considered, in good shape when he was selected in the Australian team. Jack Brake, the former University footballer and gifted all-round athlete, was also selected, in a new event: the 200-metre 'low hurdles'. Lieutenant Brake, however, was injured before the event and didn't run. Hewitt was entered in the 10,000-metre cross-country, a style of running that had suited him in Australia, but he struggled against stronger opposition in Paris and was unplaced. The marathon was cut back to 16 kilometres, and Hewitt ran again without making a place. Hewitt wasn't deterred by his performances. More training and more competition would make him more competitive, so he decided to stay on in England.

But most of the other sportsmen, by the last quarter of 1919, were headed home. Red Wing Perry was so keen to return to football that he started working in the stokehold in the transport ship on the trip home to recapture his fitness. His intentions, as always with the padre, were pure but the fates conspired against him when Norwood failed to make the finals and denied Red Wing the chance to make an appearance late in the season. It was no matter. After the ship finally arrived in Adelaide, via a stop in Sydney, it was only a few days before Perry resumed training. He lived in West Torrens, and there was speculation he would leave Norwood and play with the western suburbs club. Anyone who pondered the idea failed to understand Red Wing Perry's brand of loyalty. Norwood was Perry's club. If he played, it would be with the Redlegs.

Perry was out on the training track on 4 September 1919 but he took his time to build his condition for football. After three years away from senior football, he was a long way short of being considered for senior selection. When the club had a Welcome Home social at Norwood Town Hall for the returned soldiers three months later, Perry heard how the South Australian Football League had started the 1919 season with a £400 overdraft but by season's end had turned that into a £700 credit. It was a significant achievement because the 'Spanish Lady', the lethal influenza bug that killed more people than the war, infiltrated Australia in 1919 and curtailed crowds just as sport was getting back on its feet. The Welcome Home social included a tribute to the 13 Norwood footballers who had perished in the war and more than 70 who saw service. Chaplain Perry rose and responded with a number of others, on behalf of the returned soldiers. Norwood's reckoning of the war's cost arrived at a similar conclusion to so many football clubs – the conflict had hollowed out its talent and experience. The seasoned players were either lost to the war or still overseas, and the young players remained untested and inexperienced. Football would take some years to capture the spirit of that long-ago winter of 1914.

But there were signs of rejuvenation. Melbourne rejoined the VFL in 1919. Collingwood finished on top of the VFL and won its second premiership in three seasons, this time at Richmond's expense. A healthy crowd of 45,413 was on hand to see it. There were signs of new rivalries being established and a dynasty emerging that would help define the postwar VFL. The key figures, as it turned out, were Hughie James and Dan Minogue. While Hughie James was not known to be a prolific letter writer while he was away, he did send an important note to the Richmond Football Club secretary Bill Maybury about Minogue. James had a keen ear and after a few chats with Minogue reckoned Dan would jump from Colling-wood to Richmond with the right offer – and that meant the coaching job. Whatever coaching aspiration Minogue had at Collingwood ended when the club announced in 1918 that Jock McHale would become the non-playing coach. Richmond coach

Norman Clark was returning to his old club, Carlton, after just one season, and he wrote to Minogue while Dan was on the front about coming to the Tigers. Dan was keen.

The Magpies were blissfully unaware of the correspondence that was seducing their favoured son away. They expected Minogue to slot back in to a team that had played the past two grand finals (and won one of them). Dan would add the leadership and drive to ensure Collingwood stayed at the top. Collingwood planned to honour Minogue's return from the war – along with Doc Seddon's – with a big welcome. There was talk of a parade for Minogue down Smith Street, the retail and commercial artery that ran through the suburb. Seddon started training soon after he returned home on 22 May, and was back in the seniors less than a month later. Minogue turned up in Melbourne on 26 July. The club prepared itself for the celebration. And then Minogue said he wanted to go to Richmond.

Hughie James was still overseas and wasn't around to see the seismic impact Minogue's decision had on the two suburban football clubs. But it was instant and enduring. The celebrations were abandoned and, out of the bitterness, a deep animosity between Collingwood and Richmond was born.

Minogue's discussions with Richmond were so far advanced that the club had already arranged accommodation for Minogue in its area. The new VFL ruling for returned men was that, after three years away, a player could turn out for the club in 'whose district he first takes up residence'. Minogue was confident that it was a routine procedure that would enable him to turn out for Richmond. But the League denied him a clearance because he lodged the papers three days after the clearance deadline, which meant he had to miss the rest of the 1919 season. 'That seemed like splitting straws, and a rather raw deal for a returned soldier,' Minogue said later. 'Only my military discipline prevented me from saying what I thought at the time.'

Minogue was crestfallen at the delay. He was desperately keen to return to football. It was the game he loved, and nothing said peace had arrived more than a game of League football. 'I like other soldier-footballers at once felt a strong urge to play again the game I loved so well,' Minogue explained, 'to heave the khaki uniform joyously away and, donning football togs, career around the turf once more, without having to do this and that by "the numbers", as in the army.'

What no one, including Minogue, was talking about was the real reason he wanted to leave Collingwood. It took him 18 years to finally confess. 'Well, rightly or wrongly. I did not approve of the way that Collingwood treated a great pal of mine – a fine player for them – while I was away at the war,' Minogue said. The friend was Jim Sadler, who had been left out of Collingwood's final sides in 1917, including the grand final line-up. Minogue was unrepentant about the reason for his decision. 'I may have allowed sentiment to sway my feelings in that case – I don't know. But I have never had cause to feel sorry for my action.' Collingwood defeated Richmond for the premiership in 1919, which added further feeling to what lay ahead: in 1920, Minogue joined Hughie James in Richmond colours in what became one of the most potent Richmond sides of any era.

Many of the soldiers had already returned – some broken, some patched up, all of them exposed to sights and experiences that changed them, for good and for ill. Crowds lined the ports and the streets to welcome them home. In the Western Australian goldfields, there was a steady influx of returned men – some coming home, others in search of work. The remains of the Scullin family saw the soldiers come back to town and felt the pain of their loss all over again. 'The saddest day of our lives was to see all the boys come back and none of them ours,' the Scullins' sister Meg said later. 'It was a terrible, sad time. Our parents had us three young children and they knew they had to rear us. By clinging to us it helped them along. But the boys were missed all right, terribly missed.'

The Scullins' pain was all too common: the homecoming revealed the brutal reality that every second Australian family was bereaved by the death of a soldier. The Scullins, though, had suffered more than most. There was some material respite for everyone in the Goldfields when the federal government gave gold sellers permission to sell wherever they liked for a higher price, but the bubble of prosperity didn't last. It only succeeded in driving up wages and machinery prices. By the end of 1921, 600 jobs were gone from Boulder and Kalgoorlie. It was just another layer of pain.

Peacetime also gave rise to petty recriminations and jeal-ousies that had been silenced by the greater issue of living and dying. In the aftermath of the Armistice, the YMCA was dismissed by some critics as doing only 'backyard work' during the war. Sir John Monash, in charge of the AIF repatriation in London, took offence. Monash outlined what he considered the important role the organisation played, not only in providing recreation and entertainment but also in accompanying brigades no matter where they went. Monash singled out the cinema created by Beaurepaire, the soup kitchen in the bombed asylum in Armentières and coffee stalls at Ypres. 'Although only a small part of the association's work it was that kind of service which did so much toward building up and maintaining the wonder-ful morale of the Australian soldier,' Monash said. Monash and Beaurepaire were a formidable team, and Monash was not going to let the YMCA man, or his organisation, be publicly slighted once the war was over.

Beaurepaire managed to be reinstated as an amateur, for the first time in eight years. The significance of the change in status became important when it was confirmed in April 1919 that the Olympic Games, scheduled for Antwerp in 1920, would go ahead. Beaurepaire's great rival Billy Longworth was still in England, competing in the AIF international events. Long-worth had represented Australia in the 1912 Games, without success. The pair's main rival, Cec Healy, was arguably a better swimmer than both of them, but he was killed in the war. The talent shortage seemed acute, but Beaurepaire saw the Olympics as an opportunity to represent his country again.

By the start of the 1919–20 season, Beaurepaire was the Victorian coach for the national championships that would decide the Australian swimming team for Antwerp. Perhaps more important for him was that he had been slowly building up his fitness, getting back to the pool daily and confessing to his wife, Myra, that he had rediscovered his drive to compete. 'You know I'm not doing badly at all. I believe I am swimming faster than ever. It might be quite an idea to go in for a few races.'

Beaurepaire was not one for easing his way back in to competition. He returned in February 1920 in a head-to-head contest with the US star of the inter-Allied swimming games in Paris and world champion Norman Ross. The half-mile event was held at the St Kilda sea baths in front of 4000 people. Beaurepaire was 28 but still managed to beat Ross, who was three months shy of turning 25. It suggested that Beaurepaire was probably back at his peak and Australia's best swimmer. Even Ross thought so. 'There is not another swimmer in the world, I think, to compare with him,' the American told the excited spectators at St Kilda. Beaurepaire's resurgence was stalled when he fell ill with gastroenteritis, but he recovered so well that he swam the mile championship in Perth 14 seconds quicker than he had 11 years earlier.

After the AIF athletics competition, Hewitt continued to run in England, building up an impressive list of finishes over a five-week period. There was no shortage of athletic meetings, many of them organised under the auspices of returned soldiers or charities associated with the war. The irony was that many of the men who took part were in no great state of fitness.

On 21 June, King George V sent the marathoners on their way from Windsor Castle to Stamford Bridge in London. There had been several events billed as 'marathons' that literally failed to measure up, but this race was the correct distance: 26 miles 385 yards. Hewitt came second in two hours, 55 minutes and 29 seconds, but the full distance took a toll and Hewitt was in distress at the end.

It was remarkable that he recovered sufficiently to undertake several gruelling races in the weeks that followed. Hewitt won what was billed as a semi-marathon in July 1919 in London when he covered the 20 kilometres in one hour, 12 minutes and 25 seconds in the meeting promoted by the National Federation of Demobilised Soldiers. And he was second in the London Marathon – run over 32 kilometres in late July – and finished second again two weeks later, this time in the International Marathon (24 kilometres) in London, 40 metres behind the winner. In mid-August, he was running in another 24-kilometre event, and finished second again. By the time Hewitt boarded the *Nestor* on 11 November to return home, he had accumulated an extensive list of performances that would put him in contention for a place in the 1920 Olympics.

The war had a deep impact on English cricket. Of all the sports, prewar cricket in England extolled its virtues with a mixture of carefree charm and presumed superiority. Cricket was the Empire's game, and England was the repository of its laws, wisdom and, most tellingly, the code of genteel civility that ran through it like a grain through willow. Nothing spoke more strongly of England than its faith in the civilising influence of cricket, and its attachment to a code of behaviour intrinsic to the game itself. English cricket believed it was on top of the world after defeating South Africa and Australia in a novel triangular Test tournament in 1912, so there was an optimism fed by nostalgia that, come the peace, England would once again dominate its dominions.

But *Wisden*, the little book that became the game's manual of facts, figures, etiquette and achievement, sounded a cautionary note in 1915 that resonated four years later: 'After the War, whenever that may be, cricket will, no doubt, go on as before, but it will naturally take some time for the game to recover completely from the blow it has received.' Just how large an impact the war had on English cricket was revealed during the AIF team's tour during the 1919 summer.

Carl Willis was a talented cricketer who played five games for Victoria before the war. He made a 90 but also a 'pair', during a revolving-door selection that saw him play New Zealand on debut and Tasmania three times. He was also picked in a combined Australian and South African services team to play a strong English Navy and Army team at Lord's in 1917. Although the combined team finished up with a sizeable lead in a low-scoring match, Willis, sadly, recorded a duck at the home of cricket. Nonetheless, Willis was selected to be part of the AIF team that contained several bigger name players who went on to join one of Australia's finest-ever Test teams. The Australians' role was to restart international cricket in England, with a series of gentle contests across the country to at least try to compensate for the absence of Test cricket.

The outcome was more confronting than comfortable for the hosts. The AIF team won 12 of 28 first-class matches and lost only four games. The Australians' biggest loss was their skipper Charlie Kelleway, the noted New South Wales all-rounder, when he returned home after nine games to have a leg wound treated. Kelleway was wounded six times during the war. You didn't want to push luck like that, so he sailed home to properly recover. Herbie Collins, a cricketer whose luck earned him the nickname 'Horseshoe', took over the role. But it was Willis who dominated the batting. When the tour ended, Willis was the top run-scorer, with 1829 runs at the healthy average of 41.56. He hit four centuries, combining a watchful defence with a range of classic shots that enabled him to occupy the crease and still score heavily. Willis's important role was recognised when he was made one of the selectors.

From England, the AIF team embarked on an eight-match tour of South Africa, before returning to Australia. Willis, still wearing the AIF blazer with the rising sun emblem on the pocket, turned out at the MCG on 16 January 1920 to play against Victoria in what was Melbourne's first look at big cricket in five years.

Rain intervened on the first day and mercurial all-rounder Jack Gregory, all bounding, leaping speed, took 7–22 on a wet wicket, and Victoria was bowled out for 116. On the second day, in better weather and in front of 18,000 fans, Willis made a cool century, with a collection of 11 sweetly timed boundaries. It was his first 100 on Australian soil and helped the AIF to a 195-run first-innings lead. Victoria struggled against Allie Lampard's leg-breaks when it batted again and was left with a modest 75 runs to win the match. They made it with six wickets to spare. On the Saturday night, at Scott's hotel in the city, Donald Mackinnon, this time in his role as president of the Victorian Cricket Association, hosted a dinner for both teams. There were several high-ranking military guests, including Sir John Monash, back home after supervising the AIF's repatriation.

Monash got to his feet to sustained applause. He told the gathering all AIF commanders were impressed with the importance of sport early in the war and it became a 'powerful assistance'. No one who worked closely with Monash would have been surprised at his remarks. Then, in a moment of reflection, the general explained how sport worked for Australian troops: 'Every unit had its teams, and the keeping of the spirit of sport alive was an important factor in maintaining the morale. An appeal to the men that never failed was the appeal to their sportsmanship.' Monash went further, claiming that sportsmanship worked more powerfully than patriotism, which could become threadbare with regular use. Sportsmanship was the inspiration for many victories, Monash said. 'The appeal "It's up to you to play for your side" always told.' But there was another element that sport helped foster in the AIF, and it was teamwork. 'The reason the Australians were recognised as possessing the gift for keen work to a degree not exceeded by any other army in the war, was that they had the capacity for collective effort, which was due to the influence of sport on their life in Australia,' Monash said. Here was the nation's senior general helping to shape a powerful legacy for sport's role in what made an Australian soldier unique. Monash sat down with cheers ringing through the room.

It was Mackinnon's turn. The former national head of recruiting, the man to whom Billy Hughes had given the task of finding every way possible to drive enlistments, who had sat at the sharp edge of the conscription debates, was by 1920 living a quieter life as a state MP. There was a decided air of relief, even melancholy, about Mackinnon's speech. He admitted that sport had actually been a great aid in recruiting and he was not 'altogether dissatisfied' that the AIF remained a voluntary force. Conscription was beyond the effort of many people, he said. Those who followed Mackinnon's pronouncements during the war would not have been surprised by his comments. What Monash made of them is not recorded. But many others, those who had been demonised and vilified for sticking with their sport through the war, had a right to ask what had it all been for? All the bitter fracturing and divisions, the hostilities and the animosity – what was gained? Mackinnon made no further comment, but closed the evening with a presentation of the ball from the first day to Jack Gregory and a bat to Carl Willis for his century. The evening ended with cheers and laughter.

Willis was uncertain about playing football in 1920, and it was several months before he resumed training with South Melbourne.

He turned out for Wonthaggi just for a run and then played his first match since 1915 against St Kilda on 21 August. He had an instant effect on the South forward line, with his clever ball-handling and accurate passing. Willis's return, though, was not the main story of the 1920 football season.

There is something to be said for revenge, nurtured and polished, then served when the heat is gone. Dan Minogue met his old Collingwood teammates in round five of the 1920 season, at Richmond's home ground, Punt Road Oval. There was a lingering fog and the ground was dewy. The small oval was bursting with 20,000 fans. At one point, the roof over the verandah on the old cricket club caved in from the weight of ardent and agitated fans, narrowly avoiding dozens of spectators. The worst casualty was a returned soldier who had suffered from shell shock and apparently sustained a relapse.

The expectations around the game were high, especially among Richmond supporters. Unlike Collingwood, the Tigers had not experienced great success. They were hungry to measure themselves against their more accomplished neighbour. The pace of the game was quick, defying the damp conditions, and it was an even contest, with each team trading scores, like boxers exchanging blows. Hughie James was prominent early, marking strongly, and Minogue, the new playing coach, worked his way steadily into the game. Perhaps if Collingwood had converted three of its behinds in the final quarter, the outcome might have been different, but as the game hung in the balance, only a point separated the two teams. This was football as the crowd wanted it to be played − tense and skilful. The Magpies stole a few more seconds in the forward line and threatened to score, but Richmond ran the ball out of defence and a long kick found Hughie James. In one of those serendipitous moments, James calmly took the kick that gave Richmond victory by seven points.

It was a moment that stayed with Richmond fans. And it was reprised in the return encounter with Collingwood, at Victoria Park, when Richmond full-forward George Bayliss kicked a goal from a free kick to give the Tigers a win by two points. It was stirring stuff. What had made the difference? Well, Hughie James was back, for one, but Dan Minogue, the coach the Pies had spurned, was making a deep impression on his teammates. The team won its first minor premiership, losing only two games all season. And then, on the eve of the finals, Minogue was confined to bed with quinsy, a serious form of tonsillitis.

The newspapers understood what impact Minogue's absence would have on the team – he was considered the most influential captain-coach in the League. Minogue took himself off to Bendigo to get away from the speculation around his health. But his absence only fuelled rumours. Some suggested he was so ill that he had died. Bets were wagered on his survival, and men went to his home seeking confirmation that he was alive. It was a macabre endorsement of the strength of Minogue, the talisman in Richmond's quest for its first premiership.

Collingwood sneaked in to the grand final, against predictions, and found itself facing Richmond in a repeat of the 1919 flag-decider. Minogue, looking pale and wan, turned up at training on the Thursday night before the game. He declared himself ready to play and did some work on the skipping rope. Minogue was full of bravado but, in truth, he was struggling. 'I hardly felt equal to it, but players and officials urged me to play, for my leadership and the moral effect on the team. It didn't matter if I didn't get a kick, they said.' Minogue was the man Richmond now turned to, not just as a player but as a symbol of the disrespectful way the club believed it had been treated by the League and its member clubs. The whole episode was just part of what now seemed like a Richmond grand plan to inspire its players in the face of the Collingwood threat. Minogue, after all, had been a Collingwood captain.

Richmond club secretary Jack Archer embarked on a passion-ate address to the team before the grand final, culminating in a toe-curling diatribe against the club the Tigers were playing. 'Yes, they were good sports at social gatherings after they won, but the scene changed at Collingwood this year when we beat them, and we're going to beat them today. At Collingwood I was admiring their beautiful room and its appointments and I noticed a nice souvenir sent by Danny Minogue to the club while away in France fighting for his country. At that time all clubs wanted to boost their representation at the war. While I was admiring the souvenir, the secretary of Collingwood advised me that they had a fine photo of Minogue, which used to adorn their walls, but had been relegated to obscu-rity, with its face to the wall, on the top shelf of a cupboard. Is that sportsmanship?'

Archer's words played to the team's attachment to their coach and the deep well of insecurity that can be an endless source of inspiration for the aggrieved and disadvantaged. In the face of such rhetoric, what hope did Collingwood have? Not much, as it turned out. Minogue took up residence in the forward line to nurse himself through the game, but his influence was vital. In the end, Richmond defeated Collingwood by 17 points to secure its first flag. Hughie James kicked a goal and got his hand on the premiership cup. Minogue left the celebrations to go back to bed, where, still in a fever, he had wild dreams about the afternoon's game.

The Reverend Charles Red Wing Perry was getting married in September 1920, to a talented singer Miss Muriel Day. They had met on the Methodist church circuit, when Miss Day was singing and Reverend Perry officiating. It was a relationship that moved quickly, from courting, to engagement, to wedding. But the honeymoon was another matter. Perry was back with Norwood, and the team, showing a significant improvement in form on its prewar fortunes, was in the South Australian grand final, against North Adelaide. On the Thursday evening before the match, Perry and Miss Day were married at the Archer Street Methodist Church in Adelaide. Reverend Perry came to an arrangement with his new bride – they would have to delay the honeymoon until after the grand final on Saturday 28th. It was a clear demonstration of Red Wing's commitment to football and to Norwood. There might have been practicalities involved too – the wedding venue and arrangements had been booked well in advance of Norwood's good form, especially towards the end of the season.

The net effect was that Reverend Perry took his place in the Norwood grand final team as a freshly minted married man, without a honeymoon. He played a dominating first half at centre half-back and was thrown into the ruck for the second half. Despite his efforts, North made easy work of Norwood and won the match by 48 points. It was only then that the Perrys went on their honeymoon.

Discussions around the selection for the 1920 Olympic team were largely free of controversy, except when they concerned Thomas Sinton Hewitt. The former sergeant was not, by nature, a low-key personality. Even his choice of athletic event – the marathon – had the distinguishing feature of 'epic' about it. Hewitt recorded some good performances in the longer distance runs in England, and he had no real rivals in Australia. He emerged as Australia's best selection for the marathon in Antwerp, despite claims from other athletes in Sydney who considered themselves better runners, and were a little less zealous in the way they went about it. Hewitt's rivals wrote to the papers, protesting that he was too slow and advancing their own claims on the basis of quicker times. But Hewitt, as always, put his faith in his own performance. He lowered the national record for 20 miles by two minutes and 38 seconds, a record that had stood since 1908. And although there was still a marathon race left on the calendar, it seemed that Hewitt 's selection was inevitable and that the team for Antwerp was already picked. By 29 April, it was official. There were 13 athletes named in the Australian team – covering swimming, track and field, cycling, rowing and tennis, including Frank Beaurepaire and Thomas Sinton Hewitt, who was set to compete in the Olympic marathon. But the drama didn't quite end there. The original plan was for each sporting association to recommend athletes to the Australian Olympic Council for selection. The Council picked the team, but the number of athletes it sent depended on how much money had been raised to pay for it.

Oddly, the Victorian Amateur Athletic Association hadn't nominated any Victorian athlete, not even Hewitt. Yet, by April 1920, the Victorian arm of the Olympic Council had raised £1200 to cover costs. Once the team was announced, Hewitt let the Association know that he could not afford to go unless it paid for him. It remains a mystery who selected Hewitt – but most likely it was the Australian Olympic Council, rather than the Victorian Amateur Athletic Association, which finished up paying for his trip to Antwerp. It was a bizarre prelude to the Games.

What compounded the selection cloud that hovered over Hewitt was his withdrawal from the marathon in Melbourne, which went from Frankston in the south-east to the Wesley College Oval on St Kilda Road. Hewitt was going to use the race as a final training run and had planned to break the Victorian and Australian records for the distance, but he developed cramps at the 31-kilometre mark and abandoned the bid. There were only six men left in the field. Hewitt's withdrawal suggested he was running too much, always trying to prove himself, while increasing his physical vulnerability with every race. At least there would be some respite before the Games.

Antwerp was a terrible Olympic destination, but it had been awarded the Games for the best possible motive: to provide support and recognition for a devastated nation. The weather was cold, the facilities spartan, the competition more optimistic than eye-catching. It was remarkable that Belgium had the energy and resources to stage any sort of event so soon after the war – except the rebuilding was not complete, and there were problems for the athletes.

The Americans almost mutinied when they learnt their accommodation was in a schoolhouse, and the impoverished Australians opted for a castle out of the city and food hampers from home. Beaurepaire was accompanied by his sister Lily, who was co-opted as a swimmer and diver before the team reached Antwerp. Frank Beaurepaire qualified for the final of the 1500 metres but was well beaten by Ross and relegated to the bronze medal. Beaurepaire also made it to the final of the 400 metres but collapsed with exhaustion after the third lap and didn't finish. He did, however, collect silver in the 800-metre team race, which included Bill Herald and Harry Hay from New South Wales, and Ivan Stedman of Victoria. The revelation of the Olympics was the 100-metre gold medallist, Hawaiian Duke Kahanamoku, who used a new kick pattern to change freestyle forever. The Australian crawl that Beaurepaire had been such a successful exponent of was about to become history.

Hewitt's campaign got off to a bad start and never recovered. He took part in a London road race on his way to Antwerp and was caught up in a group of runners who took a wrong turn on the course. They had gone 32 kilometres before the error was discovered and the race was abandoned. His first event at the Games was the 10,000 metres on the fifth day of competition, but he retired after halfway. The winner was the Finnish long-distance legend Paavo Nurmi, who made his Olympic debut in Antwerp.

Hewitt's retirement might have been motivated by thoughts of the marathon in several days, where the long-distance special-ist perhaps stood the best chance of a medal. The 1920 marathon had two distinct features. One was that it started at 4 pm in cool, wet conditions, which was a first for the Olympic marathon, which had previously been held in hotter, drier temperatures.

It augured well for quick times and it suited Hewitt because it was like a Melbourne spring or autumn day. The second element was that it was the longest of Olympic marathons, measuring 42.75 kilometres.

Hewitt was one of 48 runners in the field. He started well but the Stockholm silver medallist Christian Gitsham went to the front early. Gitsham was a South African who had trained thoroughly on the Antwerp course in the preceding weeks. He made good pace but was soon joined by another Finnish runner, Hannes Kolehmainen. Together, they pushed on for another 13 kilometres before Gitsham started to lose touch with the Finn. A storm hit the runners and Hewitt, some distance behind the leaders, suffered a chill of sorts, which he never recovered from. Gitsham tore a shoe and then retired while Hewitt slipped further back.

Kolehmainen ran effortlessly. He had won three gold medals in Stockholm but not the marathon gold. In Antwerp, he crossed the line 70 metres in front, and with a record time of two hours, 32 minutes and 35 seconds, shattering the Olympic record by four minutes. Hewitt came in three minutes beyond the three-hour mark and in 30th place. That was the end of Hewitt's international athletic career.

Beaurepaire went around again, in Paris for the 1924 Olympics, but if there was one change already obvious by the end of 1920, it was the realisation that sport had evolved too – something more than just talent was required to win. The notion of the gifted amateur was all very well, but the technical changes in swimming and the evolving practice routines for track and field meant there was more required from each athlete to reach their peak. It would take many years for it to become fully 'professional' in the supposedly amateur Olympic environment, but the early manifestation of the trend was there in Antwerp. The war's profound legacy started to crack and shift the conventions of amateur sport.

Epilogue

There was nothing predictable about what happened to the other players from the 1916 Exhibition match once they came home. Most of them tried to re-establish their lives. They wanted the comfort of routine and the quietness of a life free from lethal threat, a regular night's sleep, half-decent food, a smoke and a drink, clean clothes and the vista of peace when the sun came up. The war's ugly trade-off with its survivors was that all those aspirations were possible, but there were no guarantees that the survivors were in any state to achieve it.

Several of the 1916 players, such as Carl Willis, carried physical and emotional burdens. Jack Brake, probably one of the finest footballers of his era and a gifted all-round athlete, started a career in the public service and eventually became superintendent at the Victorian Department of Agriculture. But for years he was troubled by impaired hearing, which he told the Repatriation Commission was the legacy of the constant pounding of the guns he worked with on the Western Front. The Commission, however, wasn't convinced. And Brake wasn't done with serving his country. He signed up again for the Second World War and resumed as a reservist, commanding the Melbourne University Rifles. Unlike the old days, recruits were closely assessed during their training. Brake had a lot to offer, but new soldiers on the block had some misgivings. 'Average. Rather slow especially at assimilating new ideas and a little inclined to harp back to the last war,' his training officer noted. 'Very sound and a strong personality. A good commander of men. Capable, hard working and very trustworthy. Has learned a lot in the course.' Harp back to the last war? Who wouldn't, after all they'd seen and done? Brake did, however, retain a connection to football: for more than 20 years, he chaired the VFL Tribunal.

Percy Trotter returned to Western Australia and worked his way through the Lumpers, or stevedores' union, which became, over time, the Waterside Workers Federation of Australia. He showed the same nimble approach to union politics as he did on the football field, becoming president of the union in 1935. It was through the union that he met the federal MP for Fremantle, John Curtin, whom he helped during several election campaigns that ultimately led Curtin to the Lodge. Curtin was a football fan but deferred to Trotter on his trips to Melbourne. In a nod to the past, Trotter always insisted Curtin go to Brunswick Street Oval to watch Fitzroy. Trotter took up umpiring after he retired from playing football. He was named on the interchange bench of Fitzroy's team of the twentieth century.

Hughie James left the building trade and went to work for a New Zealand manufacturer of raincoats and waterproof goods. In 1931, he and the family relocated to New Zealand, where he finished up managing the business. He occasionally came back to Melbourne, and watched Richmond play. He was rarely persuaded to pass remark on his wartime activities and his football career.

Dan Minogue's coaching career took him from Richmond to Hawthorn, Carlton, St Kilda and Fitzroy – an unparalleled record. But his peak was coaching Richmond to consecutive flags in 1920–21. He never returned to Collingwood, even if the club eventually reconciled itself to his departure and finally gave him the honoured place in its history that he was due. In 1996, he was inducted into the AFL Hall of Fame.

Frank Beaurepaire had one more Olympics in him. He captained the Australian swimming team at the 1924 Paris Games, and, at the age of 34, won silver in the 4 x 200-metre relay, and bronze behind Andrew Boy Charlton in the 1500 metres. He started his own tyre business, which became the basis of a fortune and a family dynasty. He was Melbourne lord mayor, knighted in 1942, and then a state politician who, appropriately enough, won the province of Monash, named after the general who had entrusted the 3rd Division's entertainment and recreation to him. Beaurepaire was a tireless champion of Melbourne's successful bid to host the 1956 Olympics but died earlier that year. As the doctors had warned years before, his heart was a problem no one could fix.

Thomas Sinton Hewitt managed the Australia picture theatre in Collingwood when he returned to Melbourne. His running career ebbed away and he never again ran the boundary line in a football match, although at the age of 35 he harboured hopes of getting selected for the 1924 Paris Olympics. He took part in the marathon trial but was unsuccessful. Hewitt relocated and managed the New Werribee Theatre, then moved to Geelong where he died in 1976, aged 88.

On the first anniversary of Jimmy Foy's death, his widow, Elsie, placed a notice in the 'In Memoriam' column of *The West Australian*. Events moved quickly after that. Jimmy's mother, Nora, wrote to the authorities in 1920 to correct the impression that Elsie was her son's next of kin. Mrs Foy said she hadn't seen her daughter-in-law since her son went overseas four years earlier and requested if it was possible to have Jimmy's memorial scroll sent to her. Elsie had remarried and given birth four months after she tied the knot for the second time, according to Mrs Foy. It was not an uncommon story. What else was a young widow to do?

After the Exhibition match, George Barry seemed to disappear. There are no records of any military service or indeed any evidence of George's activities anywhere. But he was overdue some quiet time. He bobbed up years later in Sefton, in New South Wales, working as a caretaker. He declared himself a 'returned man' but didn't speak publicly about his war service. He lived with his sister Mary in Sefton, and never married. He died from a range of ailments, including pneumonia, on 15 December 1959, at the age of 72. The Exhibition match in London is believed to be the last game he umpired.

Charles Perry always believed in combining faith and football. 'Some people think, especially church people, that football is really outside the pale. It lowers one's dignity, they think, and is not a fit and proper pastime for one who is a minister,' he said years later. 'Surely one can carry his Christianity with him, in his life. Is it so hard to be a Christian in a game? The closer I got to my fellow players, the easier they found it, and I found it, to converse on subjects other than football.' The war sparked in him a desire to keep offering comfort to Australian troops. When the Second World War started, he joined up and became senior chaplain to the Australian forces in the Middle East. On his return, he was the first full-time chaplain at Adelaide's Prince Alfred College.

In August 1921, George Foster Pearce was a guest at a dinner in Melbourne for the West Australian Goldfields team that was playing against the VFA. The Scullin boys were from the Goldfields, and Pearce had connections over there from his time prospecting as a young man. Pearce told the audience that much of what the AIF achieved was attributable to Australians being, at heart, sportsmen. And football was a healthy and manly sport that helped character development. By the time he released his memoirs in 1951, Australia was involved in the Korean War. Pearce again criticised spectator sport and, in the book's conclusion, once more advocated compulsory military service. The

Menzies government agreed with Pearce. Sir Robert Menzies said of the former Defence minister that he had never sat around the Cabinet table with an 'abler man'.

Tullie Sloss kept circling the globe, a peripatetic soul who never seemed to find home after she left Australia. Her work in the United States was discreet and, by the standards of the day, remarkable: she cared for the babies of Hollywood movie stars who fell pregnant at the wrong time to the wrong man. Tullie cared for the baby until the star was able to assume the role and adopt the baby. Not a word of who she worked for was ever divulged.

In time, she developed the same facility with the needle and thread her mother had shown, and made dolls' clothes for a silent movie star. Later, she would spend 16 hours a day turning out exquisite costumes made from evening-wear cut-offs sent to her by a former movie star before sending them off to charities. Tullie paid for her mother and sister May to visit her in the USA in 1925 but she didn't return to Melbourne to live until 1939. She was engaged for a time but never married. She moved in with Roy and their sisters Mary and Margaret after Christina died.

Tullie occasionally helped James, who ran a motor coach business, a safe haven from the memories of his time as a POW. Tullie was 93 when she slipped on a tram step and broke her hip. It was the beginning of the end, and her health quickly deteriorated. She had already made a deep impression on the next Sloss generation, who found her large personality vaguely intimidating and imperious. The house that was built for Bruce and Gladys is still home to a generation of the Sloss family.

Donald Mackinnon was given the job of coordinating the soldier settlement scheme in Victoria, and he worked with such urgency and effectiveness that 4000 returned men were settled within 15 months. But he lost his parliamentary seat in 1920, and although he unsuccessfully tried to enter federal politics, he eventually decided on a quiet life, occupying a number of voluntary positions, free from honours and decorations. He died in 1932, favourably remembered as a voice of reason and compassion during the conscription debates.

Munro Ferguson stayed on in his vice-regal role with an extension that enabled him to be involved in the Prince of Wales's visit to Australia in 1920. Impatience with some of his more high-handed ways of dealing with the state governments soured the experience towards the end, but he remained fond of Australia. His independent approach again crippled his political ambitions in London when he was dropped from Stanley Baldwin's government after two years as secretary for Scotland. Nonetheless, the time away from public life gave Munro Ferguson (ennobled as Lord Novar) the opportunity to wander among the landscape of his Scots homeland.

Billy Hughes displayed remarkable political survival instincts. He represented Australia at the 1919 Paris peace conference with a performance that so antagonised US President Woodrow Wilson that Wilson referred to him as 'a pestiferous varmint'. This display of will, wit and strategic gall played out on the world stage breathed more oxygen into Hughes's career, although he had to step aside for Stanley Melbourne Bruce to lead the next conservative Australian government. Hughes remained a potent political player, leading the United Australia Party in 1941 and then becoming an MP for the Liberal Party that Menzies established in 1949. It was a tumultuous political career, but Hughes was never one to shirk an argument or tug a forelock. National interest was his first defence. But for many who started their political journey with Hughes and watched him veer up and down the snakes and ladders of the political game, he remained a rat, all cunning and no loyalty. History has been kinder to him.

Gerald Brosnan resumed his sports-writing career with *The Sun News-Pictorial*, where he wrote commentary in the same fearless style he used at *The Winner.* He weighed in to the VFL when it put up admission prices in much the same way as he had years earlier. 'There is already more money in the game than is good for it. Extra revenue will mean increased payments to players, thereby fomenting jealousies and inflating suspicions that are doing a great deal of harm.' Player payments – it was a perennial problem.

If you take a walk along Honour Avenue in Kings Park, Perth, you will come across three small crosses bearing the Scullin name. Daniel, Patrick and John are commemorated there, in a simple tribute to the brothers who never made it home.

Carl Willis had every right to expect his cricketing fortunes would be bound up with the success of the AIF team. Six of the team – including the all-rounder Jack Gregory and wicketkeeper Bill Oldfield – would form part of the first postwar Australian Ashes team, in 1920–21. It would win the Ashes in Australia and then dominate England in the return series in England in 1921. But for all his success in 1919 – and the expectations that went with it – Willis experienced an inexplicable loss of form and couldn't make a case to be considered for the Test team. He barely scored a run for Victoria in the matches leading up to the first Test of the 1920–21 Ashes series, and his form never recovered. Willis was dropped from the state side before the end of the season. He was made South Melbourne captain for the 1921 VFL season but the team struggled and finished seventh out of nine teams. At the end of the season, Willis announced his retirement. He was 28 – not old for the game, but his powers, and his fitness, were fading. Willis kept playing grade cricket, captaining a strong Prahran side containing his AIF mate Allie Lampard and, for a while, leg spinner and Test legend Clarrie Grimmett, to the district cricket premiership in three consecutive seasons.

He made sporadic appearances for Victoria over the years, before his final appearance against South Australia in Adelaide in November 1928. There was a brief renaissance, when Willis hit 133 in Sydney for 'The Rest' against an Australian XI, in a benefit match. Willis also played several invitation games, most notably in Canberra in 1928 when leg-spinning cartoonist Arthur Mailey convened a team called 'The Bohemians' for a match against a combined Canberra side. Not surprisingly, Mailey picked fellow cartoonist and the creator of Ginger Meggs, Jimmy Bancks, in the team, alongside Willis and a young man from Bowral called Donald Bradman, who had been making a name for himself in New South Wales. It was the first and only time Willis played with Bradman, who did not make his Test debut until the following summer. Willis opened the batting and made nine. Bradman came in at number four and was out for seven. The Bohemians, perhaps displaying a little too much of the bohemian spirit, folded and lost by 20 runs.

Willis had a dental practice in Malvern but in April 1929 he retired from all sport and moved to Numurkah, in northern Victoria, to carry on his dentistry. Still single, and mobile because of it, Willis then moved north-east to Tocumwal, just over the New South Wales border, where he emerged from premature (cricket) retirement to captain Tocumwal, played the occasional match with Jerilderie, and even took all ten wickets in one innings and made 67 not out in an all-round performance that had the locals talking for weeks.

It was perhaps a throwback to his childhood in rural Daylesford that kept Carl searching for a small town that he could call home. As part of his dentistry practice, he travelled around the Tocumwal district and in early May 1930 was in Berrigan when he became ill with what appeared to be influenza. Willis was too sick to be moved and was kept at Berrigan. The news reached Willis's brother Jack, who was a doctor in Mount Gambier. Willis's younger brother Alan was working in Papua New Guinea, and while both his parents were alive, in Melbourne, his father had been unwell, so Jack was the only relative who could get to Carl.

Dr Willis approached a local pilot to fly him to Berrigan. The plane was at Terang in Victoria when the call came through on Sunday morning, 11 May, but the pilot flew to Mount Gambier, picked up Dr Willis and was in the air again at 9 am, heading for Berrigan. But the weather was rough and the flying difficult. Instead of going over the Grampians to New South Wales, the pilot flew around the mountains, taking up precious time. They stopped at Echuca, just 70 miles from their destination, and spent Sunday night there. Three times they tried to leave Echuca the next day, but the weather was too bad each time. In the end, the mercy mission proved fruitless – Carl Willis deteriorated quickly and died late on the Sunday, before his brother arrived. Dr Willis got to Berrigan in time to help arrange his brother's funeral, to be held in Melbourne.

Although Carl Willis was believed to have died from influenza complications, the family thought the damage the gas did to his lungs in 1917 haunted his health from then on. His AIF paperwork only gives a rudimentary insight into the effect of the gas – ten days in hospital. But perhaps the most telling decision was that, once Willis was released from hospital, he was sent straight to the Dental Corps. He never saw action again. Some who were gassed were not so lucky as to have a profession to fall back on, but dentistry might well have saved Willis, for a time at least.

At the Victorian Cricket Association meeting held after Willis's death, association president Donald Mackinnon asked members to stand for two minutes in Willis's memory. The pallbearers at his funeral included his old Wesley mate – and University and Victorian cricket teammate – Roy Park, and fellow cricketers Allie Lampard and E.J. 'Chappie' Dwyer. The sporting fraternity, once again, came out to honour one of its own.

Willis's rapid promotion during the war to lieutenant caused his local paper to comment, 'He left Melbourne as a private, but a University education coupled with unswerving loyalty, inexhaustible energy and all-round capability that comes of devotion to athletics, were responsible for his rapid advancement . . .' It was a resilient view of success at the time – a good education, solid character and a commitment to exercise were the ingredients for a virtuous life. None of them, however, could protect anyone from the vile legacies of the war itself. Willis died at 37, another life cut short among the thousands of men who survived the war to come home to confront a drastically changed existence – a personal world inhabited by visions of hell that never went away, and encased in bodies that could never do what they used to.

The impetus for keeping the details of the Exhibition match alive fell to an unlikely source: the man who made the match footballs, Claude McMullen. He helped with the occasional story, detailing some of the events of the day, which appeared sporadically in the Melbourne press. McMullen also kept a stash of the distinctive jumpers in his house. But after he died, the jumpers, like many souvenirs, were lost. A rallying call for players from the match to get in touch with *The Sporting Globe* lured a few men to reflect again on the game, including 'Bill' Cesari, who was a trainer at South Melbourne at the time, Percy Jory, who became an umpire when he returned to Melbourne, and Harold Moyes, who was also in the 3rd Division team.

'If we could only turn back the years I'd go so far as to say it was the best team ever,' Moyes said. It was the one element of the match that remained constant in the players' recollection – the quality of the game, and the high standard of the players who took part. Years later, the men who played were singled out in various histories of Australian football for what they did on that day in London. The game became something remarkable and the players pioneers in their own way.

It didn't take long for people to forget how vitriolic the campaign to recruit sportsmen had been. The pressure exerted on them, and especially footballers, during the First World War was left to quietly slide away. It was replaced by a version of history that proved more resilient, arguably because it was more palatable. As early as 1931, *The Sporting Globe* in Melbourne was publishing a story headlined 'Sportsmen Lent Dash to the Ranks of the AIF – Champions Quick to Respond to Call'. The front-page story read:

> It was only to be expected that when the call came to Australia to stake 'the last man and the last shilling' in the great war, there should be a bold and ready response from her sportsmen, including hundreds of those who reached the pinnacle of popular fame in cricket, football, tennis, boxing, rowing and all the other games.

Perhaps it was just the inevitable passage of time that allowed the sting and spite to be leached from the picture, like a faded photograph, leaving only a hazy outline of what really happened. Or then again, it was perhaps the understanding that sportsmen did indeed respond promptly and that those agitators years earlier had misjudged them.

Inevitably, the war swept dozens of talented footballers from the game. Some who had served their country returned to football but many were physically and emotionally changed by the war experience. The game's development was hermetically sealed from major changes during the war, and it took some years before football recovered its dash and poise. But the triumph of football in Australia during the war was that the game played on.

Rugby union, the amateur game, was shut down in New South Wales, and so many of its players enlisted, ceding the ground to the working-class rugby league. It took until the late 1920s for union to recover the players and patronage it lost during the war. But Australian Rules still had a core of players and supporters, many of them from working-class suburbs. It reached a farcical low-point in 1916, but the VFL, in particular, never surrendered its place in the state's calendar or in its emotions. It is highly likely that football would have survived anyway, even if all the main competitions ceased, but its future would have been more unpredictable, and its capacity to resist the eruption of social changes that followed the war might have been compromised. Instead, the national game underlined its deep connections to its origins by its very continuity at the time of its greatest challenge. The game had a role to play as entertainment and diversion, just as its supporters claimed at the time.

It is entirely appropriate now to see those men who took part in the Exhibition match as footballers first and soldiers second. It was football that linked them. Their military service gave them an opportunity to play the game somewhere else and in different conditions. But, of course, being a soldier was their inescapable daily duty. That was why the Exhibition match was a contest that captured the players' imagination: it was about a time when the result of a game mattered. Notions of winning and losing were redundant when life was precious. Football was the light relief that made the confronting issues of life and death momentarily tolerable; it helped banish the sights of torn-apart men and lost lives, broken minds and shattered families. In that circumstance, football became the most powerful fraternity of all.

Yet it wasn't just the oppressive mortal threat that the footballers defied; it was the public clamouring before they left home to enlist and do their duty, which compromised footballers' enjoyment and made the idea of playing the game so contested. They were fit men with a physical ability, and that was part of what supposedly made a good soldier. Australians were 'a race of athletes', according to the mythmakers, and footballers had an obligation to prove it. Footballers understood teamwork too, and soldiers needed that kind of cooperation to achieve success in battle.

Some of it, of course, was misguided mythology, hatched in the early days of the war when the nation was struggling to find itself, desperately keen to help the Empire, and hoping the best specimens were in khaki. As the war became the awful burden at home – and a grinding mess of death and mayhem at the Front – it was obvious that footballers, and any sportsmen, were not more or less valuable than any other recruit.

The footballers themselves, of course, already knew that. The pigskin fraternity were pragmatists. They were not taken in by any cockeyed notions of being special or a race apart. They were just blokes who played footy. But they did feel football gave them something nothing else did; it connected them all to a landscape of innocence, where there were no trenches, mortars, tanks or endless vistas of mud. And it was an Australian game, distinctive, unique and their own. It was a simple reminder of home. For one day in 1916, there was a time again to feel the thrill of it, the running, jumping, kicking and tackling. And for that one day, those soldiers became footballers again. None of them could know what lay ahead in the Western Front, but, for all of them, it proved to be the game of their lives.

Acknowledgements

A project like this inevitably relies on extensive cooperation with the families of those who are at the centre of the story. But it was a long time ago and the direct connections to the men who played in the 1916 Exhibition match are diminishing. Nonetheless, there were many relatives who were tremendously helpful. I'm indebted to John Sloss, who was unfailingly polite and always helpful, despite some very trying personal circumstances he was dealing with at the time. The end result is immeasurably better for his cooperation and for the opportunity to tell the Sloss story. I also want to thank relatives of other men: Ken McInnes, Helen Blanckensee, Peter Cesari, the De Crespigney family, the Lester family, Susan Mack, the Morgan family, Jan Coffey, Janet and Richard Willis, Ken James, Peter Couzens and Jennifer McMullen.

There were, in addition, a range of researchers who pointed me in the right direction: Col Hutchinson at the AFL; Greg Wardell-Johnston, Perth football historian; Anne-Marie Conde at the National Archives of Australia; Mairead Foley, Catholic Archdiocese of Perth; Tom Reynolds at the State Records Office in Western Australia; Annette Shiell at the Royal Agricultural Society of Victoria; Melinda Clarke at the Friends School; Margot Vaughan at Wesley College; Alex Browne at Trinity in

Cambridge; Baden Pratt, Andrew Pittaway and Wayne Koch in Perth; Michael Roberts at Collingwood; Steve Howell and Tim Lethorn at the State Library of Western Australia; Fred Pratt at RSL Victoria; David Studham at the MCC Library, and Katie Wood at the University of Melbourne archives. Alf Batchelder and John Richardson provided information at vital times.

Tackling this subject during the centenary of the First World War meant that I was lucky enough to stand on the shoulders of some new research that made my work so much easier, so hats off to Barb Cullen, for her exhaustive (and, I suspect, exhausting) book on VFL footballers who served in all Australia's wars. And Michael Coligan, Trevor Gyss and Ian Granland, whose work was extremely helpful. And although I have never met Lenore Frost, her terrific local history website (The Empire Called and I Answered) helped illuminate some of my research. Other researchers, Bruce Coe and Les Everett, also provided important information, while Graeme Haigh was a tremendous help in tracking down and making sense of family trees that took root across states and countries. Michael Molkentin's work on the training units in England was important and helped me make sense of what had been a somewhat mystifying part of the story.

It's important to note that projects such as this have to start somewhere, and Dale Blair's work, particularly around football in the First World War, deserves special mention. David Allen and Jim Main's *The Fallen* broke new ground when it was published and was the starting point for some of the research in this book.

One of the great assets for researchers is the digitised archives that enable us to find material so easily. I well remember my fishing expeditions in the National Library of Australia 20 years ago, hunting through sometimes imperfect microfilm. Trove has thankfully made that just a memory, and the NLA's decision to digitise many smaller newspapers from the First World War era was a huge help to my research. Any Federal Government attempt to cut funding to the NLA and Trove is a bone-headed piece of misplaced parsimony. No matter how good the material, researchers still need guidance and I was fortunate to find expert help at the NLA, the Australian War Memorial, the NAA and the State Library of Victoria when required. None of this would have been in clear view, however, without Richard Lindsay's expert help.

I'm particularly grateful to John Rosling at British Pathé, who was keen to help with identifying and accessing the original film footage of the Exhibition match. A version of the film, with some different edits, also exists at the National Film and Sound Archive in Australia. Zsuzsi Szucs, with Simon Smith, at the NFSA were also very cooperative in helping me access the Australian film version.

My history mentor June Senyard was once again enlisted to help with this, and I'd like to thank her for her willingness to keep an eye on a former student's progress. She was once again penetrating in her observations and the book is better for her learned eye. And my apologies if I still haven't answered some of those questions! One of the other fellow-travellers in the sports history area – Rob Hess – deserves special mention for supporting my early steps in the field. And Michael McKernan's enthusiasm to read a draft of the work was a massive vote of confidence in the project. Michael's own research over many years touches several key themes of this book, so his response to the draft significantly sharpened and enlightened the final version.

The whole project really wouldn't have started without Peter Blunden, the Victorian managing director of editorial at News Corp, and Damon Johnston, the editor of the *Herald Sun*, asking me to coordinate the *Herald Sun*'s centenary coverage of the First World War. Without that invitation and act of faith, I wouldn't have turned up the story of the Exhibition match. Once I had, there were several people within the building who helped its progress: Patrick Carlyon (for also standing in for me during a TV interview on the topic), and Andrew Rule, who has been the soul of common sense and writing wisdom. And a special thanks to Glenn McFarlane, who was on a similar journey with his own project and has always been interested in the Exhibition match. Robert Moseley helped me when this project's life was still confined to newspaper pages.

Jacinta DiMase is a delightful agent to have, and I'm glad we have a stress-free working association. At Pan Macmillan, Angus Fontaine has been a publisher and journo rolled into one, which, after all my time in journalism, makes me feel very secure. Alex Lloyd is an editor blessed with an ocean of patience, a keen eye and quiet persistence. It just makes the process of actually finishing a book so much easier. While Kevin O'Brien was an empathetic and measured copy editor, who, thankfully, saved me when I lost my way.

Closest to home, Sue Westwood has put up with some crankiness, and I relied on her cups of tea and home-baked biscuits to effectively soothe the savage lurking in the bungalow at the bottom of the garden. Her last-minute work on the endnotes made my life significantly easier. That's, of course, only part of the story of her constant support. And Patrick's frequent checking on my progress was a reminder that, although I was doing it, this was a project we all had a stake in.

The book is dedicated to my grandfather, Private Charles Henry White, who was wounded at Gallipoli and invalided home. I was privileged to have known him and, towards the end of his life, hear his stories. Without him, the inspiration for *The Game of Their Lives* would have never existed.

Endnotes

Prologue

Page
2. 'There had been numerous attempts . . .': Leonie Sandercock and Ian Turner, *Up Where Cazaly?*, p. 69.
2. 'Alfred Deakin told an audience . . .': Rob Hess, Matthew Nicholson, Bob Stewart and Gregory De Moore, *A National Game*, p. 147.
5. 'Attentive . . . industrious . . .': Sloss family archive, personal reference for Bruce Sloss, 30 June 1909.
5. 'Visiting warriors . . .': *The Sydney Sportsman*, 5 August 1914, p. 7.
6. 'Exercise, for the King's Man . . .': Chris Cunneen, *The King's Men*, pp. 107–9.
7. 'We have been to the Races . . .': Lord Novar Papers, letter to Colonial Secretary Lewis Harcourt, 7 June 1914.
7. 'If any part of what one hears . . .': Ibid.
9. 'It is impossible to conduct business . . .': Lord Novar Papers, letter to Colonial Secretary Lewis Harcourt, 2 August 1914.
11. 'The Government is full of zeal . . .': Ibid.
12. '[W]ith the notification that war had been declared . . .': *The Argus*, 6 August 1914, p. 9.

1: Where it Began

Page
17. 'In time, there would be plenty . . .': Hugh Anderson, *The Rise and Fall of Squizzy Taylor, Larrikin Crook*, pp. 12–14; *The Argus*, 8 January 1913, p. 13; *The Age*, 8 January 1913, p. 9; *The Argus*, 21 February 1913, p. 7.
18. 'At a big circus show . . .': John Devaney, 'Percy Trotter', www.australian football.com.

18. 'The one system that tells . . .': *Daily News* (Perth), 13 June 1911, p. 2.

19. 'Dejected. Delusion that he is unclean . . .': Case book of male patients, Victorian Public Records Office, VPRO/VPRS 7398/P0001/22.

20. '[I]t was his custom to count . . .': *The West Australian*, 8 January 1913.

20. 'My wife and I had always lived carefully . . .': John Connor, *Anzac and Empire*, pp. 2–9.

21. 'He was buffeted from side to side . . .': Commonwealth Parliamentary Debates, 7 November 1907, p. 5683.

21. 'Our White Australia legislation . . .': Ibid.

22. 'For every hundred youths . . .': Ibid.

23. 'Football playing – and watching . . .': Geoffrey Blainey, *A History of Victoria*, pp. 79–80.

23. 'Absentee numbers were often large . . .': *The Essendon Gazette and Keilor, Bulla and Broadmeadows Reporter*, 4 June 1914.

24. 'His uncle George . . .': John Barrett, *Falling In*, p. 201.

24. 'Hard to pass the Collingwood football ground': Dale Blair, 'Beyond the metaphor: football and war, 1914–1918', *Journal of the Australian War Memorial*, Issue 28, April 1996, www.awm.gov.au/journal.

24. 'It does not follow . . .': *The Essendon Gazette and Keilor, Bulla and Broadmeadows Reporter*, 12 March 1914, p. 6.

24. 'I would have looked upon [training] . . .': Ibid.

25. 'He said he didn't know much . . .': *Daily News* (Perth), 16 October 1913, p. 10; *The West Australian*, 17 October 1913, p. 11.

26. 'Not surprisingly, the umpire . . .': Ross McMullin, 'Heyday of the larrikin spectator', in John Ross (ed), *100 Years of Australian Football*, p. 99.

26. 'It is being pointed out . . .': *The Winner*, 23 June 1915, p. 7.

26. 'No one objects to a strenuous game . . .': Leonie Sandercock and Ian Turner, *Up Where Cazaly?*, pp. 62–3.

26. 'The umpiring task was already difficult . . .': Blainey, *A Game of Our Own*, pp. 179–180.

27. 'Umpiring my first few games . . .': *The Sporting Globe*, 14 September 1935, p. 7.

27. 'Why? Simply because . . .': *The Geraldton Guardian*, 8 June 1911, p. 1.

28. 'There is no doubt about his impartiality . . .': *Goomalling-Dowerin Mail*, 7 June 1912, p. 4.

28. 'The reporter backed Barry . . .': *Goomalling-Dowerin Mail*, 5 July 1912, p. 3.

29. 'Barry continued to complain . . .': *Goomalling-Dowerin Mail*, 2 August 1912, p. 3.

29. 'If Barry wishes a recommendation . . .': *Goomalling-Dowerin Mail*, 6 September 1912, p. 1.

30. 'His improvement continued . . .': West Australian State Archives Cons 752, file 760/1914 (George Barry).

31. 'Did the actions of the accused . . .': *Daily News* (Perth), 10 March 1914, p. 10.

31. 'The only way to deal with it . . .': *The West Australian*, 11 March 1914, p. 10.
31. 'You are no more mad . . .': *Daily News* (Perth), 26 March 1914, p. 5.
32. '[I] am only 23 . . .': West Australian State Archives Cons 752, file 760/1914 (George Barry).
32. 'I do not think [he] has criminal inclinations . . .': Ibid.
33. 'It is a great pity . . .': Ibid. (letter, 16 July 1914).
33. 'A warm welcome awaits you . . .': *The Weekly Times*, 19 September 1914, p. 33.
34. 'All the adventurous roving natures . . .': C.E.W. Bean, *Official History of Australia in the War of 1914–18, Vol. I*, p. 43.
34. 'What is the good of games . . .': *The Pastoral Review*, quoted in Michael McKernan, *The Australian People and the Great War*, p. 98.
35. 'But the working class saw sport . . .': See McKernan, *The Australian People and the Great War*, for more detail, pp. 94–115.
36. 'Sports lessons for character development . . .': Martin Crotty, *Making the Australian Male*, pp. 80–1.
36. 'It was true in the British Army . . .': Tony Mason and Eliza Riedi, *Sport and the Military*, p. 83.
37. 'His salary was an exceptional . . .': *The Australasian*, 18 April 1905, p. 37.
38. 'A brilliant footballer . . .': *Wesley Chronicle*, Michaelmas term, 1908, p. 29.
38. 'A great Public School was not complete . . .': *The Argus*, 14 September 1908.
39. 'It sparked a minor kerfuffle . . .': *The Argus*, 3 September 1909, p. 9.
40. 'In December 1910, Martin sat examinations . . .': Student archive, Stanley Carlton Martin, University of Melbourne.

2: The Believers
Page
46. 'I have wandered over many parts . . .': Christina Ellen 'Tullie' Sloss, diary, Sloss family archive, p. 6.
47. 'When tired and weary . . .': Ibid.
47. 'Home to Christmas – minus its spirit . . .': Ibid., p. 7.
49. 'You freak! . . .': Ibid., p. 18.
50. 'On the same evening as hearing . . .': *The Argus*, 2 July 1910, p. 19.
51. 'Willis's representative at the hearing . . .': *The Age*, 23 May 1912, p. 8.
52. 'Two years later . . .': 'A Riot on the "G"', *The Argus*, 9 August 1915, p. 8.
53. 'Troops in training could also use . . .': *The Argus*, 28 November 1914, p. 19.
53. 'To help the sturdy sons of Britain . . .': *Melbourne's Manhood*, Vol. 1, 25 June 1915, p. 1.
54. 'The opportunity of linking of men . . .': Ibid.
54. 'Even a debilitating bout of rheumatic fever . . .': Harry Gordon, *Australia and the Olympic Games*, p. 66; Graham Lomas, *The Will to Win*, p. 5.
55. 'If Frank had time to follow football . . .': Lomas, p. 12.
55. '[He] has plenty of football in him . . .': *Wesley College Chronicle*, 1909, p. 34.

55. 'He carried all before him . . .': Lomas, p. 35.

55. 'He had given up his amateur status . . .': Ibid., p. 44.

56. 'I remember him playing . . .': Perry family archive.

57. 'Most telling, though . . .': *The Observer* (Adelaide), 8 May 1909, p. 17.

57. 'A football association was established in Adelaide . . .': Rob Hess, Matthew Nicholson, Bob Stewart and Gregory De Moore, *A National Game*, p. 136.

57. 'Norwood's biggest rivals . . .': Hess et al., p. 137.

58. 'In 1888, Norwood defeated South Melbourne . . .': Mike Coward, *Men of Norwood*, p. 14.

59. 'If anyone has any reason to get wild . . .': *The Chronicle* (South Australia), 27 July 1912, p. 18.

59. 'One female fan became notorious . . .': *The Advertiser* (Adelaide), 17 July 1912, p. 8.

59. 'He had some other messages . . .': *The Register*, 22 July 1912, p. 5.

60. 'If they couldn't attend . . .': *The Advertiser* (Adelaide), 22 July 1912, p. 12.

60. 'If sport was "clean" . . .': *The Advertiser* (Adelaide), 18 February 1913, p. 18.

61. 'When a man failed in life . . .': *The Barrier Miner*, 7 July 1913, p. 5.

61. 'Why, that young minister must be . . .': *The South-Eastern Times*, 22 July 1913, p. 2.

62. 'Despite some desperate attempts . . .': *The Chronicle* (South Australia), 11 July 1914, p. 43.

62. 'But such was Norwood's respect . . .': Michael Coligan, *Norwood Men Who Served 1914–18*, p. 114.

62. 'En route on the SS *Katoomba* . . .': Meagan Dillon, 'From Perth Tour to the World War I Battlefront for Eight Norwood Football Club Players', *Eastern Courier Messenger*, 11 August 2014, www.news.com.au.

62. 'The military authorities recognised that football . . .': Coligan, p. 8.

63. 'It is understood that the authorities . . .': *Leader*, 26 September 1914, p. 19.

63. 'There was no doubt that . . .': Leonie Sandercock and Ian Turner, *Up Where Cazaly?*, pp. 94–5.

63. 'In April 1915, Melbourne approached . . .': University of Melbourne Sports Council Minutes, 28 April 1915.

64. 'Nine university players finished . . .': Alf Batchelder, *Playing the greater game: the Melbourne Cricket Club and its ground in World War I*, MP Publications, Brighton, 1998, pp. 71–72.

64. 'The committee huffed and puffed . . .': University Sports Council Minutes, 10 September 1915.

65. 'The MCC responded to the call . . .': Alf Batchelder, 'MCC Roll of Honour 1914–18', MCC research paper, MCC, 1998.

65. 'Within two weeks . . .': L.L Robson, *The First AIF*, pp. 28–9.

65. 'In consequence of the mobilisation of the troops . . .': *The Advertiser* (Adelaide), 13 August 1914, p. 9.

65. 'Ten days later, lacrosse . . .': *The Weekly Times*, 29 August 1914, p. 22.

66. 'Some well-known figures were absent . . .': *The Winner*, 26 August 1914, p. 8.

66. 'Silently, automatically . . .': *Saturday Referee and the Arrow*, 15 August 1914, p. 4.

67. 'Admirable admiration for the pluck of Belgium': *Daily News* (Perth), 9 April 1915, p. 7.

67. 'The football public . . .': *The Argus*, 11 September 1914, p. 5.

68. 'Lester Kelly, another old Wesleyan . . .': *The Argus*, 7 October 1914, p. 9.

3: Taking the Shilling

Page

70. 'We had sports at Rabaul recently . . .': Paul Macpherson and Ian Granland, *A Game to Be Played*, p. 9.

71. 'In his first political meeting . . .': *The Daily Standard*, 16 December 1916, p. 15.

71. 'Very little reflection will make us see . . .': *The Age*, 9 February 1915, p. 8.

72. 'This is a real opportunity . . .': *Woman Voter*, 5 July 1917, p. 2.

72. 'Forty years ago when I was your age . . .': Mackinnon family papers, State Library of Victoria, letter to Brice Bunny Mackinnon, 9 January 1917.

73. 'Mackinnon added that . . .': *Geelong Advertiser*, 11 February 1915, p. 3.

73. '[T]he captain had called . . .': *The Age*, 25 February 1915, p. 7.

73. 'Come along, be a man . . .': *The Argus*, 11 February 1915, p. 6.

74. 'There were a number of special . . .': Andrew Riddoch and John Kemp, *When the Whistle Blows*, p. 9.

74. 'The esprit de corps . . .': *Leader*, 20 February 1915, p. 19.

75. '[T]he players of field games . . .': *The Register*, 5 March 1915, p. 7.

75. 'There were estimates of 241 enlistments . . .': Ian Syson, 'Behind the Lines: Victorian Soccer and WWI', Football Federation Victoria, www.footballfed vic.com.au.

75. 'And the Victorian Amateur Swimming Association recorded . . .': *The Weekly Times*, 27 February 1915, p. 19.

75. 'The East Sydney athletics club . . .': Athletics Australia, 'The Greater Game', 24 April 2015, http://athletics.com.au.

75. 'By the end of September, 1100 men . . .': Murray G. Phillips, 'Sport, War and Gender Images: The Australian Sportsmen's Battalions and the First World War', *International Journal of the History of Sport*, Vol. 14. No. 1, March 2007, p. 79.

77. 'Unless it is regarded also as a moral training . . .': *The Argus*, 8 May 1911, p. 6.

77. '[A]s public school people . . .': *The Argus*, 22 April 1915, p. 5.

78. 'He was our wartime leader . . .': Brian Lewis, *Our War*, p. 209.

78. 'The general enlistment rate . . .': Dale Blair, 'War and Peace', in Rob Hess and Bob Stewart, *More than a Game*, p. 117.

79. 'The VFA wanted to talk about . . .': Blair, p. 118.

79. 'I thought I gave you to understand . . .': Bruce Sloss, letter to Tullie, 9 September 1914, Sloss family archive.

80. 'The reports came from British war correspondent . . .': Fred and Elizabeth Brenchley, *Myth Maker*, p. 85.

81. 'Recruitment figures jumped in May . . .': L.L. Robson, *The First AIF*, p. 9.

81. 'Who is the hero . . .': *The Argus*, 11 June 1915, p. 10.

81. '[Y]et at a time when more men were required . . .': *The Australasian*, 22 May 1915, p. 15.

82. 'The atmosphere in the dressing rooms . . .': *The Australasian*, 17 July 1915, p. 25.

82. 'Even Donald Mackinnon agreed . . .': Blair, p. 117.

83. 'I am in a convalescent home . . .': MCC Library, Anzac Day factsheet, April 2010.

84. 'Eventually, a doctor who saw Derrick . . .': *Richmond Guardian*, 9 June 1917, p. 2.

84. '"What irony! What a reply . . .': *Punch*, 22 April 1915, p. 42.

84. 'As casualties mounted, standards dropped': Michael Tyquin, 'Unjustly Accused? Medical Authorities and Army Recruitment in Australia 1914–1918', *Journal of Military and Veteran's Health*, Vol. 22, No. 2, June 2014, pp. 21–3.

84. 'The acting head of the Army Medical Services . . .': *The Argus*, 16 July 1915, p. 18.

84. 'Before Gallipoli, the League claimed . . .': *Geelong Advertiser*, 6 April 1915, p. 3.

85. 'People who go to football . . .': *The Argus*, 29 May 1915, p. 20.

85. 'No doubt many people . . .': *Geelong Advertiser*, 11 May 1915, p. 7.

85. 'The League dismissed the players' request . . .': *Kyabram Guardian*, 30 July 1915, p. 2.

86. 'Three weeks after winning the medal . . .': Trevor Gyss, *1915 South Australian Football and the First World War*, p. 202.

87. 'The Rugby Union footballers seem . . .': *The Referee*, 16 September 1914, p. 16.

87. 'It was a total commitment . . .': Waratahs, 'About Us: History: 1914–1919', www.waratahs.com.au.

89. 'He was his usual funny self . . .': Christina Ellen 'Tullie' Sloss, diary, Sloss family archive, p. 17.

89. 'It was quite a statement . . .': *The Argus*, 5 July 1915, p. 10.

89. '[T]his is intended as a reproof . . .': *Mercury*, 19 July 1915, p. 4.

89. 'The census identified 600,000 fit . . .': Joan Beaumont, *Broken Nation*, p. 147.

90. 'There was not any justification . . .': *The Winner*, 15 March 1916, p. 6.

90. 'All the players are men . . .': *The Argus*, 10 May 1915, p. 10.

90. 'McLennan was peeved . . .': Ibid.

91. 'It was felt that the playing of football . . .': Howard Kotton and Tony DeBolfo, 'Carlton, 1915', in Geoff Slattery, *Grand Finals, Vol. 1, 1897–1938*, pp. 190–1.

91. 'At a club event to farewell . . .': *Richmond Australian*, 25 September 1915, p. 3.

92. 'Treated very well . . .': Bruce Sloss, letter, 10 September 1915, Sloss family archive.

93. 'Hundreds [who] streamed into the members' reserve . . .': *The Australasian*, 11 September 1915.

93. 'When soldiers are misbehaving . . .': *The Age*, 25 October 1915, p. 13.

93. 'Local authorities in the aftermath . . .': Marilyn Lake, 'The Power of Anzac', in Michael McKernan and Margaret Browne, *Australia: Two Centuries of War and Peace*, pp. 194–222.

94. 'Unselfishly made their desires . . .': Glenn McFarlane, *Jock*, pp. 171–2.

94. 'Seddon recalled years later that the adjutant . . .': Ibid., p. 175.

94. 'The [Collingwood] club secretary whirled out . . .': Blair, pp. 122–3.

95. 'In what looked like a tacit acknowledgement . . .': *The Age*, 30 July 1915, p. 5.

95. 'He donated £50 . . .': *The Advocate*, 11 September 1915, p. 26.

96. 'He told the players that cricket helped . . .': VCA Minutes, 20 September 1915, accessed at Cricket Victoria's Jolimont (Melbourne) HQ.

96. 'The mood was similar in Sydney . . .': Phillip Derriman, *True to the Blue*, p. 139.

97. 'Most of them were senior players . . .': *The Australian Statesman and Mining Standard*, 7 October 1915.

97. 'He also had elderly parents . . .': Gideon Haigh, *The Big Ship*, p. 252.

97. 'Ryder's reasons for not enlisting . . .': Marc Fiddian, *A Life-Long Innings*, p. 36.

97. 'Ted McDonald, who became one . . .': Nick Richardson, *The Silk Express*, pp. 43–4.

97. 'Because it did not want to do anything . . .': VCA Minutes, 13 December 1915.

4: The Larrikins

Page

101. 'There were similar performances . . .': Hewitt family archive (courtesy of Sue Mack).

101. 'The athletes exercised to music . . .': Trevor Robbins, *Running into History*, pp. 12–13.

101. 'But the athlete who would become best known . . .': Graem Sims, *Why Die?*, p. 17.

102. 'We waited at the pier . . .': Christina Ellen 'Tullie' Sloss, diary, Sloss family archive, p. 23.

102. 'We were leading . . .': Private Victor Laidlaw, diary, 18 January 1915, State Library of Victoria, MS11827.

103. '[He] would have developed in to a champion . . .': *The Australasian*, 10 April 1915, p. 21.

104. 'But it seems they mixed me up . . .': *The Argus*, 28 January 1916.

105. 'There was no allowance or pension . . .': Janet McCalman, *Struggletown*, p. 52.

106. 'Willis was given an inscribed silver cigarette case . . .': *The Winner*, 16 February 1916, p. 6.

107. 'He was prone to quoting the poets . . .': Richard and Patrick Morgan, *The Morgan Family of 'Niddrie'*, Richard Spillane, Melbourne, 1990, pp. 143–4.

107. 'When the shoot commences . . .': *The Winner*, 26 April 1916, p. 4.

108. 'To arrange no football program . . .': *The Argus*, 19 January 1916, p. 5.

109. 'To view the execrable football-as-usual decision . . .': *The Argus*, 16 February 1916, p. 9.

110. 'Their matches, after the first one or two . . .': *The Winner*, 15 March 1916, p. 6.

110. 'A yell was raised by the morning papers . . .': *The Football Record*, round 1, 1916, pp. 3–10.

110. 'We are going to play the game . . .': Ibid., p. 13.

111. 'I said to myself: You'd better get out . . .': Michael Roberts, *A Century of the Best*, p. 211.

112. 'Nonetheless, he was sanguine . . .': *The Sporting Globe*, 7 August 1937, p. 8.

113. 'Fancy telling a man . . .': Ibid.

114. 'Perry's experience was unusual . . .': Michael McKernan, *Padre*, pp. 14–15.

114. 'Perry decided that he would share . . .': *The Register*, 11 December 1915, p. 11.

114. 'Why should we withhold our hand . . .': *Daily Herald* (Adelaide), 2 March 1916.

115. 'As hard as a stout wire nail': *The Telegraph* (Launceston), 12 May 1916, p. 3.

116. 'Last-minute attempt to patch up the shortage . . .': *The Referee*, 19 May 1915, p. 13.

116. 'Even the usual season-opening tradition . . .': Paul Macpherson and Ian Granland, *A Game to Be Played*, pp. 18–19.

116. 'The best umpire ever seen here': *The Daily Advertiser* (Wagga Wagga), 13 August 1915, p. 4.

116. 'Paddington accounted for Newtown . . .': *The Sydney Morning Herald*, 13 September 1915, p. 11.

116. 'When Country and Metropolitan returns are finalized . . .': Macpherson and Granland, p. 20.

117. 'Altogether the period spent in Maribyrnong . . .': 8th Field Artillery Brigade Diary, April 1916, AWM 4, sub-class 13/36.

118. 'But he kept pretty much to himself . . .': *Westralian Worker*, 13 March 1914, p. 8.

119. 'Hoft was a footballer of great promise . . .': *Western Mail*, 6 June 1916, p. 36.

119. 'Their hardness in withstanding the rigors . . .': *Western Mail*, 28 April 1916, p. 36.

120. 'An anonymous donor . . .': *Fitzroy City Press*, 5 February 1916, p. 2.

120. 'You really don't know how important Fitzroy is . . .': Chris Donald, *For the Love of the Jumper*, Pennon Publishing, Melbourne, 2002, p. 38.

120. 'Goodbye to football . . .': *The Sporting Globe*, 14 August 1937, p. 8.

121. 'He told Christina how pleased he was . . .': Harold Ordish to Christina Sloss, letter, 7 January 1917, Sloss family archive.

121. 'We have just got word through . . .': Bruce Sloss, letter, 14 June 1916, Sloss family archive.

123. 'The DAC boys went mad': *The Winner*, 15 November 1916, p. 8.

5: 'These Big Chaps'
Page

125. '[W]e were all down-hearted . . .': *Gippsland Mercury*, 12 September 1916, p. 3.

126. 'The soldiers' only joy . . .': *Sea Lake Times and Berriwillock Advertiser*, 21 October 1916, p. 3.

126. 'After seven weeks . . .': M.B.B. Keatinge, *War Book of the Third Pioneer Battalion*, 3rd Pioneer Battalion, Melbourne, 1922, pp. 24–5.

126. '[W]e then commenced a journey . . .': *The Winner*, 11 October 1916, p. 8.

127. 'It almost seems as if some one had designed . . .': Ibid.

128. 'Always mindful of the spiritual obligations . . .': James Brunton Gibb, State Library of New South Wales, 28 January 1916, MLMSS 3446.

128. 'And how Beaurepaire loves swimmin' . . .': *The Kiama Independent and Shoalhaven Advertiser*, 25 March 1916, p. 2.

128. 'In the years to come . . .': Michael McKernan, *Beryl Beaurepaire*, p. 62.

129. 'Last night I put on a boxing entertainment . . .': *The Winner*, 3 May 1916, p. 7.

129. 'The VFL asked football manufacturer Syd Sherrin . . .': *The Referee*, 2 February 1916, p. 13. Sherrin only accepted payment for the cost of making the footballs.

130. 'Back home, recruitment numbers . . .': L.L. Robson, *The First AIF*, p. 11.

130. 'One of Monash's instructions . . .': Graham Lomas, *The Will to Win*, pp. 49–50.

131. 'The tournaments required a sentry . . .': *The Winner*, 19 July 1916, p. 9.

131. 'And as the Australians waded in . . .': Lomas, p. 51.

132. 'The Fromelles attack was . . .': Les Carlyon, *The Great War*, p. 51.

132. 'Poor old George . . .': *The Winner*, 8 November 1916, p. 8.

133. 'The noise [of the shells] is terrific . . .': *The Winner*, 25 October 1916, p. 8.

133. 'The savage and debilitating fighting . . .': Peter Dennis, Jeffrey Grey, Ewan Morris and Robin Prior, *The Oxford Companion to Australian Military History*, p. 655.

134. 'George Foster Pearce – acting prime minister . . .': John Connor, *Anzac and Empire*, pp. 80–1.

135. 'The most recent list for eleven days . . .': Commonwealth Parliamentary Debates, Vol LXXIX, p. 8402, 30 August 1916.

135. 'There would be separate training requirements . . .': Michael Molkentin, *Training for War*, p. 7.

136. '[I]t helps very much . . .': *The Winner*, 4 October 1916, p. 9.

136. 'All the men I have seen . . .': Monash, letter, 22 July 1916, Sir John Monash Papers, AWM, Series 3, Folder 42.

136. 'But lack of equipment in Australia . . .': Molkentin, p. 10.

136. 'The men had never met . . .': Geoffrey Serle, *John Monash*, p. 269.

137. '[N]o recollection is more bitter . . .': Peter Pedersen, 'The AIF on the Western Front: The Role of Training and Command', in Michael McKernan and Margaret Browne (eds), *Australia*, p. 169.

138. 'There is no prospect of our going . . .': Monash, letter, 16 September 1916, AWM, Series 3, Folder 42.

138. 'The bomb-throwing school . . .': Thomas Alexander White, diary, State Library of New South Wales, http://ww1.sl.nsw.gov.au/content/thomas-alexander-white.

138. 'Will be glad when it's all over . . .': Bruce Sloss, letter, 16 August 1916, Sloss family archive.

139. 'Most of the AIF trainers were selected . . .': Robert Stevenson, *The War with Germany*, Oxford University Press, Melbourne, 2015, p. 59.

140. 'Excellent bayonet-fighting instructor': Cyril Longmore, *Eggs-A Cook: The Story of the Forty-Fourth*, Hesperian Press, Perth, 2010, p. 28.

140. 'One Australian forecast the bayonet . . .': Molkentin, p. 20.

140. 'They were also trained in . . .': Martin Brown and Peter Osgood, *Digging Up Plugstreet*, p. 37.

140. 'Rain swept the open country . . .': Ibid.

140. 'A day a week was devoted . . .': 8th Field Artillery Brigade War Diary, August 1916, AWM 4, sub-class 13/36.

140. 'Never has a division been so hardly tested . . .': *The Adelaide Mail*, 18 November 1916, p. 10.

141. 'My dear fellow . . .': Ibid.

141. '"Don't" is a word the Aussies . . .': Longmore, p. 10.

141. 'I am writing to [Defence Minister] Pearce . . .': Monash, letter, 26 July 1917, in *War Letters of General Monash*, p. 182.

141. 'All the old units are still fighting . . .': *Cootamundra Herald*, 28 November 1916, p. 3.

142. 'Minogue was restless . . .': Batchelder, *Playing the greater game: the Melbourne Cricket Club and its ground in World War I*, p. 244.

142. 'As regards the questions of keeping men fit . . .': Monash, lecture 2, Larkhill, 25 October 1916, AWM, Sir John Monash Papers, Series 3, Folder 44.

142. 'Unlike many of his troops, Monash . . .': Serle, p. 21.

142. 'Instinct for sport and adventure': Ibid., pp. 391–2.

143. 'The Australian is unaccustomed . . .': George Cuttriss, *Over the Top with the Third Division*, p. 108.

143. 'The Divisional Sports Committee, with the approval . . .': Monash, memo, 2 September 1916, AWM25 897/10.

144. 'The Allies believed the Germans had . . .': Molkentin, pp. 20–1.

144. 'Johnny The Turk treats all our boys . . .': Bruce Sloss, letter, 6 September 1916, Sloss family archive.

146. 'Officers to start with a night white dress . . .': Beaurepaire, memo, 14 September 1916, AWM25 897/10.

146. 'It is to be hoped that all Units . . .': Ibid.

146. 'Any point that seems debatable . . .': Ibid.

147. 'Beaurepaire told Longworth . . .': *The Australasian*, 9 December 1916, p. 19.

147. '[W]e kicked till we were tired . . .': *The Winner*, 29 November 1916, p. 8.

147. 'We (the King and I) . . .': Bruce Sloss, letter to Tullie, 3 October 1910, Sloss family archive.

147. '[The King] expressed his great appreciation . . .': Newton Moore report, AWM AIF 369/1/262, p. 23.

148. 'Less than a third of the eligible men . . .': Joan Beaumont, *Broken Nation*, p. 236.

148. '[T]here are many rumours . . .': Monash, letter, Larkhill, 26 October 1916, Sir John Monash Papers, AWM, Series 3, Folder 44.

148. 'They are a fine, bright lot . . .': *The Winner*, 8 November 1916, p. 8.

6: The Game

Page

151. 'The result was that, after a few noggies . . .': *The Sporting Globe*, 30 April 1938, p. 8.

152. 'For all those interested in Football . . .': AIF Depots in the United Kingdom, Miscellaneous (re: football matches), AWM 15, 7950.

154. 'All officers and men in this division . . .': Wootten, memo, 12 October 1916, AWM25 897/10.

154. 'He showed good form . . .': *The Record – Emerald Hill*, 18 November 1916, p. 2.

155. 'They were all fit': Bruce Sloss, letter, 22 October 1916, Sloss family archive.

155. 'They were as good as any ball . . .': *The Winner*, 23 August 1916, p. 9.

155. 'Hewitt's runners at Epsom . . .': *The Winner*, 22 November 1916, p. 6.

157. 'It was there that Barry, somehow . . .': UK National Archives, ADM/188/585.

157. 'It was about ten metres too short . . .': *The Winner*, 10 January 1917, p. 4. The MCG, for example, is 170 metres x 146 metres.

157. 'The Queen's Club was actually keen . . .': *The Daily Telegraph*, 30 December 1916.

158. 'I never cease to marvel . . .': Ross McMullin, 'Will Dyson: Australia's Radical Genius', *Papers on Parliament*, No. 59, April 2013.

158. 'Interpret in a series of drawings . . .': Ross McMullin, *Will Dyson*, pp. 126–7.

159. 'Pictorial records embodying the spirit . . .': Ibid., p. 129.

159. 'The entrance fee was set . . .': *The Sporting Globe*, 28 October 1939, p. 5.

159. 'To be selected from . . .': Pioneer Exhibition Game, Australian Football, 28 October 1916, official program. The final Training Units' line-up is not known. Photographs of the team are only captioned with the list of names from the program. As a result, it has not been possible to identify all the players in the Training Units' photographs. The 3rd Division team photograph caption is not accurate but the players can be identified from their playing records.

162. 'Carl Willis's, Bill Sewart's and Ned Alley's . . .': Beaurepaire, memo, 25 October 1916, AWM25 897/10.

162. 'But the threat of disbanding the 3rd Division . . .': Ernest Scott, *Official History of Australia in the War of 1914–18, Vol. XI*, pp. 339–40; Ken Inglis, 'Conscription in Peace and War 1911–1945', in Roy Forward and Bob Reece, *Conscription in Australia*, p. 35.

163. 'It is pleasing for us to know . . .': *The Record – Emerald Hill*, 15 January 1916, p. 2.

163. 'What helped to create a confused picture . . .': Joan Beaumont, *Broken Nation*, p. 243.

163. 'I can hardly forbear . . .': Peter Cochrane, *Australians at War*, p. 65.

165. 'Many and devious were the dodges . . .': *The Sporting Globe*, 21 August 1937, p. 8.

167. 'By 1910, the stab kick was . . .': *The Argus*, 27 June 1910, p. 6.

167. '[H]e showed us that he still retains his old dash . . .': *The Winner*, 10 January 1917, p. 4.

169. 'Moyes was a successful goalsneak . . .': *The Argus*, 26 April 1915, p. 10.

170. 'Perry, the footballing padre . . .': *The Winner*, 20 December 1916, p. 7.

172. 'For my part, I know I never played harder . . .': *The Sporting Globe*, 21 August 1937, p. 8.

172. 'There have been fugitive matches . . .': *The Winner*, 20 December 1916, p. 7.

172. 'It betrayed the newspaper's mistaken assumption . . .': Ibid.

173. 'Footballers have answered the call . . .': *The Australasian*, 4 November 1916, p. 26.

173. 'Brake was so attached to the jumper . . .': *The Winner*, 7 March 1917, p. 8.

173. 'The New Division v The Old Heads': *Wesley Chronicle*, May 1917, p. 23.

173. 'Sloss could not conceal . . .': Bruce Sloss, letter to Tullie, 9 September 1914, Sloss family archive.

174. 'Big hulking soldiers': *The Sporting Globe*, 21 August 1937, p. 8.

174. 'Two weeks after the Exhibition match . . .': Geoffrey Serle, *John Monash*, p. 275.

175. 'My batman is here . . .': Bruce Sloss, letter, 13 November 1916, Sloss family archive.
175. 'What do you think of the house?': Ibid.
175. 'On Sloss's final night . . .': Christina Ellen 'Tullie' Sloss, diary, Sloss family archive, p. 29.
175. 'I addressed the men for half an hour . . .': *Western Mail*, 29 December 1916, p. 17.

7: The Greater Game

Page

177. 'Their reputation in Europe . . .': Robert Stevenson, *The War with Germany*, p. 102.
177. '[T]he Australians hate being called "Anzacs" . . .': Monash, 15 January 1917, in *War Letters of General Monash*, p. 161.
178. '[T]hey made such a success . . .': Quoted in *The Aussie*, Australian Variety Theatre Archive, http://ozvta.com/troupes-digger-companies.
179. 'I know you are going off at me . . .': Bruce Sloss, letter, 11 December 1916, Sloss family archive.
179. 'I am sorry to say . . .': Ibid.
180. 'Really did not know what the day was . . .': Ibid., 25 December 1916.
181. 'It is rather a queer sensation . . .': *Moorabbin News*, 31 March 1917, p. 2.
182. 'It killed him': *The Record – Emerald Hill*, 17 November 1917, p. 2.
183. 'I don't know what happened . . .': Christina Ellen 'Tullie' Sloss, diary, Sloss family archive, p. 26.
183. 'His beautiful body was riddled . . .': Ibid., p. 29.
183. 'The committee and players feel keenly . . .': Howson, letter, 17 January 1917, Sloss family archive.
183. 'He is as versatile as he is brilliant . . .': *The Record – Emerald Hill*, 20 January 1917, p. 2.
184. 'Risk has never entered my mind . . .': Tullie, diary, 15 February 1917, p. 27.
185. 'When all but three boatloads . . .': Tullie, diary, 25–26 February 1917, pp. 27–8.
185. 'The previous year, 1000 people . . .': Blair, 'War and Peace', p. 127.
185. 'Every effort has been made . . .': *The Record – Emerald Hill*, 3 March 1917, p. 2.
185. 'If they are I think a suitable idea . . .': *The Winner*, 26 September 1917, p. 8.
186. 'Within two weeks . . .': L. Broinowski (ed), *Tasmania's War Record 1914–1918*, pp. 1–9, 40th Battalion 1st AIF 1916–18, http://40th-bn.org/40thbn.html.
188. 'There were 30 soldiers wounded . . .': *The Daily Telegraph* (Launceston), 8 December 1917, p. 11.
188. 'His personality, his soldierly qualities . . .': *The Examiner* (Launceston), 31 May 1917, p. 6.

188. 'His 44th Battalion had impressed . . .': *Camp Chronicle*, 16 November 1916, p. 6.

189. 'And the artillery barrage was to be . . .': Cyril Longmore, *Eggs-A Cook*, p. 46.

189. 'The Circus would support the 44th . . .': Neville Browning, *Westralian Battalion*, pp. 74, 78.

189. 'In the days before the raid . . .': Ibid., p. 79.

190. 'Under the artillery cover . . .': Ibid., pp. 80–1.

190. 'But Foy was hit in the right thigh . . .': 'Sgt James Francis Foy', Wounded and Missing Enquiry Files, Australian Red Cross Society, IDRL/0428.

190. '[T]he operation failure can . . .': Longmore, p. 49.

190. 'The raid was not actually a success . . .': 'Sgt James Francis Foy', Australian Red Cross Society.

191. 'I can hardly express the esteem . . .': Ibid.

191. 'Sgt Foy was a personal friend of mine . . .': Ibid.

191. 'Foy's death became part of a tale . . .': *Daily News* (Perth), 10 December, 1917, p. 6.

192. 'Geelong claimed its return was based on . . .': Blair, 'War and Peace', p. 128.

192. 'Carlton was the worst example . . .': Ibid., p. 129.

192. 'The Blues put £99 towards . . .': Michael McKernan, 'Sport, War and Society', in Richard Cashman and Michael McKernan, *Sport in History*, p. 12.

192. 'Fitzroy paid £152 from £918 . . .': John Ross (ed), *100 Years of Australian Football*, p. 92.

193. 'He went to the federal election . . .': Donald Horne, *Billy Hughes*, p. 137.

193. 'It has come under my notice . . .': *The Age*, 3 May 1916, pp. 9–10.

194. 'Through you, if your executive . . .': *The Age*, 23 January 1917, p. 5.

194. 'These are narratives in plain language . . .': Quoted in *Daily News* (Perth), 30 May 1917, p. 1.

195. 'I . . . listened, with others . . .': *The Winner*, 23 May 1917, p. 7.

196. 'The harm has been done . . .': *The Winner*, 6 June 1917, p. 10.

196. 'The reporters do not miss . . .': *The Argus*, 26 May 1917, p. 17.

196. 'The State War Council wrote to the League . . .': *The Age*, 26 May 1917, p. 12.

197. 'The Council would also approve . . .': *The Argus*, 19 June 1917, p. 6.

197. 'How well that misunderstanding . . .': *The Age*, 23 June 1917, p. 13.

197. 'The League also pointed out . . .': Michael McKernan, *Victoria at War 1914–1918*, p. 81.

197. 'But Brownlow did note . . .': Batchelder, *Playing The Greater Game*, p. 373.

198. 'The Government is of the opinion . . .': *Forbes Advocate*, 3 July 1917, p. 4.

199. 'The playing field was within shell range . . .': *The West Australian*, 4 August 1917, p. 7.

200. 'It is impossible to chronicle . . .': *The Argus*, 10 May 1917, p. 8.

8: Those Who Are Left

Page

201. 'James well at latest': *Richmond Guardian*, 20 January 1917, p. 2.

202. 'All Richmondites, I know . . .': *Richmond Guardian*, 21 April 1917, p. 2.

202. 'The match took place . . .': Batchelder, *Playing The Greater Game*, p. 245.

202. 'One team wore shirts . . .': Ibid, p. 246.

204. 'A magnificent instrument recklessly shattered . . .': C.E.W. Bean, *Official History of Australia in the War of 1914–18, Vol IV*, p. 354, https://www.awm.gov.au/images/collection/pdf/RCDIG1069499--1-.pdf.

204. 'Martin's 22nd Battalion was on the left . . .': Les Carlyon, *The Great War*, p. 378.

204. 'For no other struggle . . .': Eugene Gorman, *With the 22nd*, p. 53.

205. 'The noise of the bullets . . .': Ibid., p. 54.

206. 'Slater was hit by shrapnel . . .': Paul Kendall, *Bullecourt 1917*, pp. 175–6.

206. 'One Digger waited 16 hours . . .': Ibid.

206. 'Compelled to retire . . .': 22nd Battalion War Diary, May 1917, AWM 4, sub-class 23/39.

206. 'The 22nd was all but wiped out . . .': Gorman, p. 56.

207. 'He was shot through the chest . . .': 'Hector Martin', NAA B2455.

208. 'My wife is in a deplorable state . . .': *Richmond Guardian*, 21 April 1917, p. 2.

208. 'The Minister desires me to convey . . .': Ibid.

209. 'To go for water means . . .': Ibid.

209. 'They beat us by seven points . . .': *The Record – Emerald Hill*, 11 August 1917, p. 2.

209. 'In an engineering lecture theatre . . .': Grantlee Kieza, *Monash*, p. 352.

209. 'The YMCA paid £170 for the projectors . . .': *The Age*, 16 June 1917, p. 3.

209. 'You might stroll one evening . . .': Ibid.

210. 'Many of the jokes were at Monash's expense . . .': Kieza, p. 353.

210. 'The Anzac Coves . . .': Robert Holden, *And the Band Played On*, pp. 157–64.

210. 'One correspondent estimated 150,000 Diggers . . .': *The Register*, 18 December 1917, p. 8.

210. 'It appears I had been sickening for weeks . . .': *The Record – Emerald Hill*, 11 August 1917, p. 2.

211. 'I need not say how very sorry . . .': Graham Lomas, *The Will to Win*, pp. 52–3.

211. 'Had I been severely gassed . . .': *The Referee*, 27 February 1918, p. 9.

212. 'Mason was so incapacitated . . .': *The Weekly Times*, 29 December 1917, p. 22.

214. 'But Lee declined the offer . . .': *Camberwell and Hawthorn Advertiser*, 1 March 1918, p. 3.

214. 'A frontal attack would be madness . . .': Martin Brown and Peter Osgood, *Digging Up Plugstreet*, p. 55.

215.	'As we went up thro [sic] wood . . .': Carlyon, p. 409.

215.	'There is no chance of mistaking the gas shell . . .': *The Winner*, 22 August 1917, p. 8.

215.	'I can honestly say that I got . . .': *The Winner*, 26 September 1917, p. 8.

215.	'Somehow in war you expect . . .': *The Winner*, 22 August 1917, p. 8.

216.	'Nothing could have withstood . . .': Andrew Richardson, 'The Battle of Messines 1917', Army (website), 18 March 2015, www.army.gov.au.

216.	'It was a complicated task . . .': *The Kalgoorlie Miner*, 22 August 1917, p. 2.

217.	'A pioneer battalion is a unit of specialists . . .': *The Register*, 3 July 1917, p. 8.

217.	'In desperation, Lee's aunt . . .': *The Graphic*, 30 November 1917, p. 21.

218.	'What Coffey found out later . . .': 'Private Edward Lee, 10th Machine Gun Company', Wounded and Missing Enquiries File, Australian Red Cross Society, 1DRL/0428.

219.	'My son made Mr George Lee . . .': 'Leslie Edward Lee', NAA B2455, pp. 47–8.

220.	'In loving remembrance of my dear Leslie . . .': *The Argus*, 9 June 1919, p. 1.

220.	'The Richmond Football Club, the committee and members . . .': *Richmond Guardian*, 20 April 1918, p. 2.

221.	'We regret to announce the death . . .': 'A Salute to Les Lee', 24 April 2015, Richmond FC, www.richmondfc.com.au.

221.	'The Pioneers buried him . . .': 'Private Edward Lee, 10th Machine Gun Company', Australian Red Cross Society.

9: The Great Brotherhood of Sport

Page

223.	'McMullen became so good . . .': *The Australasian*, 31 March 1917, p. 38.

224.	'Owing to the training necessary . . .': *The Winner*, 28 February 1917, p. 4.

226.	'I am going back to France . . .': *The Winner*, 4 July 1917, p. 9.

226.	'I could do with a good game . . .': *The Winner*, 19 December 1917, p. 8.

226.	'Collingwood kept in touch . . .': *The Winner*, 28 March 1917, p. 8.

226.	'Brosnan claimed there were . . .': Batchelder, *Playing The Greater Game*, p. 372.

227.	'Sportsmen of Australia . . .': *The Sydney Morning Herald*, 27 July 1917, p. 7.

227.	'Fritz knew that it was coming off . . .': *The Winner*, 22 August 1917, p. 8.

228.	'That all governing bodies or committees of clubs . . .': Sportsmen's Recruiting Committee minutes, 31 January 1917, RSL Victoria Archives.

229.	'Arousing of interest among the womenfolk . . .': Sportmen's Recruiting Committee minutes, 17 March 1917, RSL Victoria Archives.

229.	'Mackinnon understood . . .': Ashley Browne, 'For Women, Too', in *The Australian Game of Football Since 1856*, p. 253.

229.	'South Melbourne members . . .': *The Record – Emerald Hill*, 14 February 1914, p. 2.

229. 'Games were played . . .': Rob Hess, 'Missing in Action? New Perspectives on the Origins and Diffusion of Women's Football in Australia during the Great War', *International Journal of the History of Sport*, Vol. 31, No. 18, p. 2329.

229. 'In preparation for the national Win the War day . . .': *The Sydney Morning Herald*, 10 February 1917, p. 4.

230. 'She circulated a letter . . .': Sportsmen's Recruiting Committee minutes, 3 March 1917, RSL Victoria Archives.

232. 'Enlist one man by appealing . . .': Murray G. Phillips, 'Sport, War and Gender Images: The Australian Sportsmen's Battalions and the First World War', *International Journal of the History of Sport*, Vol. 14, No. 1, March 2007, p. 90.

232. 'This duty will not interfere . . .': *Northern Times*, 30 October 1917, p. 1.

232. 'It seems incongruous and callous . . .': Carmel Shute, 'Heroines and Heroes: Sexual Mythology in Australia 1914–18', in Joy Damousi and Marilyn Lake, *Gender and War: Australia at War in the Twentieth Century*, p. 26.

232. 'Taking in to account the great influence . . .': Sportsmen's Recruiting Committee minutes, 7 March 1917, RSL Victoria Archives.

233. 'A recruiting rally held in West Melbourne . . .': *The Argus*, 17 March 1917, p. 12.

233. 'St Kilda Town Hall fared a little better . . .': Sportsmen's Recruiting Committee minutes, November 1917, RSL Victoria Archives.

233. 'Many were discouraged from enlisting . . .': L.L. Robson, *The First AIF*, pp. 123–45.

233. 'The fact that the club cabled . . .': *The Referee*, 30 August 1916, p. 12.

234. 'At the unfurling of the 1913 premiership flag . . .': Chris Donald, *For the Love of the Jumper*, p. 37.

234. 'I am in the best of health . . .': *The Winner*, 25 October 1916, p. 8.

234. 'He was indeed recalled . . .': *The Winner*, 6 December 1916, p. 8.

235. 'The new plan involved . . .': Robert Stevenson, *The War with Germany*, p. 141.

235. 'An unprecedented artillery attack . . .': Robin Prior and Trevor Wilson, *Passchendaele*, p. 115.

235. 'Low cloud hampered . . .': Ibid., p. 117.

236. 'German aircraft tried to bomb . . .': 8th Battalion War Diary, 19–20 September 1917, AWM 4, sub-class 23/8.

236. 'Hop out and lads done well . . .': Peter Liddle (ed), *Passchendaele in Perspective*, p. 234.

237. 'It is gratifying to the proprietor . . .': *The Football Record*, 22 September 1917, p. 10.

237. 'Mr Cooper was a native of Fitzroy . . .': *Sporting Judge*, 27 April 1918, p. 4.

238. 'Personally, I think it would be . . .': *The Kalgoorlie Miner*, 13 April 1916, p. 6.

238. 'The season finally got under way . . .': *The Kalgoorlie Miner*, 15 May 1916, p. 3.

238. 'In 1907, five mining companies . . .': Geoffrey Blainey, *The Golden Mile*, p. 77.

239. 'The absence of 600 mainly . . .': Ibid., p. 106.

239. 'From Scullin's team . . .': *The Kalgoorlie Miner*, 18 April 1917, p. 4.

241. 'Dan and Patrick Scullin were each given . . .': 51st Battalion War Diary, 2 October 1917, AWM 4, sub-class 23/68.

241. 'At 5.50 am, the Australian gunners . . .': 51st Battalion War Diary, 2 October 1917, AWM 4, sub-class 23/68, and Neville Browning, *Fix Bayonets*, pp. 97–103.

242. 'Dan had written home earlier . . .': *The Kalgoorlie Miner*, 16 November 1917, p. 5.

242. 'The boys' sister, Meg . . .': Les Everett, interview with the author, October 2015.

242. 'In sad and loving memory . . .': *The Kalgoorlie Miner*, 26 September 1918, p. 2.

10: 'The Boys Are Dead Against It'

Page

243. 'I hope this shoe . . .': Glenn McFarlane, *Jock*, p. 186.

244. 'It was not considered necessary . . .': *Brisbane Courier*, 13 September 1917, p. 6.

245. '[W]e have the liquor trade against us . . .': Michael McKernan, *The Australian People and the Great War*, p. 113.

246. 'It was the final evidence to compel . . .': Robert Stevenson, *The War with Germany*, pp. 145–7.

246. 'A series of three-man sub-committees . . .': Sir John Monash Papers, 25 November 1917, AWM, Series 3, Folder 53.

246. 'Put another way, 35 Australians died . . .': Peter Cochrane, *Australians at War*, p. 70.

247. 'A gallant officer . . .': Letter to Christina Sloss, 23 January 1917, Sloss family archive.

247. 'He was known more widely . . .': Ordish, letter, 1 January 1917, Sloss family archive.

248. 'In loving memory of my dear friend . . .': *The Argus*, 15 January 1917, p. 1.

248. 'On a shipboard cruise . . .': Christina Ellen 'Tullie' Sloss, diary, 7 June–17 November 1921, Sloss family archive, p. 33.

249. 'Hours before we stopped . . .': Sloss family archive, section 7, p. 16.

250. 'Roy and Jock go back to France . . .': Tullie, diary, December 1916, p. 29.

250. 'He had been vocal about conscription . . .': *The Camperdown Chronicle*, 26 July 1917, p. 3.

250. 'Emphatically declined to allow themselves . . .': *Brisbane Courier*, 22 September 1917, p. 6.

251. 'Businesses that took a tough line . . .': Joan Beaumont, *Broken Nation*, pp. 334–5.

251. 'I am now worn with the storm . . .': L.S. Fitzhardinge, *The Little Digger 1914–1952*, p. 201.

251. 'The three Cs . . .': *The Armidale Express and New England General Advertiser*, 22 January 1918, p. 3.

252. 'Mannix was not archbishop . . .': Brenda Niall, *Mannix*, p. 86.

252. 'If you surrender your freedom . . .': *The Advocate*, 8 December 1918, p. 14.

252. 'Like a swimmer in a vast ocean . . .': Beaumont, p. 377.

253. 'Was very pleased to see that . . .': *The Record – Emerald Hill*, 21 April 1917, p. 3.

253. 'The boys are dead against it . . .': *The Record – Emerald Hill*, 23 February 1918, p. 2.

253. 'So Munro Ferguson rehired Hughes . . .': Les Carlyon, *The Great War*, p. 530.

254. 'He has all the arts of a crab . . .': Ernest Scott, *Official History of Australia in the War of 1914–18, Vol. XI*, p. 175.

254. 'In April, it was announced . . .': *Daily News* (Perth), 16 April 1918, p. 2.

254. 'He had already approached Monash . . .': Letters of Harry Joseph Cave, State Library of New South Wales, MLMSS 1224.

255. 'But the doctor's recommendation was clear . . .': 'Frank Beaurepaire', NAA MT1486/1 and B73.

255. 'My troupes are real artists . . .': Monash, letter, 15 March 1918, in *War Letters of General Monash*, pp. 212–3.

255. 'Both have beautiful clear soprano voices . . .': Ibid.

256. 'I did not know of [Aaron's] death . . .': *Leader*, 6 October 1917, p. 24.

256. '[P]oor old Jack . . .': *The Weekly Times*, 5 January 1918, p. 22.

256. 'There were even plans to establish a "barometer" . . .': *The Sydney Morning Herald*, 25 June 1917, p. 6.

256. 'Part of the reason was a lingering tension . . .': Sportsmen's Recruiting Committee minutes, 27 August 1917.

257. 'A prominent member of the Victorian Parliament . . .': Sportsmen's Recruiting Committee minutes, 22 January 1918.

257. 'The classless nature . . .': Newton Wanliss, *The History of the 14th Battalion AIF, being the vicissitudes of an Australian Unit during The Great War*, Arrow Printery, Melbourne, 1929, p. 263.

258. '[A]m deadly sick of it already . . .': *The Record – Emerald Hill*, 5 January 1918, p. 2.

258. 'It became a significant problem . . .': Ross Bastian, 'Dentistry: the Cinderella of health services', in Jacqueline Healy (editor), *Compassion and Courage*, p. 29.

259. 'Rather than try to offer regular services . . .': Chaplain's Department, War Diary, 1918, AWM 4, sub-class 6/5.

260. 'We saw R[ichthofen] overhead . . .': P.J. Carisella and James W. Ryan, *Who Killed the Red Baron?*, p. 145.

260. 'The orderly declared the pilot dead . . .': Gunner Hugh S. Hawes, 'The Last Flight of the "Red Baron", Baron Manfred von Richthofen, 21 April 1918', 1976, State Library of Victoria, MS4434/7.

261. 'Lieutenant John Warneford, of the 3rd Squadron . . .': 'Left Flying Overboot: Baron M von Richthofen', AWM RELAWM00705, www.awm.gov.au.

261. 'Association clubs had an ulterior motive . . .': Leonie Sandercock and Ian Turner, *Up Where Cazaly?*, p. 78.

262. 'The Association's vice president . . .': *Brunswick and Coburg Leader*, 12 April 1918, p. 1.

262. 'An analysis of the total number . . .': Data compiled from www.australian football.com.

262. 'Everything else went to the patriotic funds': *Richmond Guardian*, 6 April 1918, p. 2.

262. '*The Argus*, that paragon . . .': Jim Main, 'Flag tinged with blood' in Browne, Ashley, (ed), *Grand Finals volume I, 1897-1938*, Slattery Media Group, Docklands, 2011, p. 221.

263. 'Enlist and Play The Game . . .': *The Winner*, 12 June 1918, p. 8.

263. 'The military authorities have decided . . .': *The Football Record*, 22 September 1917, pp. 3–4.

265. 'It gets very monotonous . . .': *The Record – Emerald Hill*, 2 November 1918, p. 2.

266. 'I am afraid that I would not last long . . .': Ibid.

266. 'I knew he'd do it': *Richmond Guardian*, 6 April 1918, p. 2.

267. 'The Australian Corps was exhausted . . .': Robert Stevenson, *The War with Germany*, p. 198.

11: The Final Siren

Page

269. 'While it is freely admitted . . .': *The Australasian*, 21 September 1918, p. 26.

270. '*The Football Record* was lobbied . . .': Stuart Macintyre, 'Football weathers the storms of war' in Ross (ed), *100 Years of Australian Football*, Viking, Ringwood, 1996, p. 91.

270. 'I'm feeling terribly sad today . . .': Gladys, letter to Tullie, 22 March 1918, Sloss family archive.

271. 'It is about the only thing . . .': Tullie, letter to Christina, 17 April 1918, Sloss family archive.

271. 'How I prayed that the Germans . . .': Christina Ellen 'Tullie' Sloss, diary, 2 June 1918, Sloss family archive, p. 30.

271. 'WAR IS OVER! . . .': Tullie, diary, 11 November 1918, p. 31.

271. 'SON: On the way from Turkey . . .': Ibid.

272. 'James McKenzie Sloss was free . . .': Sloss family archive, section 7, p. 21.

272. 'What greater problem . . .': E.H. Goddard, *Soldiers and Sportsmen*, p. 7.

273. 'By the end of the year, 15 troopships . . .': Joan Beaumont, *Broken Nation*, p. 522.

273. '[W]hile the [Australian] Corps was . . .': Goddard, p. 9.

274. 'The Victorian Racing Club gave £100 . . .': *The Age*, 13 February 1919, p. 4.

274. 'The AIF Headquarters in London's Horseferry Road . . .': Goddard, p. 12.

275. 'I have had a great time . . .': *The Record – Emerald Hill*, 17 May 1919, p. 2.

275. '[N]othing but lack of funds . . .': Ibid., p. 3.

276. 'That was only the start . . .': *The Sporting Globe*, 30 April 1938, p. 8.

276. 'I can't understand what has happened . . .': *The Record – Emerald Hill*, 17 May 1919, p. 2.

277. 'The YMCA Australian Corps Sports Cup . . .': *Australian Corps News Sheet*, No. 15–19, 1919.

277. 'The one thing the Americans couldn't . . .': Goddard, p. 51.

278. 'The marathon was cut back . . .': Ibid., p. 57.

278. 'After three years away . . .': *Daily Herald* (Adelaide), 12 September 1919, p. 7.

279. 'Chaplain Perry rose . . .': *The Register*, 11 December 1919, p. 11.

279. 'James had a keen ear . . .': Richard Stremski, *Kill for Collingwood*, p. 77.

279. 'Richmond coach Norman Clark . . .': *The Sporting Globe*, 10 July 1937, p. 8.

280. 'There was talk of a parade . . .': Glenn McFarlane, *Jock*, p. 197.

280. 'Whose district he first takes up residence . . .': Stremski, p. 77.

280. 'That seemed like splitting straws . . .': *The Sporting Globe*, 10 July 1937, p. 8.

281. 'I like other soldier-footballers . . .': *The Sporting Globe*, 28 August 1937, p. 8.

281. 'The saddest day of our lives . . .': Les Everett, *Gravel Rash*, p. 65.

282. 'The Scullins' pain . . .': 'If we count as family, a person's parents, children, siblings, aunts and uncles and cousins, then every second Australian family was bereaved by the war. The most unusual aspect of this bereavement, in Australia as in all those belligerent countries where increased expectation of life had made death an event of old age, was that so many of the mourners were a generation older than their dead. The news was broken most often to mothers and fathers who had lost sons, less often – for more than 80 per cent of the AIF were unmarried – to women who had been made widows.' K.S. Inglis, *Sacred Places*, p. 97.

282. 'By the end of 1921 . . .': Geoffrey Blainey, *The Golden Mile*, p. 114.

282. 'Although only a small part . . .': *Maitland Weekly Mercury*, 31 May 1919, p. 9.

283. 'You know I'm not doing badly . . .': Graham Lomas, *The Will to Win*, p. 54.

283. 'There is not another swimmer . . .': Ibid., p. 56.

283. 'Beaurepaire's resurgence was stalled . . .': Ibid., p. 57.

284. 'There had been several events . . .': *The Referee*, 27 August 1919, p. 12.

284. 'Hewitt won what was billed . . .': *The Referee*, 8 October 1919, p. 12.

284. 'English cricket believed . . .': Ronald Mason, *Warwick Armstrong's Australians*, p. 12.

285. 'After the War, whenever that may be . . .': Quoted in Andrew Renshaw, *Wisden on The Great War*, p. 6.

287. 'It was Mackinnon's turn . . .': *The Age*, 19 January 1920, p. 8; *The Australasian*, 24 January 1920, p. 19.

288. 'In one of those serendipitous moments . . .': *The Age*, 27 May 1920, p. 7.

289. 'The newspapers understood . . .': *The Advocate*, 30 September 1919, p. 23.

289. 'I hardly felt equal to it . . .': *The Sporting Globe*, 28 August 1937, p. 8.

290. 'Yes, they were good sports . . .': Paul Daffey, 'Richmond Eats Magpies Alive', in Geoff Slattery (ed), *Grand Finals, Vol. I*, p. 246.

291. 'Hewitt's rivals wrote to the papers . . .': *The Referee*, 31 March 1920, p. 10.

291. 'And although there was a marathon . . .': *The Referee*, 5 May 1920, p. 10.

292. 'Yet, by April 1920 . . .': *The Barrier Miner*, 30 April 1920, p. 4.

292. 'There were only six men left . . .': *The Age*, 10 May 1920, p. 8.

293. 'The Americans almost mutinied . . .': Harry Gordon, *Australia and the Olympic Games*, p. 99.

293. 'Beaurepaire was accompanied . . .': Ibid., p. 98.

293. 'The revelation of the Olympics . . .': Lomas, p. 60.

293. 'They had gone 32 kilometres . . .': *The Referee*, 4 August 1920, p. 8.

294. 'In Antwerp, he crossed the line . . .': Charlie Lovett, *Olympic Marathon*, pp. 31–3.

Epilogue

Page

296. 'Average. Rather slow . . .': 'John Brake', NAA, B884, V52492.

297. 'On the first anniversary of Jimmy Foy's . . .': *The West Australian*, 14 March 1918, p. 1.

297. 'Elsie had remarried . . .': 'James Francis Foy', NAA, B2455.

298. 'Some people think, especially church people . . .': Perry family archive.

298. 'Pearce told the audience . . .': *The Argus*, 8 August 1921, p. 6.

298. 'Pearce again criticised spectator sport . . .': John Connor, *Anzac and Empire*, p. 168.

299. 'Sir Robert Menzies said of the former . . .': Sir Robert Menzies in Peter Heydon, *Quiet Decision*, p. 2.

300. 'He represented Australia at the 1919 Paris . . .': Margaret MacMillan, *Paris 1919 – Six Months That Changed The World*, Random House, New York, 2003, p. 48.

301. 'There is already more money . . .': Richard and Patrick Morgan, *The Morgan Family of 'Niddrie'*, pp. 143–4.

302. 'Still single, and mobile . . .': *The Jerilderie Herald*, 15 May 1930, p. 3.

303. 'In the end, the mercy mission . . .': *Border Watch*, 13 May 1930, p. 6.

303. 'At the Victorian Cricket Association meeting . . .': *The Prahran Telegraph*, 22 May 1930, p. 4.

304. 'He left Melbourne as a private . . .': *The Record – Emerald Hill*, 15 September 1917, p. 3.

304. 'If we could only turn back the years . . .': *The Sporting Globe*, 20 August 1949, p. 11.

305. 'Sportsmen Lent Dash . . .': *The Sporting Globe*, 22 April 1931, p. 1.

306. 'It took until the late 1920s . . .': Chris Cunneen, 'The Rugby War: The Early History of Rugby League in NSW, 1907–15', in David Headon, *The Best Ever Australian Sports Writing*, pp. 321–2.

Select Bibliography

Books

Anderson, Hugh, *The Rise and Fall of Squizzy Taylor, Larrikin Crook*, Pan Books, Sydney, 1981

Barrett, John, *Falling In: Australians and 'Boy Conscription' 1911–1915*, Hale & Iremonger, Sydney, 1979

Batchelder, Alf, *Playing the Greater Game: The Melbourne Cricket Club and its Ground in World War I*, MMP Publications, Brighton, 1998

Bean, C.E.W., *Official History of Australia in the War of 1914–18, Vol. I, The Story of Anzac*, Angus & Roberston, Sydney, 1941

Beaumont, Joan, *Broken Nation*, Allen & Unwin, Sydney, 2013

Blackburn, Kevin, *War, Sport and the Anzac Tradition*, Palgrave, Basingstoke, 2016

Blainey, Geoffrey, *A Game of Our Own*, Black Inc, Melbourne, 2003

——*The Golden Mile*, Allen & Unwin, Sydney, 1993

——*A History of Victoria*, Cambridge University Press, Melbourne, 2006

Brenchley, Fred and Elizabeth, *Myth Maker: Ellis Ashmead-Bartlett*, Wiley, Brisbane, 2005

Brown, Martin and Peter Osgood, *Digging Up Plugstreet: The Archaeology of a Great War Battlefield*, Haynes Publishing, Sparkford, Somerset, 2009

Browne, Ashley (ed), *The Grand Finals: The Stories Behind the Premier Teams of the Victorian Football League, Vol. 1, 1897–1938*, Slattery Media Group, Docklands, 2011

Browning, Neville, *Fix Bayonets: The History of the 51st Battalion, AIF*, self-published, Perth, 2000

——*Westralian Battalion: The History of the 44th Battalion, AIF, 1916–1919 and the Western Australian Rifles*, self-published, Perth, 2004

Cardwell, Ronald, *The AIF Cricket Team*, Greenwood Press, Balgowlah Heights, 1980

Carisella, P.J., and James W. Ryan, *Who Killed the Red Baron?*, Fawcett, New York, 1969

Carlyon, Les, *The Great War*, Pan Macmillan, Sydney, 2006

Cochrane, Peter, *Australians at War*, ABC Books, Sydney, 2001

Coleman, Robert, *Seasons in the Sun: The Story of the Victorian Cricket Association*, Hargreen Publishing, North Melbourne, 1993

Coligan, Michael, *Norwood Men Who Served 1914–18*, NFC History Group, Adelaide, 2015

Connor, John, *Anzac and Empire: George Foster Pearce and the Foundations of Australian Defence*, Cambridge University Press, Melbourne, 2011

Cordner, John, *Black and Blue: The Story of Football at the University of Melbourne*, Melbourne University Football, Melbourne, 2007

Coward, Mike, *Men of Norwood: The Red and Blue Blooded*, Lane Print Group, Camden Park, 1992

Crotty, Martin, *Making the Australian Male: Middle Class Masculinity 1870–1920*, Melbourne University Press, Melbourne, 2001

Cullen, Barbara, *Tougher Than Football: League Players at War*, Slattery Media Group, Richmond, 2015

Cunneen, Chris, *The King's Men: Australia's Governors-General from Hopetoun to Isaacs*, Allen & Unwin, Sydney, 1983

Cuttriss, George P., *Over the Top with the Third Division*, Project Gutenberg ebook, originally published 1918

Dennis, Peter, Jeffrey Grey, Ewan Morris and Robin Prior, *The Oxford Companion to Australian Military History*, Oxford University Press, Melbourne, 1995

Derriman, Phillip, *True to the Blue: A History of the NSW Cricket Association*, Richard Smart Publishing, Sydney, 1985

Donald, Chris, *For the Love of the Jumper*, Pennon Publishing, Melbourne, 2002

Dyrenfurth, Nick, *Mateship*, Scribe, Melbourne, 2015

Everett, Les, *Gravel Rash: 100 Years of Football on the Goldfields*, Goldfields Football League, Fremantle, 1996

Fiddian, Marc, *A Life-Long Innings: The Jack Ryder Story*, Packenham Press, Melbourne, 1995

Fitzhardinge, L.F., *The Little Digger 1914–1952: William Morris Hughes, A Political Biography Vol. II*, Angus & Roberston, Sydney, 1979

Forward, Roy and Reece, Bob (eds), *Conscription in Australia*, University of Queensland Press, St Lucia, 1968

Gammage, Bill, *The Broken Years*, Penguin, Ringwood, 1974

Goddard, E.H. *Soldiers and Sportsmen*, AIF Sports Control Board, London, 1919

Gordon, Harry, *Australia and the Olympic Games*, University of Queensland Press, St Lucia, 1994

Gorman, Eugene, *With the 22nd: A History of the Twenty-Second Battalion*, AIF HH Champion, Melbourne, 1919

Gyss, Trevor, *1915 South Australian Football and the First World War*, self-published, Adelaide, 2015

Haigh, Gideon, *The Big Ship: Warwick Armstrong and the Making of Modern Cricket*, Text, Melbourne, 2001

Hess, Rob, Matthew Nicholson, Bob Stewart and Gregory De Moore, *A National Game*, Viking, Melbourne, 2008

Select Bibliography

Heydon, Peter, *Quiet Decision: A Study of George Foster Pearce*, Melbourne University Press, Melbourne, 1965

Holden, Robert, *And the Band Played On*, Hardie Grant, Melbourne, 2014

Horne, Donald, *Billy Hughes*, Black Inc., Melbourne, 2000

Inglis, Ken, *Sacred Places: War Memorials in the Australian Landscape*, The Miegunyah Press, Melbourne, 1999

Keatinge, M.B.B., *War Book of the Third Pioneer Battalion*, 3rd Pioneer Battalion, Melbourne, 1922

Kendall, Paul, *Bullecourt 1917: Breaching the Hindenburg Line*, Spellmount, Stroud, 2010

Kieza, Grantlee, *Monash: The Soldier Who Shaped Australia*, ABC Books, Sydney, 2015

Larsson, Marina, *Shattered Anzacs*, UNSW Press, Sydney, 2009

Lewis, Brian, *Our War: A View of World War I from inside an Australian Family*, Penguin, Melbourne, 1980

Liddle, Peter (ed), *Passchendaele in Perspective: The Third Battle of Ypres*, Leo Cooper, London, 1997

Lomas, Graham, *The Will to Win: The story of Sir Frank Beaurepaire*, Heinemann, Melbourne, 1960

Longmore, Cyril, *Eggs-A Cook: The Story of the Forty-Fourth, War as the Digger Saw It*, Hesperian Press, Perth, 2010

Lovett, Charlie, *Olympic Marathon: A Centennial History of the Games' Most Storied Race*, Prager, Connecticut, 1997

MacMillan, Margaret, *Paris 1919 – Six Months That Changed The World*, Random House, New York, 2002,

Macpherson, Paul and Ian Granland, *A Game to Be Played*, NSW Australian Football History Society, Sydney, 2015

Main, Jim and David Allen, *The Fallen: The Ultimate Heroes – Footballers Who Never Returned from War*, Crown Content, Melbourne, 2002

Main, Jim and Russell Holmesby, *The Encyclopedia of League Footballers*, Wilkinson Books, Melbourne, 1992

Mason, Ronald, *Warwick Armstrong's Australians*, Epworth Press, Newton Abbott, 1973

Mason, Tony and Eliza Riedi, *Sport and the Military: The British Armed Forces 1880–1960*, Cambridge University Press, Cambridge, 2010

McCalman, Janet, *Struggletown: Public and Private Life in Richmond 1900–1965*, Melbourne University Press, Melbourne, 1985

McFarlane, Glenn, *Jock: The Story of Collingwood's Greatest Coach*, Slattery Media, Melbourne, 2011

McKernan, Michael, *The Australian People and the Great War*, Thomas Nelson, Melbourne, 1980

——*Beryl Beaurepaire*, University of Queensland Press, Brisbane, 1999

——*Padre: Australian Chaplains in Gallipoli and France*, Allen & Unwin, Sydney, 1986

——*Victoria at War 1914–1918*, New South Publishing in association with the State Library of Victoria, Sydney, 2014

McKernan, Michael and Margaret Browne (eds), *Australia: Two Centuries of War and Peace*, AWM with Allen & Unwin, Canberra, 1988

McMullin, Ross, *Farewell Dear People*, Scribe, Melbourne, 2012

——*Will Dyson: Australia's Radical Genius*, Scribe, Melbourne, 2006

Molkentin, Michael, *Australia and the War in the Air*, Oxford University Publishing, South Melbourne, 2014

Monash, John, *War Letters of General Monash*, Black Inc, Melbourne, 2015

Morgan, Richard and Patrick, *The Morgan Family of 'Niddrie'*, Richard Spillane, Melbourne, 1990

Niall, Brenda, *Mannix*, Text, Melbourne, 2015

Perry, Roland, *Monash: The Outsider Who Won a War*, Random House, Sydney, 2014

Prior, Robin and Trevor Wilson, *Passchendaele: The Untold Story*, Scribe, Melbourne, 2003

Renshaw, Andrew, *Wisden on The Great War*, John Wisden and Co., Bloomsbury, London, 2014

Richardson, Nick, *The Silk Express: The Story of E.A. 'Ted' McDonald*, cricketbooks. com.au, Melbourne, 2015

Riddoch, Andrew and John Kemp, *When the Whistle Blows: The Story of the Footballer's Battalion in the Great War*, Haynes Publishing, Yeovil, 2011

Robbins, Trevor, *Running into History: A Centenary Profile of the Malvern Harriers Athletic Club 1892–1992*, Malvern Harriers, Melbourne, 1996

Roberts, Michael, *A Century of the Best: The Story of Collingwood's Favourite Sons*, CFC, Melbourne, 1991

Robson, L.L., *Australia and the Great War*, Macmillan, South Melbourne, 1970

——*The First AIF: A Study of its Recruitment 1914–1918*, Melbourne University Press, Melbourne, 1979

Rodgers, Stephen, *Every Game Ever Played: VFL Results 1897–1982*, Lloyd O'Neil, Melbourne, 1983

Ross, John (ed), *100 Years of Australian Football*, Viking, Ringwood, 1996

Sandercock, Leonie and Ian Turner, *Up Where Cazaly? The Great Australian Game*, Granada, Sydney, 1981

Scott, Ernest, *Official History of Australia in the War of 1914–18, Vol. XI, Australia During the War*, Angus & Robertson, Sydney, 1941

Senyard, June, *The Ties that Bind: A History of Sport at the University of Melbourne*, Walla Walla Press, Petersham, 2004

Serle, Geoffrey, *John Monash: A Biography*, Melbourne University Press, Melbourne, 1985

Sims, Graem, *Why Die? The Extraordinary Percy Cerutty, the Maker of Champions*, Lothian Books, Melbourne, 2003

Stevenson, Robert, *The War with Germany*, Oxford University Press, South Melbourne, 2015

Stremski, Richard, *Kill for Collingwood*, Allen & Unwin, Sydney, 1986

Wanliss, Newton, *The History of the 14th Battalion AIF, being the vicissitudes of an Australian Unit during the Great War*, Arrow Printery, Melbourne, 1929

Webster, Ray and Miller, Allan, *First-Class Cricket in Australia*, Vol. 1, 1850–51 to 1941–42, Ray Webster, Glen Waverley, 1991

Select Bibliography

Articles and Chapters

Allen, David G., 'The Anzac Match in London 1916: Australian Football's Greatest Exhibition', *The Yorker*, MCC, Autumn 2000, No. 25

Bastian, Ross, 'Dentistry: The Cinderella of Health Services', in Jacqueline Healy (ed), *Compassion and Courage: Australian Doctors and Dentists in the Great War*, Medical History Museum and University of Melbourne, Melbourne, 2015

Batchelder, Alf, 'MCC Roll of Honour 1914–18', MCC research paper, MCC, 1998

Blair, Dale, 'War and Peace, 1915–1924', in Rob Hess and Bob Stewart, *More than a Game*, Melbourne University Press, Melbourne, 1998

Browne, Ashley, 'For Women, Too', in Slattery, Geoff and Weston, James (eds), *The Australian Game of Football Since 1858*, Slattery Media, Melbourne, 2007

Cunneen, Chris, 'The Rugby War: The Early History of Rugby League in NSW, 1907–15', in David Headon, *The Best Ever Australian Sports Writing: A 200 Year Collection*, Black Inc., Melbourne, 2001

Daffey, Paul, 'Richmond Eats Magpies Alive', in Browne, Ashley (ed), *Grand Finals, Vol. 1, 1897–1938*, Slattery Media, Docklands, 2011

Hess, Rob, 'Missing in Action? New Perspectives on the Origins and Diffusion of Women's Football in Australia during the Great War', *International Journal of the History of Sport*, Vol. 31, No. 18

Inglis, Ken, 'Conscription in Peace and War 1911–1945', in Roy Forward and Bob Reece, *Conscription in Australia*, University of Queensland Press, Brisbane, 1968

Kotton, Howard and DeBolfo, Tony, 'Carlton, 1915', in Browne, Ashley (ed), *Grand Finals, Vol. 1, 1897–1938*, Slattery Media, Docklands, 2011.

Lake, Marilyn, 'The Power of Anzac', in Michael McKernan and Margaret Browne, *Australia: Two Centuries of War and Peace*, AWM with Allen & Unwin, Canberra, 1988

Macintyre, Stuart, 'Football weathers the storm of war' in Ross, John (ed), *100 years of Australian Football*, Viking, Ringwood, 1996

McKernan, Michael, 'Sport, War and Society', in Richard Cashman and Michael McKernan, *Sport in History: The Making of Modern Sporting History*, University of Queensland Press, Brisbane, 1979

McMullin, Ross, 'Heyday of the larrikin spectator', in John Ross (ed), *100 Years of Australian Football*, Viking, Ringwood, 1996

——'Will Dyson: Australia's Radical Genius', *Papers on Parliament*, No. 59, April 2013, Department of the Senate, Canberra

Main, Jim, 'Flag Tinged With Blood' in Browne, Ashley (ed), *Grand Finals, Vol. 1, 1897–1938*, Slattery Media, Docklands, 2011

Menzies, Sir Robert, in Peter Heydon, *Quiet Decision: A Study of George Foster Pearce*, Melbourne University Press, Melbourne, 1965

Molkentin, Michael, 'Training for War: The 3rd Division AIF at Larkhill, 1916', AWM Summer Scholar Paper, 2005

Pedersen, Peter, 'The AIF on the Western Front: The Role of Training and Command', in Michael McKernan and Margaret Browne (eds), *Australia: Two Centuries of War and Peace*, AWM with Allen & Unwin, Canberra, 1988

Phillips, Murray G., 'Sport, War and Gender Images: The Australian Sportsmen's Battalions and the First World War', *International Journal of the History of Sport*, Vol. 14, No. 1, March 2007

Shute, Carmel, 'Heroines and Heroes: Sexual Mythology in Australia 1914–18', in Joy Damousi and Marilyn Lake, *Gender and War: Australia at War in the Twentieth Century*, Cambridge University Press, Melbourne, 1995

Tyquin, Michael, 'Unjustly Accused? Medical Authorities and Army Recruitment in Australia 1914–1918', *Journal of Military and Veterans' Health*, Vol. 22, No. 2, June 2014

Archives

Australian Red Cross Wounded and Missing Enquiry Bureau Files
James Francis Foy, No. 809, 1DRL/0428
Leslie Edward Lee, No. 224, 1DRL/0428
James McKenzie Sloss, No. 11, 1DRL/0428

Australian War Memorial
8th Battalion War Diary, AWM 4, sub-class 23/8
8th Field Artillery Brigade Diary, AWM 4, sub-class 13/36
22nd Battalion War Diary, AWM 4, sub-class 23/39
51st Battalion War Diary, AWM 4, sub-class 23/68
AWM 25 897/10 [Sports] Correspondence regarding arts and crafts exhibition, boxing tournament, cross country racing, cricket, football, horse racing, mule racing. Instructions for divisional sports etc, 3rd Australian Division
Chaplain's Department, War Diary, AWM 4, sub-class 6/5
Sir John Monash Papers, AWM, Series 3

Cricket Victoria
VCA Minutes 1915–1919

Mitchell Library, State Library of New South Wales
Harry Joseph Cave, letters, MLMSS 1224
James Brunton Gibb, diaries and papers, 14 January 1916–15 June 1919

National Archives of Australia
'Frank Beaurepaire', NAA MT1486/1 and B73
'John Brake', NAA, B884, V52492
'James Francis Foy', NAA, B2455
'Leslie Edward Lee', NAA B2455
'Hector Martin', NAA B2455
Also, service records for: Italo Vincent Cesari, Francis Ignatius Joseph Coffey, John Thomas Cooper, Thomas Sinton Hewitt, John Hugh James, Stanley Carlton Martin, Daniel Thomas Minogue, Charles Julius Perry (chaplain), James Pugh, Daniel Scullin, John Joseph Scullin, Patrick Scullin, Bruce Moses Farquhar Sloss, Percy George Trotter, Carl Bleackley Willis

National Library of Australia
Lord Novar Papers
Program, Pioneer Exhibition Game, Australian Football, at Queen's Club, 28 October
1916

Private Papers (held by the family)
Hewitt family archive (courtesy of Sue Mack)
Perry family archive
Sloss family archive

Public Records Office Victoria
Case book of male patients, Victorian Public Records Office, VPRO/VPRS 7398/
P0001/22

RSL Victoria Archives
Sportsmen's Recruiting Committee minutes, 1917

State Library of Victoria
Hawes, Gunner Hugh S., 'The Last Flight of the "Red Baron", Baron Manfred von
Richthofen, 21 April 1918', 1976, State Library of Victoria, MS4434/7
Laidlaw, Private Victor, diary, State Library of Victoria, MS11827
Mackinnon family papers, State Library of Victoria, MS9470

University of Melbourne Archives
Student Administration Collection 1988.0051, Stanley Carlton Martin academic
record
Sports Union Minute book: Minutes of Melbourne University Sports Union,
14 April 1909–1920

West Australian Archives
West Australian State Archives Cons 752, file 760/1914 (George Barry)

Newspapers, Magazines and Periodicals
The Adelaide Mail, The Advertiser (Adelaide), *The Advocate, The Age, Anzac Bulletin,
The Argus, The Armidale Express and New England General Advertiser, The Aussie,
The Australasian, The Australian Statesman and Mining Standard, The Barrier Miner,
Border Watch, Brunswick and Coburg Leader, The Bulletin, Camberwell and Hawthorn
Advertiser, Camp Chronicle, The Camperdown Chronicle, The Chronicle* (South Australia),
Cootamundra Herald, The Daily Advertiser (Wagga Wagga), *Daily Herald* (Adelaide),
Daily News (Perth), *The Daily Standard, The Daily Telegraph, The Daily Telegraph*
(Launceston), *The Essendon Gazette and Keilor, Bulla and Broadmeadows Reporter, The
Examiner* (Launceston), *The Football Record, Geelong Advertiser, The Geraldton Guardian,
Gippsland Mercury, Goomalling-Dowerin Mail, The Graphic, The Herald, Herald Sun,*

The Jerilderie Herald, The Kalgoorlie Miner, The Kiama Independent and Shoalhaven Advertiser, Kyabram Guardian, Leader, Maitland Weekly Mercury, Melbourne's Manhood (YMCA), *Mercury, Moorabbin News, Northern Times, The Observer* (Adelaide), *The Pastoral Review, The Prahran Telegraph, The Record – Emerald Hill, The Referee, The Register, Richmond Australian, Richmond Guardian, Saturday Referee and the Arrow, Sea Lake Times and Berriwillock Advertiser, The South-Eastern Times, The Sporting Globe, Sporting Life, The Sun News-Pictorial, The Sydney Morning Herald, The Sydney Sportsman, The Telegraph* (Launceston), *The Times, Weekly Despatch, The Weekly Times, Wesley College Chronicle, The West Australian, West Oz, Western Mail, Westralian Worker, The Winner, Woman Voter, The Yorker*

Online Sources

Athletics Australia, 'The Greater Game', 24 April 2015, http://athletics.com.au

The Aussie, Australian Variety Theatre Archive, http://ozvta.com/troupes-digger-companies

Bean, C.E.W., *Official History of Australia in the War of 1914–18*, Vol. IV, The Australian Imperial Force in France 1916–18, Angus & Robertson, Sydney, 1935, https://www.awm.gov.au/images/collection/pdf/RCDIG1069499--1-.pdf

Blair, Dale, 'Beyond the metaphor: football and war, 1914–1918', *Journal of the Australian War Memorial*, Issue 28, April 1996, www.awm.gov.au/journal

Broinowski, L. (ed), *Tasmania's War Record 1914–1918*, J. Walch & Sons Ltd, Hobart, 1921, 40th Battalion 1st AIF 1916–18, http://40th-bn.org/40thbn.html

Devaney, John, 'Percy Trotter', www.australianfootball.com

Dillon, Meagan, 'From Perth Tour to the World War I Battlefront for Eight Norwood Football Club Players', *Eastern Courier Messenger*, 11 August 2014, www.news.com.au

Frost, Lenore, 'The Empire Called And I Answered', http://empirecall.blogspot.com.au/

'Left Flying Overboot: Baron M von Richthofen', AWM RELAWM00705, www.awm.gov.au

Oz Sports History, 'The Melbourne Rules: University Football Club', www.ozsportshistory.com

Parliament of Australia, 'Commonwealth Parliamentary Debates', http://parlinfo.aph.gov.au/parlInfo/download/hansard80/hansards80/1907-11-07/toc_pdf/19071107_senate_3_41.pdf;fileType=application%2Fpdf#search=%221900s%201907%22

Richardson, Andrew, 'The Battle of Messines 1917', Army (website), 18 March 2015, www.army.gov.au

Riley, Michael, 'Class and Warfare: The MAFA and the VFL Seconds', Boyles Football Photos, http://boylesfootballphotos.net.au/article47-Class-and-Warfare-The-MAFA-and-the-VFL-Seconds

'A Salute to Les Lee', 24 April 2015, Richmond FC, www.richmondfc.com.au

Syson, Ian, 'Behind the Lines: Victorian Soccer and WWI', Football Federation Victoria, www.footballfedvic.com.au

Waratahs, 'About Us: History: 1914–1919', www.waratahs.com.au

White, Thomas Alexander, diary, State Library of New South Wales, http://ww1.sl.nsw.gov.au/content/thomas-alexander-white

Image Credits

Front Cover
AWM H16689 3rd Division team for the 1916 Exhibition match; Peter Couzens; Aussie Rules Collectables (http://aussierulescollectables.com.au/).

Back Cover
AWM H16688 Training Units team for the 1916 Exhibition match; Sloss family archive.

Inside Cover
Top left, middle left, middle right and bottom right: From the National Film and Sound Archive of Australia.

Bottom left and top right: Courtesy of British Pathé.

Picture Section
Page 1: AWM ARTV07583.

Pages 2–3: Brake, Sewart, Trotter, Sloss, James and Minogue cards courtesy of Aussie Rules Collectables (http://aussierulescollectables.com.au/); Orchard card courtesy of Peter Couzens; Cesari card courtesy of Peter Cesari; Willis, Heinz, Cooper and Jory cards sourced by Nick Richardson.

Page 4: Sloss family archive.

Page 5: *Donald Mackinnon*, Miles & Kaye Photographers, State Library of Victoria; *Man. You are wanted! In the Sportsmen's 1000*, Troedel & Cooper, State Library of Victoria; Janice Coffey (Scullin image); AWM H05990 (Lee image).

Page 6: AWM 511567 (Robertson image); sourced by Nick Richardson (Pugh and James images); Richard Willis (Willis image).

Pages 7–10: Sloss family archive.

Page 11: Courtesy of British Pathé.

Page 12: From the National Film and Sound Archive of Australia.

Page 13: Courtesy of British Pathé (top image); from the National Film and Sound Archive of Australia (middle and bottom images).

Page 14: Courtesy of the Minogue, Bergin, French and Slyjp families (Minogue jumper); courtesy of Richard Willis (Willis image); AWM H16071 (Hughes image); Mitchell Library, State Library of New South Wales, P3/54/2 (Monash portrait).

Page 15: Courtesy of Melbourne Cricket Club (Beaurepaire image); AWM E04919 (Hughes dummy image); Sloss family archive (Tullie image).

Page 16: Sloss family archive (Sloss grave image); courtesy of Richard Willis (Willis image); courtesy of Aussie Rules Collectables (http://aussierulescollectables. com.au/ – Minogue card); National Archives of Australia: M1218, 3 (Beaurepaire image).